BEYOND THE GREAT GLEN

BEYOND THE GREAT GLEN

A WAYFARING GUIDE TO THE NORTH-WEST
HIGHLANDS

BY

F. REID CORSON

OLIVER AND BOYD
EDINBURGH: TWEEDDALE COURT
LONDON: 98 GREAT RUSSELL STREET, W.C.1
1950

First Published 1934
Second Edition 1950

PRINTED IN GREAT BRITAIN BY
ERIC BEMROSE LTD., LIVERPOOL

TO

G.C. H.M.G.C. J.R.C.

WHO NO LONGER TREAD
THE HIGHLAND HILLS

FOREWORD

I HAVE no hesitation in recommending this book to the wayfaring public who desire to explore the North-West Highlands.

It is a most interesting and reliable guide to all the hill-paths and cross-country routes in that fascinating region.

It is quite the fullest and most detailed account from the walker's point of view of the region be-north and be-west of the Great Glen, that has yet been published, so far as I am aware, and as such it is peculiarly valuable and welcome in these days when so many are anxious to get off the beaten track, but don't know where to go or what to do.

This book contains just the information that will help them.

A. E. ROBERTSON

PUBLISHER'S NOTE TO THE
SECOND EDITION

The author's untimely death, combined with the region's inaccessibility during the war years, and the difficulty of producing those books most desperately needed, caused us regretfully to allow this fine and useful work to lapse. Now the walker and the cyclist are on the move north again, all asking for the information this book gives.

With such care, thoroughness, and deep knowledge was the work first done that only superficial corrections have been found necessary, on details such as communications and accommodation. In addition, notes are included on the undertakings of the North of Scotland Hydro-Electric Board, particularly where these affect accessibility.

CONTENTS

ILLUSTRATIONS

MAPS

INTRODUCTION

It is the considered opinion of qualified judges that the finest scenery in Britain lies north and west of the Great Glen of Scotland. The great sea-lochs of the west, the hundred peaks of Ross-shire, the three unrivalled Inverness-shire glens, the Coolins of Skye and the strange isolated mountains of Sutherland are all to be found in that part of Scotland, which can also boast Loch Shiel, Loch Arkaig and the queenly Loch Maree. Yet in this crowded Twentieth-century Britain, with its throngs of summer holiday-makers, its hikers and campers and cyclists, how few are familiar with the wonderful region which lies beyond the Caledonian Canal!

Intensive advertising has, it is true, made the island of Skye known to the outer world; the new road through Glencoe is bringing motorists along the Great Glen to Inverness, and reliability trials occasionally penetrate to Applecross and Dundonnell. But even so, to the vast majority of English and Scottish holiday-makers the glories of North-West Scotland are still a sealed book. To remedy this lack of information is the aim of the present guide. It is designed to smooth the path of intending visitors, to help them to explore the glens and lochs and mountain passes and the splendid sea-lochs of the West Coast. It is, therefore, primarily a book for walkers and cyclists, and for those car-owners who have not yet lost the use of their legs.

Each of its nineteen chapters is devoted to a separate district, or group of districts, deals with its history, communications and accommodation, and describes its roads, hill-tracks and mountain passes.

The district of Lochaber, though situated south-east of

the Great Glen, is the southern gateway to the North-West Highlands, and has, therefore, been included. Its capital, Fort William, is the best centre for Locheil and Ardgour.

Although the ascent of a few prominent mountains is described, the book is not a climber's guide. The mountaineering fraternity has already, in the excellent guidebooks of the Scottish Mountaineering Club, all that can be desired.

The sketch maps are intended to help the reader in the planning of excursions. They cannot, of course, take the place of maps of adequate scale, which are essential to the real enjoyment of mountain tramps. Those published by the Ordnance Survey, on the scale of one inch to the mile, are the best for the walker. On the smaller scale of half an inch to the mile there is nothing better than the excellent series published by Bartholomew of Edinburgh. The system of layer colouring employed in these maps facilitates the estimating of heights and of the rise or fall of mountain paths. A reference to the appropriate sheets of each of the above series of maps will be found at the beginning of each chapter.

To Mr Alexander Smith, whose *Hill-paths and Drove-roads of Scotland* has been his companion on many a mountain tramp, the author is indebted for much valuable information. His knowledge of the byways of Scotland is extraordinarily wide, and is reflected in his book, which is a classic in the literature of the open air.

Since the immediate post-war years there has been a great development of public motor services in the North-West Highlands. These are often exceedingly useful to the walker, who is enabled by their aid to reach his centre of operations, or to send on his kit, while he himself crosses the hills to his destination. It is, however, seldom safe to count on securing a seat at a wayside halting-place, especially in the season: the wise man makes use of the motor-bus from its starting point if at all possible. Particulars of these motor services will be found in each chapter, under the heading of " Communications."

To facilitate reference to the maps of the Ordnance Survey, all place-names have been spelt as far as possible in accordance with those maps. In a few cases, however, the anglicised version of well-known names has been used to avoid confusion. Ben Attow, for example, appears instead of A' Bheinn Fhada, and Loch Beneveian instead of Beinn a' Meadhoin. In other cases the English pronunciation has been added in brackets after the Gaelic name; *e.g.* Ladhar Bheinn (Larven).

The author gratefully acknowledges the kindly help received from the Rev. A. E. Robertson, ex-president of the Scottish Mountaineering Club and president of the Scottish Rights of Way Society, who has read and corrected the typescript, and suggested a number of improvements in the book.

BRACKLEY, *5th April, 1934*

CHAPTER I

LOCHABER AND LOCHEIL

MAPS.—*O.S. Popular Edition, 1 inch, sheets 47 and 48.
Bartholomew's Half Inch, sheets 50 and 51.*

LOCHABER is a district in southern Inverness-shire, extending from Glen Spean to Loch Leven, and containing the range of mountains of which Ben Nevis is the chief height. It takes its name from a loch which used to exist in the swampy plain at the head of Loch Linnhe, Loch Aber signifying the " Loch of the Swamp."

The capital of Lochaber is Fort William, a small town by the seashore at the nothern end of Loch Linnhe, the long straight sea-loch which divides Lochaber from Ardgour. At this strategically important spot a fort was built in 1650 by General Monk, with the object of over-awing the Camerons of Lochaber, and of garrisoning the southern end of the Great Glen. Round this fort rose the town of Maryburgh, which has grown into the modern Fort William, a name given to the fort in the days of Dutch William. It is now a flourishing town of shops and banks, the most important between Oban and Inverness, and is well provided with hotels and private accommodation for the summer visitor. The establishment of aluminium works at Inverlochy has increased the importance of Fort William, and a new town of workers' houses now stands on the site of the battle of Inverlochy.

The chief rivers of Lochaber are the broad, rushing Lochy, which flows out of Loch Lochy to Loch Linnhe, and its tributary the Spean, coming from far Loch Laggan, and roaring down by gorge and rapid to join the Lochy

near the Falls of Muccomer. Loch Treig, in the valley
to the east of the Ben Nevis group of mountains, and Loch
Lochy in the Great Glen, are the chief fresh-water lochs.
The former, which is well seen from the West Highland
Railway, lies at a height of some 830 feet and is about 7
miles long. Loch Lochy is the southernmost of the chain
of three lochs which stretch between Fort William and
Inverness, and help to form the Caledonian Canal.

The Ben Nevis group of mountains, with its three summits of 4000 feet, covers a wide expanse of country to the
east of Fort William. The deep and narrow trench of Glen
Nevis curves round its western and southern flanks and
separates it from the peaks of the Mamore Forest, which
look across Loch Leven to Glencoe and Appin. North of
Glen Spean rise the lesser heights around Glen Roy, with
the mighty mass of Creag Meaghaidh above Loch Laggan,
the latter, however, being outside the bounds of Lochaber.

Lochaber, together with the neighbouring district of
Locheil, is the country of the Camerons, whose chief still
resides at Achnacarry, by Loch Arkaig side. In the old
fighting days of the fourteenth century one branch of the
clan occupied Glen Nevis, where a few fallen stones still
mark the site of the chief's house, and serve to remind us
of a tragedy of long ago. The story goes that a party of
Macintoshes from Badenoch had been entertained by the
Cameron chief, and had taken their leave, when the chief's
piper struck up the battle pibroch of the clan, known as
" Sons of the dogs, come and get flesh." Stung by what
they considered to be a studied insult, the Badenoch men
returned during the night and slew their late host with
almost all his family. One child alone was saved by the
devotion of a clansman, to grow up in obscurity and later
to assume the chieftainship of the Glen Nevis branch of
the clan. At a later period the head of the house of Lochiel
was the acknowledged chief of Clan Cameron, which is still
the case. Sir Ewen Cameron, who fought successfully
against Cromwell's men, and the " Gentle Lochiel " of the

'Forty Five, were notable chiefs in the seventeenth and eighteenth centuries.

Lochaber was also the home of the Keppoch Macdonalds, a branch of the great Clan Donald. Their country was in Glen Roy and Glen Spean, and was held by right of conquest, in face of the chief of the Macintoshes, who claimed that he alone had a good title to the lands in question. This claim was the cause of the fight at Mulroy, near the modern Roy Bridge, notable as the last clan battle in the Highlands. It took place in 1688, between the Macdonalds, under their chief Coll of the Cows, and a force of Macintoshes under Lachlan Macintosh. The Macintoshes were supported by a company of Government troops under Mackenzie of Suddie, but in spite of this reinforcement the day went against them, and their chief fell into the hands of Keppoch. After the battle was decided a force of Macphersons came up, and by the menace of their presence were able to secure the release of the Macintosh chief; they did not, however, attack the victorious Macdonalds. Coll of the Cows afterwards fought with Dundee at Killiecrankie, and was in the end reconciled to the rule of Dutch William, while the old feud with Macintosh was peacefully settled in the year 1700.

On the south bank of the Lochy, surrounded by the houses of the new settlement of aluminium workers, stands the ancient castle of Inverlochy. Built by a Comyn in the thirteenth century, its venerable walls have seen two great battles. In 1441, a royal army under the Earl of Mar was put to flight at Inverlochy by Donald Balloch and his islesmen. Two centuries later, in 1645, the Marquis of Monrose, with a royalist force of Macdonalds, Macleans, Stewarts and Camerons, surprised the Marquis of Argyll, and cut to pieces his army of Campbells and Lowlanders. Montrose was at Kilcumin, now known as Fort Augustus, when news was brought that Argyll was at Inverlochy. By a wonderful forced march through the mountains in snowy weather, the king's general was able to take the Campbells by surprise, and win a resounding victory. The story of the battle forms part of the fine romance of *John Splendid* by Neil Munro, the late gifted Highland novelist. Locheil and Lochaber also form the background of Miss Broster's *Flight of the Heron, Gleam in the North*, and other West Highland novels.

Accommodation in Lochaber and Locheil

Hotels and boarding-houses at Fort William, Gairlochy, Spean Bridge, Roy Bridge, Banavie, Corpach, Corran, Onich, North Ballachulish, Kinlochleven. Rooms at private houses at most of these places, also at Kinlocheil.

Youth Hostels

1. At Loch Ossian, 1 mile east of Corrour Station, on the L.N.E.R. line from Glasgow to Fort William. Not available during stalking season, i.e., from 12th August till 31st October.

2. In Glen Nevis, 3 miles from Fort William.

Communications

Railways.—1. L.N.E.R. from Glasgow (Queen Street) and Edinburgh to Spean Bridge and Fort William.

2. L.N.E.R. from Mallaig, Arisaig and Glenfinnan to Fort William.

3. L.N.E.R. from Spean Bridge to Gairlochy, Invergarry and Fort Augustus. This line was closed from December, 1933. A service of road motors now runs between Spean Bridge and Fort Augustus in connection with L.N.E.R. trains.

4. L.M.S. from Oban to Ballachulish, thence motor-bus to Fort William.

Steamers (in season only).—1. From Oban to Ballachulish and Fort William.

2. From Banavie to Fort Augustus and Inverness, via Caledonian Canal.

Road Services.—1. Fort William to Fort Augustus and Inverness.

2. Fort William to North Ballachulish.

3. Fort William to Onich, Kinlochleven and South Ballachulish.

4. Fort William to Spean Bridge, Roy Bridge and Tulloch.
5. Spean Bridge to Invergarry and Fort Augustus.

Hill Walks in Lochaber and Locheil

1. Through Glen Nevis to Loch Treighead and Corrour Station, 19 miles. Take the north road out of Fort William, turning off to Glen Nevis at Nevis Bridge. Lower Glen Nevis is a broad green glen, some 5 miles long, with the slopes of Ben Nevis above on the east. The road keeps to the true left bank of the River Nevis, passing the farm of Achintee, on the right bank, where the pony track up the mountain begins. Three miles from Fort William is the Youth Hostel, and in another 2 miles the glen bends sharply to the east beyond the farm of Poll Dubh, and begins to ascend between the lower slopes of Cairn Dearg and Sgurr a Mhaim. Crossing the river by a fine waterfall, the road becomes rougher and the scenery wilder, the huge boulders and picturesque Scottish pines being especially striking. Two miles further on the road becomes a narrow track, which presently turns south-east across the face of a cliff, and climbs through a gorge above the rushing stream to the green levels of Upper Glen Nevis. Leave the suspension bridge to the right, keeping to the north side of the river, past the cottage at Steall with the magnificent waterfall behind, and continue for 4 miles to Tom-an-Eite, a small round hill which marks the summit of the pass. Here the track ceases, and it is best to cross to the south bank of the river. From this point the route descends gradually for 6 miles, following the course of the River Rath, and reaches the head of Loch Treig, where is a lodge, a farm and some keepers' houses. By keeping round the head of the loch to the east, the walker will cross three bridges and eventually reach the railway line by a steep road up the hill-side. This track leads in about 2 miles more to Corrour Station.

2. Spean Bridge to Kinlochleven by the Lairig nan Leacan, 18½ miles. This walk takes one round the eastern side of the Ben Nevis range by the wild pass of the Lairig nan Leacan, and east of the Mamore Forest down to Loch

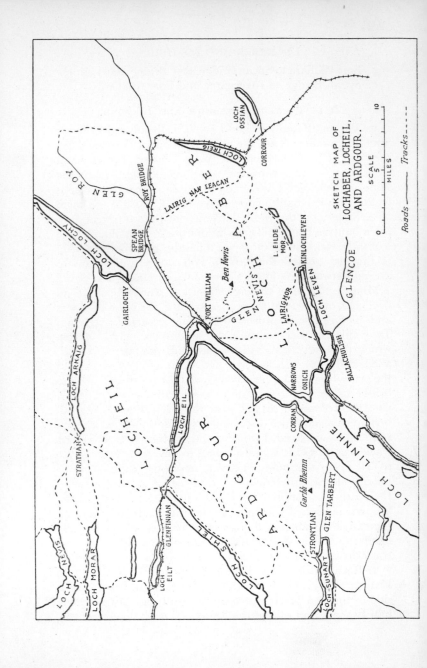

SKETCH MAP OF
LOCHABER, LOCHEIL,
AND ARDGOUR.

SCALE

0   5   10
        MILES

Roads ——— Tracks - - - - -

Leven. It is best started from Spean Bridge Station, which is reached from Fort William by the morning train. On leaving the station at Spean Bridge, turn *right* along the road on the south side of the River Spean. At the bridge over the Cour (2 miles), take a path to the right which leads south, past Corrychoillie Farm, and then begins to climb towards the opening in the hills ahead. Crossing the construction railway track of the British Aluminium Co., Ltd. (which is laid along the line of the Southern Parallel Road of Glen Spean), continue by the well-made path up into the hills, cross the stream and climb along the eastern slope of the glen to the summit of the pass at a height of 1656 feet. Half a mile further on, after passing a shooting bothy in a hollow by the stream, the track crosses a plank bridge and begins to ascend across the eastern slopes of Stob Ban, then passes between Meall a' Bhuirich and Meall Mor before descending into the glen of the Rath River close to the cottage of Lubeilt. Here the Loch Treig-Glen Nevis track is crossed at right angles (see Route 1). Still keeping southwards the path now crosses a low watershed to Loch Eilde Beag, and continues along its north-west shore and past the two-mile long Loch Eilde Mor, at the foot of which begins the steep descent to Kinlochleven. A walk of 2 miles, passing Mamore Lodge, will take one down to the main road of the town, where a bus to Fort William can be obtained. The aluminium works, to which the town owes its rise from a hamlet, are on the south side of the River Leven.

Note.—By crossing to the left bank of the burn *before* reaching the bothy mentioned above, and following a rough and wet track below the western slopes of Stob Coire an Easain Mor (3658 feet), the walker can reach Loch Treighead and Corrour Station (see Route 1). By this route the distance from Spean Bridge to Corrour is 16 miles.

3. Tulloch Station to Leichroy, Turret Bridge and Glen Roy, 21 miles. Train from Fort William to Tulloch, walk up to main road and go west along it for one mile as far as the junction with a road coming up from the left from

Inverlair and Fersit. At this point a track strikes off north-east across the hill-slopes, and soon turns north along the Allt a Chaoruinn, with the heights of Ben Teallach and Ben a Chaoruinn above to west and east. Follow this track up into the hills until it comes to an end at a height of 2000 feet, then strike due north until the headwaters of the Burn of Agie are reached. After about 1½ miles of hill-side another track is reached in a glen descending to the north, and trending north by west, and later north-west, into Glen Roy, where the cottage of Annat is reached in 4 miles. On the opposite side of the glen is the ruined cottage of Leich-roy, the famous Parallel Roads showing distinctly on the hill-side beyond. Keeping westward along the left bank of the Roy, Turret Bridge, where the Turret joins the Roy, is soon reached. Here is the head of the narrow road which runs down Glen Roy to Roy Bridge (9 miles), with its hotel and railway station. This Glen Roy track was the route taken by Montrose in 1645 on his way to surprise Argyll at Inverlochy. He is thought to have pushed up Glen Tarff, across the hills into Glen Turret, and down Glen Roy, finishing his march by the old track along the north-west base of the Ben Nevis range. The modern road keeps to the right bank of the Roy, and affords good views of the Parallel Roads at different points along the sides of the glen. At Roy Bridge the train can be joined for Fort William.

Note.—If this Glen Roy circuit is considered too long for one day's walk, it may be possible to secure a night's accommodation at a keeper's house at Annat. This cannot, however, be expected during the shooting season.

4. Loch Arkaig, by Spean Bridge and Gairlochy, 16 miles. Loch Arkaig, though not so well known, ranks with Loch Maree, Loch Shiel and Loch Lomond, as one of the most beautiful of inland lochs. The twelve-mile walk along its northern shore is recommended to good walkers, but if it is intended to return the same day to Fort William, only the eastern end of the loch can be visited. If time is of importance a car is advisable and can be hired at Fort

William or Spean Bridge. The *best* way to see Loch Arkaig is a two-days' expedition, with a night spent at Strathan, as set out below:—

Train to Spean Bridge, thence by road to Gairlochy Lock, across the canal, and northward to the west shore of Loch Lochy to Clunes, whence it is about 2 miles through the " Dark Mile " to Loch Arkaig foot. Achnacarry House, the seat of Lochiel, stands among the trees to the south of the road. There is a shorter route back to Gairlochy which crosses the Arkaig River near the loch, and goes south-east behind Achnacarry to emerge on the main road at a point 2 miles from Gairlochy.

It is 12 miles to Strathan at the head of the loch, and the road is passable for cars as far as Glen Dessary Farm. There is no hotel at Strathan, but it is sometimes possible to obtain a night's lodging at the sheep-farm. If this is done, the next day's walk can be to Kinlochiel, through the hills, and on to the railway at Locheilside Station, whence Fort William can easily be regained.

Leave Strathan and cross the River Pean, go up the glen of the Allt a Chaoruinn for about a mile, and climb round the western end of Leac nan Carnaich to the head of Glen Camgharaidh, then south-east over the high " Panting Pass " west of the double-peaked mountain Gulvain, and down into the glen of the Allt a Choire Reidh. Follow the stream down into Glen Fionnlighe, and join the path which leads southwards to the Mallaig road. Turn east along the road to Kinlocheil, a mile beyond which is the station of Locheilside. If the last train has gone, accommodation can be had at Kinlocheil from 1st April through the summer season.

5. Fort William to Kinlochleven by the Lundavra road, 14 miles. This hill-road, with its splendid views, and freedom from motor traffic, leaves the main road to North Ballachulish a short way south of the station at Fort William, and climbs steadily to the clachan and school-house of Blarmachfoldach. From this point there are specially fine views of Ben Nevis seen from the south. Still

climbing, with the Kiachnish River in the glen below, the
road leaves on the right the Loch of Lundavra, said to have
been the site of Macbeth's castle, trends more and more
east, and then makes a sharp bend round the flank of the
mountain Meall a Chaoruinn (Hill of the Rowan Tree).
Passing the cottage of Larigmor, the road at length reaches
the summit at the Tigh nam Sloc, a lonely dwelling at a
height of nearly 1000 feet. From the other side of the pass
begins the steep descent through the Nathrach Glen to Loch
Leven, lying in its deep trough below the mountains of
Glencoe. Kinlochleven is reached in 14 miles from Fort
William, and here buses to Fort William or to Ballachulish
may be joined.

Note.—By leaving the above road at Larigmor, and taking a track
leading south-west, it is possible to reach the main road at Callart
House, 3 miles east from North Ballachulish Ferry, and on the bus route
to Fort William. The mileage by this route is reduced to 11 miles.

6. Down the western shore of Loch Linnhe to Ardgour,
and back by Corran Ferry, 20 miles. Take the ferry boat
across Loch Linnhe to Camusnagaul, opposite Fort William.
From this bay a narrow road follows the shore to Ardgour
and beyond, commanding fine views of the Ben Nevis range
and the Mamore peaks across Loch Linnhe. Three miles
from Camusnagaul, Stronchreggan House and glen are
passed, and some miles beyond begin the woods of the
Conaglen Estate, the property of the Earl of Morton.
Conaglen House stands back from the bay of Inverscaddle,
where the two glens of Cona and Scaddle converge. It was
on the rocks of Inverscaddle that Glengarry was killed in
1828, when leaping from the stranded steamer *Stirling
Castle*. Beyond Inverscaddle Bay the road hugs the shore
of the narrowing Loch Linnhe, and at 5 miles from Conaglen
reaches the Ardgour Hotel. Here, at the Corran Narrows,
8 miles below Fort William, the tides of Loch Linnhe pour
through a strait 2 furlongs wide. A white lighthouse guards
the passage, and the Ardgour Hotel looks across to that of
Nether Lochaber beyond the ferry. Crossing by the ferry

boat it is but a short walk up to the main road with its buses to Fort William.

Ascent of Ben Nevis

The summit of Ben Nevis is 7 miles distant from Fort William, and is reached by road and by a good pony track, which leaves the former at the farm of Achintee in Glen Nevis. In good weather the ascent is easily made, and the magnificent views obtained on the way up, and from the summit will be ample recompense for the toil involved.

Leave Fort William by the road to Nevis Bridge, cross the bridge, and turn off by the road into Glen Nevis. In 2½ miles, at the farm of Achintee, the pony track begins, winding upwards along the flanks of Meall an t' Suidhe, an outlying hill which hides Ben Nevis itself. In the hollow behind this hill is the loch of the same name, along which comes the old track from Banavie, joining the present track near the ruined shelter known as the half-way house. At this point the pony track turns south and begins to ascend Ben Nevis, winding up the slopes in a series of long zigzags, which eventually bring the climber due east to the summit. The latter part of the ascent is across a chaos of huge boulders and shattered rocks, which stretches away eastward to the neighbouring height of Carn Mor Dearg. On the flat summit plateau of the mountain is the observatory, now for many years disused, and the ruins of the little inn for summer visitors.

The view from the summit on a clear day is very extensive: southward from Loch Linnhe to Mull, Islay and Jura, and across the Mamore peaks to the mountains of Glencoe, and Ben Cruachan, above Loch Etive. Westward beyond Loch Eil is the sea, with the islands of Rhum, Eigg and the Outer Isles. North-west are the savage peaks of Skye and the ranges of Inverness and Ross-shire. Northward runs the line of the Great Glen, driving like a giant furrow towards the Moray Firth. Eastward there is little to be seen, the huge bulk of the Aonachs shutting out the hills of Badenoch and of Athol.

The most impressive feature of Ben Nevis is the great northern precipice, the longest and highest in Britain. It drops vertically to 1900 feet, and is best seen from the summit of Carn Dearg Mor, or from the floor of the deep corrie below the cliffs. This can be reached by a track which descends in an easterly direction from near the junction with the Banavie track above Loch Meall an t' Suidhe. The scramble up this glen will disclose more of the grandeur of Ben Nevis than the ascent to the summit.

CHAPTER II

Ardgour, Morvern, Sunart and Ardnamurchan

Maps.—*O.S. Popular Edition*, 1 *inch, sheets* 46 *and* 53.
Bartholomew's Half Inch, sheets 47 *and* 50.

West of Loch Linnhe and extending to the Sound of Mull stretches the large irregularly-shaped peninsula containing the districts of Ardgour, Morvern, Sunart and Ardnamurchan. Washed on three sides by the Atlantic, the Sound of Mull and the waters of Loch Linnhe, the peninsula is almost cut in two by the long sea-loch of Sunart, which separates Morvern from Ardnamurchan. The latter consists of a promontory some 20 miles long, extending westwards into the Atlantic. On its furthest point stands the great light-house, whose powerful beam warns shipping off the most westerly rocks of the mainland of Great Britain. The surface of the district of Ardnamurchan is mainly rough moorland, devoted to grouse and deer; there are few mountains.

Morvern is a country of low mountains and green glens, lying between Loch Sunart and the Sound of Mull. The former is the southernmost of the great sea-lochs which penetrate the Western Highlands; it winds for 20 miles deep into the land, and at its head is only separated by some 6 miles from Loch Linnhe. From the southern shore of Loch Sunnart, through a narrow strait behind the island of Carna, the fiord-like Loch Teacuis penetrates into Morvern. From its head extends the depression in which lies the fresh-water Loch Arienas, from which Loch Aline is only 3 miles distant.

The district of Sunart lies to the north of the loch of that name and south of Loch Shiel; it contains the townships of Salen, Acharacle and Strontian, and its chief mountain is the imposing Ben Resipol. North of Sunart, with the long fresh-water Loch Shiel for its western boundary, is the rugged district of Ardgour, with its series of deep glens opening on to Loch Linnhe. It is a land of mountains and hill-tracks, traversed by one road only, and is almost entirely given up to deer and grouse. The salt-water Loch Eil, stretching westward from the head of Loch Linnhe, forms its northern boundary; through the gap between Kinlocheil and the head of Loch Shiel enters the road which encircles Ardgour and continues to Loch Sunart and Morvern.

In the old clan days Ardgour and Morvern were held by the Macleans, who had wrested the district from its earlier lords of the Clan MacMaster. This was achieved by Ewen Maclean, a scion of the Macleans of Mull; he held his conquered lands as a vassal of Somerled, first Lord of the Isles. The castle of Ardtornish, which stands near the entrance to Loch Aline on the Sound of Mull, was one of the strongholds of the Lords of the Isles, and the place of assembly of their feudal parliaments. It is the scene of the opening cantos of Scott's poem, *The Lord of the Isles*.

Clan Gillian, as the Macleans were known in Gaelic, was ever a turbulent race, at war with Macdonalds, with Campbells, or with the royal forces. The armies of Montrose and Dundee were swelled by Macleans, and the clan was out with Prince Charlie in the 'Forty Five. Their territory, like that of their neighbours in Ardnamurchan, was coveted by the Campbells, who eventually dispossessed them either by force or by fraud.

Ardnamurchan and Sunart were the home of the MacIans of Ardnamurchan, a branch of the great Mac-donald clan. Mingarry Castle, which still frowns from its sea-washed rock across the Sound of Mull, was the seat of their chiefs. But the MacIans fell on evil days. Argyll attacked Ardnamurchan with his Campbell clansmen, driving out or slaying the inhabitants, and settling the land with hungry men of Clan Diarmaid. The MacIans were crushed and Mingarry became a Campbell fortress.

In 1644 it was the Campbell's turn to suffer, when Alasdair Macdonald with his Irish clansmen swept Ardnamurchan and Morvern with fire and sword, besieged and took Mingarry and the castle of Lochaline from their Campbell garrisons, and passed on to join Montrose at Blair Atholl. A century later, after the rising of 1745, Mingarry was garrisoned by King George's troops. It has now for many years been ruinous and deserted.

COMMUNICATIONS

Railways.—There are none in the district, but Glenfinnan Station, on the Fort William-Mallaig line, is the rail-head from which goods and passengers reach Sunart and Ardnamurchan. There is a daily steamer service on Loch Shiel from Glenfinnan to Acharacle, whence a mail motor-bus runs to Salen and Kilchoan.

Steamers.—1. On Loch Shiel between Acharacle and Glenfinnan.

2. From Oban to Lochaline daily.

3. From Kilchoan to Oban thrice weekly.

4. *In summer season only.* From Ardgour to Oban, and to Fort William. Glasgow steamers call occasionally at Salen and Strontian.

Road Services.—1. From Ardgour Hotel (Corran Ferry) to Strontian on Loch Sunart.

2. From Acharacle Pier to Salen and Kilchoan.

Ferries.—Corran Ferry gives access from Fort William and Ballachulish. There is a ferry from Drimnin to Tobermory.

ACCOMMODATION

Hotels at Ardgour, Lochaline, Strontian, Acharacle, Salen and Kilchoan.

Accommodation in private houses at Shiel Bridge and Kilchoan.

WALKS

(a) *By Road*

Distances are so great and roads so few that these districts are on the whole better suited to the cyclist than to the walker. Ardgour, being far more rugged, offers a number of fine hill-walks, but in Morvern, Sunart and Ardnamurchan the roads themselves are the best means of seeing the country. The following routes are recommended to the cyclist and the walker; they are definitely not suitable for fast motoring:—

1. Ardgour and Clovulin to Inversanda, thence by Glen Tarbert to Strontian, 15 miles. This road skirts Loch Linnhe for 7 miles, with fine views across to Appin, and turns at Inversanda up Glen Tarbert, a straight, narrow trough running between sharply-peaked mountains. Garbh Bheinn (Garven), though not more than 2900 feet in height, is a wild, rocky peak affording excellent rock-climbing to mountaineers. It is one of the most shapely mountains in Scotland, and can be tackled by way of Coire an Iubhair, the fine glen opening off the road to the north. Glen Tarbert is nearly 7 miles long; its western end opens on the head of Loch Sunart, where the road divides, the main branch going along the northern shore to Strontian, with its hotel, post-office and churches. This was once a centre for lead-mining, and several deserted mines are to be seen in the hills up the course of the Strontian River. Another road leads along the southern shore for some 4 miles, then turns south up the glen of the Liddesdale Burn and climbs over a pass of 800 feet to join the Lochaline road, mentioned in the next route. This road affords a ready means of returning to Ardgour by way of Kingairloch.

2. Inversanda and Kingairloch to Lochaline and Drimnin, 35 miles. Leaving the Glen Tarbert road at Inversanda, this route goes south along the base of the mountains, with the shores of Loch Linnhe a mile away on the left hand. At Kilmalie the road reaches the shore and runs for 3 miles on a ledge between the mountains and the

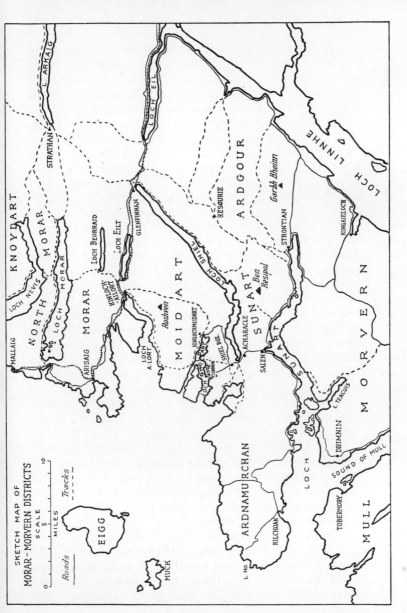

SKETCH MAP OF
MORAR-MORVERN DISTRICTS
SCALE
MILES
0   5   10
Roads
Tracks

KNOYDART

L. ARKAIG

STRATHAN

LOCH NEVIS

NORTH   MORAR

LOCH MORAR

MALLAIG

ARISAIG

Loch Beorraid

MORAR

LOCH EIL

GLENFINNAN

Loch Eilt

LOCH SHIEL

RESOURIE

ARDGOUR

Garbh Bheinn

STRONTIAN

KINGAIRLOCH

LOCH LINNHE

KINLOCH-
AILORT

Roshven

MOIDART

LOCH A'LORT

KINLOCHMOIDART

LOCH
CASTLE
TIORAM

SHIEL BGE.

ACHARACLE

SUNART

Ben
Resipol

SALEN

LOCH   SUNART

EIGG

MUCK

ARDNAMURCHAN

L. HO.

KILCHOAN

L. TEACUIS

DRIMNIN

MORVERN

TOBERMORY

SOUND OF MULL

MULL

B

sea. At this point the rocky slopes above, with the huge boulders strewn along the shore, contrast effectively with the expanse of sea below the narrow road. Rounding the headland at the entrance to Glen Galmadale, the road crosses that glen and turns north-east along the shore of Loch a Choire, at the head of which is Kingairloch House. The next 3 miles are up the glen of the Coinnich River, a beautiful stretch of tree-clad winding road, with the stream in the gorge below. The road goes on climbing over open moorland, passes the junction of the direct Strontian road (see Route No. 1), and descends in another 9 miles to Kinlochaline. The scenery of the glen of the Aline River is pleasantly pastoral, and after the bare moorlands the trees and shrubs are very welcome. The road keeps high up on the slopes above Loch Aline, leaving the pier and hotel to the left, and presently reaches the shore of the Sound of Mull at Fuinary, the place made famous by Dr Norman Macleod. From Fuinary to Drimnin is 7 miles, by a road which skirts the shore, sometimes passing through wooded stretches, and almost all the time affording glorious views of Mull across the water. On a point about half-way to Drimnin stands the ruined fort known as Caisteal nan Con (Dog's Castle), and further on is an ancient Dun by the seashore. Drimnin is a village with post-office and pier and a ferry to Tobermory, in Mull. A steamer calls regularly on the way to and from Oban.

3. Acharacle to Salen and Strontian, 12 miles. This road climbs up from the foot of Loch Shiel and descends through a wooded defile to the pleasant bay of Salen, with its hotel and steamer pier on Loch Sunart. Thence to the east, along the northern shore of the loch, the road passes through shady wooded levels, with fine views of the hills of Morvern across the water.

4. Salen to Kilchoan, 19 miles. This is a narrow hilly road, with splendid sea views. It skirts the shore of Loch Sunart for 10 miles, then turns inland to make a detour round the base of Ben Hiant, before striking south-west down a wide glen and past Mingarry to Kilchoan. Kil-

choan is a township on a southward-facing bay; it has steamer services from Oban and Tobermory, and accommodation for visitors. From it the lighthouse of Ardnamurchan Point is a five-mile walk. Faskadale and Kilmory on the north shore of the peninsula can be reached by road or path, and there are many walks along the rockbound coast. The ascent of Ben Hiant to the east, and of Ben na Seilg to the west, can easily be made, and from each the seascapes are exceedingly fine.

(b) *By Hill-track and Path*

1. Kinlochaline to Salen, via Loch Teacuis, 16 miles. North from Kinlochaline by road for just over a mile, then by a track along the west side of Loch Arienas, and the east side of the little Loch Durinemast to Kinlochteacuis, thence along Loch Teacuis for nearly a mile, and north across the hill to the foot of Glen Cripesdale on Loch Sunart. From here a boat must be obtained to cross the loch to Port nan Gall on the north shore, whence Salen is 4 miles north-east by the loch-shore road.

2. Strontian to Glenfinnan by Loch Shiel, 20 miles. Go north from Strontian Free Church for 2 miles, then north by west past the old Corrantee lead-mine to Loch Doilate, and across the ford to Polloch. Cross the next stream by a foot-bridge and go north and then north-east to Gorstanvorran on Loch Shiel. A loch-side track leads from here to the Callop River at the head of the loch, a distance of 10 miles. If it is not possible to get a boat across to the steamer pier, it will be necessary to go a mile up-stream in order to ford the river and gain the road to Glenfinnan. Another half mile will bring one to a bridge, if the stream is too high for easy fording.

3. Strontian to Glenfinnan by Resourie, 20 miles. This is a real mountain walk, which crosses the pass from Resourie at a height of 2200 feet. Go north from Strontian by Scotstown, and north-east over the Druim Glas and down to Glen Hurich, then along this glen to Resourie at its head. Thence the track climbs over a high pass and drops to the

head of Cona Glen, crosses the Cona River and again climbs by the east of the mountain Glac Gharbh and by Doire Ban over to the headwaters of the Allt na Cruaiche and the Callop River. The latter is crossed at Craigag, which is 2 miles east of Glenfinnan.

4. Ardgour to Glenfinnan, 24 miles. North by road to Aryhoulan at the mouth of Glen Scaddle, then west along the Scaddle River for 7 miles, past the waterfall at Sron Beinne Mheadhoin, and over a pass by the Lochan Dubh down to Resourie at the head of Glen Hurich. From here to Glenfinnan the route is that described in Route No. 3.

5. Ardgour to Glenfinnan via Conaglen, 20 miles. This is an alternative and somewhat shorter route than No. 4. North by road to Aryhoulan, cross the bridge over the combined streams of the Cona and Scaddle, and take a path which goes north to join one coming from Conaglen House. This latter path goes west up Cona Glen, keeping north of the river, and in 10 miles joins the track to Doire Ban and Craigag described in Route No. 3.

6. Ardgour to Strontian through the hills, 14 miles. Go south-west through Clovulin to Salachan, at which point the road is left for a track running along the south shore of Loch nan Gabhar (Loch of the Goat) and up Glen Gour. Just north of the mountain Sgurr mhic Eacharna the Gour is crossed to its northern bank, and in another 2 miles the track fades out. Climbing west by north for half a mile a small lochan is reached, from which flows the Strontian River. By following the course of the latter down to lower ground and crossing to its western bank at a point 3 miles from the lochan, it is possible to reach the head of a track leading down to the village of Strontian, on Loch Sunart.

Ascent of Ben Resipol (2774 feet)

From Salen: 6 miles.—By Strontian road to Resipol Farm, thence by path along west side of Allt Mhic Chiarain and along north side of stream (no path) up to its source in

Lochan Bac an Lochain, 1893 feet. Thence to the summit is a climb of 881 feet. The view from the summit is very fine, Morvern, Ardnamurchan, Loch Shiel and Moidart, Loch Sunart and the Sound of Mull, the Hebrides and the western sea all being visible.

CHAPTER III

MOIDART, ARISAIG AND MORAR

MAPS.—*O.S. Popular Edition, 1 inch, sheets 35 and 46.
Bartholomew's Half Inch, sheet 50.*

BETWEEN Loch Shiel and the Sound of Arisaig is the district
of Moidart, separated from Ardnamurchan by the River
Shiel. Except for a small portion south of Loch Moidart
it is a land of mountains, penetrated by the sea-lochs of
Moidart and Ailort, and looking westward to the Hebrides
and the Atlantic. Along its northern boundary runs the
road to Morar and Mallaig, in the south a short road
connects Kinlochmoidart with Shiel Bridge; with these
exceptions it is a roadless district, given up to deer and
grouse. Two glens give access to the mountains, Glen
Moidart running east and north from the head of Loch
Moidart, and Glen Aladale north from the middle reach of
Loch Shiel. The mountains are higher than those of
Morvern or Ardnamurchan; they extend south-west and
west from the head of Loch Shiel in two diverging ranges.
Fros Bheinn (Roshven) in the range south of Loch Ailort,
attains a height of 2887 feet: the two sister peaks of Ben
Odhar Mhor and Ben Odhar Bheag rise from the north-
western shore of Loch Shiel to heights of 2853 and 2895 feet
respectively.

To the north of Moidart lies the sea-washed district of
Arisaig, which stretches from Loch Ailort to Loch nan
Cilltean. It is a place of low hills and wooded shores, of
wide sea-lochs and sandy bays looking across the sea to
the islands of Eigg and Rhum and the jagged peaks of
Skye. The peninsula of Ardnish, projecting into the Sound

of Arisaig, separates Loch Ailort from the wider Loch nan Uamh (Loch of the Caves), which is divided from Loch nan Cilltean by the long promontory on which is the pier of Arisaig. Through the district runs the road to Morar, and the railway from Fort William, both passing through some of the most beautiful scenery in the Highlands.

Morar stands at the foot of the fresh-water Loch Morar, which has given its name to the district. North Morar is the long peninsula between Loch Nevis and Loch Morar; it contains the fishing port and railway terminus of Mallaig. South Morar lies between Loch Morar and the district of Arisaig; it is a mountainous strip of land containing the secluded Loch Beoraid and the beautiful islet-studded Loch Eilt. Both districts are rugged and broken, with a strip of low ground along the western coast, where are the sands of Morar, famous for their dazzling whiteness Loch Morar, with its maximum depth of 1080 feet, is the deepest lake in Britain: it is connected with the sea by the short and rapid River Morar. A new hydro-electric scheme, completed late in 1948, utilises Loch Morar as its reservoir, the water level having been raised three feet by a weir. The power station is excavated out of a mass of rock rising above the south bank of the River Morar, so that little more than the doorway is seen. The water returns to the river below the main fall. A fish-pass has been provided.

Moidart, Arisaig and Morar were territories of the Macdonalds of Clanranald; Castle Tioram, on an islet in Loch Moidart, was the stronghold of their chiefs. Built in the fourteenth century, it had seen many wars and sieges when it was burnt in 1715 by Red Alan, the Clanranald of that day. He was about to join the rising which ended at Sheriffmuir, where he fell, and feared that in his absence the castle might be taken and garrisoned by the Campbells. The Clanranald chiefs came of a warlike stock, and had no lack of foes: all through the centuries there was fighting in Moidart or beyond its bounds. Frasers, Macintoshes and Macleans in turn felt the Macdonald broadswords, Mackay of Strathnaver and Macleod of

Dunvegan lay in the dungeons of Castle Tioram, the proud Earl of Atholl and MacCailean Mor himself recoiled from its walls in despair, and Huntly felt the Queen Mother's wrath after his failure to take the castle at her command. Once only, by a clever stratagem, did the Campbells take Castle Tioram, but its capture brought them little good. Clanranald speedily retook his own fortress from his ancient foes, and slew all the remaining defenders.

At the Battle of the Shirts, in 1544, when the Frasers were almost exterminated by Camerons and Macdonalds, the clan was led by John of Moidart. He was chief for fifty-four years, defied the whole power of Scotland during his long life, and died quietly in his bed. Another Clanranald was with Montrose at Inverlochy, and Red Alan fell at Sheriffmuir in the 'Fifteen. The clan was out in the 'Forty Five under young Clanranald, and it was at Borrodale House that Prince Charles stayed after his landing in Loch nan Uamh in August 1745. From there he went to Kinlochmoidart and Dalilea, and sailed up Loch Shiel to Glenfinnan, where, on 19th August, the Royal Standard was unfurled by the aged Marquis of Tullibardine. After the disaster of Culloden, the Prince was for some time in hiding in Moidart, and it was from Loch nan Uamh that he sailed for Roscoff on 20th September 1746.

After Culloden came the still-remembered " Year of the Great Wasting," when Moidart was ravaged by the Government troops, and the inhabitants treated with great barbarity. The glens at that time were thick with houses and crofts, where now hardly a house is to be seen. It was the Government policy to break down the clan system, and to destroy the ties which bound the clansmen to their chiefs. This policy was successful, but at a terrible cost to Scotland. The chiefs became landlords, their clansmen tenants. Then came the era of the great sheep-farms, and the crofters had to make way for flocks of sheep, which brought in greater profits for the landlord. This meant emigration for the displaced, or migration to the growing towns of the south, so that to-day in the glens around Loch

PLATE I   THE GLENFINNAN HILLS

View over Loch

e Gluibsachan

Photograph by R. M. ADAM

Shiel the human habitations are few. Sheep have given place to deer and grouse, and shepherds to stalkers and gillies, but the glens are empty and the sheilings deserted. Principal Shairp tells the story in his well-known lines:—

" On the braes around Glenfinnan fast the human homes are thinning,
    And the wilderness is winning to itself those graves again;
    Name nor date here no man knoweth; o'er grey headstones heather
      groweth,
    Up Loch Shiel the sea-wind bloweth over sleep of nameless men."

In the narrows of Loch Shiel, on the little Eilean Fhianain, are the remains of the ancient church of St Finnan, one of the early Pictish missionaries. Close by, in the quiet graveyard, lie the old chiefs of Clanranald with their clansmen around them. Above them rises a tall grey cross of stone, for the holy isle of Loch Shiel is still used as a burying-place. Across the water to the south towers Ben Resipol, fit guardian of the last sleep of the Clanranalds.

ACCOMMODATION

Hotels at Glenfinnan, Acharacle, Loch, Ailort, Arisaig, Morar and Mallaig. Other accommodation in private houses at Shiel Bridge, Arisaig and Mallaig.

COMMUNICATIONS

Railway.—L.N.E.R. from Fort William to Mallaig. Stations at Glenfinnan, Loch Ailort, Arisaig and Morar.

Steamers.—1. From Glenfinnan down Loch Shiel to Dalilea and Acharacle (for Shiel Bridge and Kinloch-moidart) once daily in connection with train from Mallaig.

2. From Mallaig to Kyle of Lochalsh, Broadford, Applecross, Portree and Stornoway daily, and to Armadale and Glenelg once a week.

3. From Mallaig to Eigg, Rhum and the Outer Hebrides twice a week.

4. Motor launch from Mallaig to Inverie and head of Loch Nevis on certain days.

5. Motor launch to Armadale daily in summer.

WALKS BY ROAD AND HILL-TRACK

Although recently widened and improved in surface, the road from Banavie and Glenfinnan to Mallaig has not been spoiled for the pedestrian and cyclist, and should certainly be traversed from Glenfinnan to Mallaig. Winding as it does by gorge and pass and wooded defile, now beside a rushing burn amid birches and bracken, now by Loch Eilt or the sandy bays of Arisaig and Morar, now high above lovely Loch Ailort and Loch nan Uamh, there is beauty in each of the 27 miles which separate Mallaig from Glenfinnan.

1. Leaving Glenfinnan the road crosses the railway, ascends to the low watershed between Loch Shiel and Loch Eilt, and skirts the northern shore of the latter, the railway following the south shore. Beyond the loch, road and rail descend together to Loch Ailort Station, overlooking the head of that loch. Thence the road turns inland for 3 miles, to emerge on the shore of Loch nan Uamh, with glorious views to seaward. Here it turns abruptly up Glen Beasdale, diving beneath the railway line, and swings once more westward past the private station of Beasdale, and through the woods to Arisaig, where a branch road leads round the southern shore of Loch nan Cilltean to the pier opposite the Island of Eigg. Beyond Arisaig road and railway part for some miles, the former making for the coast and keeping by the shore, until it swings east and south to round the bay of Morar. Crossing the Morar River immediately south of Morar Station, the road goes east under the railway, passes the hotel and recrosses the line, then goes northwards to Glasnacardoch Bay and on to Mallaig.

Notes.—(1) The island of Eigg, which is so prominent in the offing from the Arisaig coast, can easily be visited from Mallaig. The Outer Islands steamer calls at regular intervals, and launches can be hired to take a party over. The grand basaltic cliffs of the Scuir, the cave where the Macdonalds were suffocated by the Macleods, and the ancient chapel of Kildonnan are worthy of a visit. Accommodation might be obtained if required, but there is now no inn on the island. Eigg was the scene of the martyrdom, in 617, of the Pictish missionary, St Donnan the Great. He was a contemporary of Columba who, however, refused to welcome him when he paid a visit to Iona on his way to Eigg. He and his followers were murdered by the inhabitants at the instigation of the Queen of Moidart, who was averse to having her herdsmen in the island converted from heathendom.

(2) The large and mountainous island of Rhum, which lies north-west of Eigg, is rarely visited by strangers, though possessing in its glens and splintered peaks some of the finest rambling ground in Britain. It was for many years strictly forbidden to land upon the island, and no accommodation was to be had for visitors. The same steamer which serves Eigg also calls at Rhum, and if landing is permitted it should be possible for camping trampers to spend some days among the glens and on the peaks. Loch Scresort, with pier and post-office, is on the eastern side of the island, and is connected by road with Kilmory on the north coast. The highest peaks are in the south and west of the island; they are exceedingly rocky and should afford good climbing. The western coast is ringed by high cliffs, except where two wide glens debouch on the shore. Halleval, Haskivall, Ashvall and Sgor nan Gillean are the chief southern mountains, with heights ranging from 2363 to 2659 feet; Orval in the west rises to a height of 1869 feet.

2. Shiel Bridge to Lochailort, by the coast, 16½ miles. This is, in fine weather, one of the finest sea-coast walks in the Highlands, the route lying between the mountains and the sea, with wonderful views of the Hebrides. The islands and wooded shores of Loch Moidart are very lovely on a calm day, when their reflections in the glassy water resemble those of an inland lake.

Cross the River Shiel by New Shiel Bridge and go north by road to the path which leads northwards along the Blain Burn and over the hill to Port a Bhata on Loch Moidart. From this point a boat is necessary to carry the walker across the South Channel to the island of Shona Beag, which is crossed to its north side. If the tide is low cross by the ford through the North Channel to the foot of Glen Uig, which is muddy but safe. If the tide is not suitable it is best to cross Loch Moidart by boat from Port a Bhata, or to make a detour on foot round the head of Loch Moidart, which will add 5 miles to the length of the walk. From the foot of Glen Uig the route is north over the low pass and down to the Sound of Arisaig, thence east along the coast to the mouth of Loch Ailort. The sea views from this part of the walk are exceedingly fine, embracing the islands of Rhum, Eigg and Muck and the opposite shores of Arisaig. The track continues along the south shore of Loch Ailort below the slopes of Roshven, climbs over the Beallach Breac to the head of the loch, crosses the Ailort River and reaches the main road close to the hotel and station of Lochailort.

Note.—An alternative route, which permits of a visit to Castle Tioram on its island in Loch Moidart, is to take the road from Shiel Bridge to Dorlin pier, where a boat to the castle should be obtained. After visiting the castle, go on by boat to Shona Beag, as already described. When the tide is high, it may be possible to cross by boat to the north shore of Loch Moidart, passing the islet of Riska and rounding Shona Beag, thus avoiding the long walk round the head of the loch.

3. Shiel Bridge to Loch Ailort, through the hills, 14 miles. By road east, and then north past Ardmolich to Kinlochmoidart, thence up Glenmoidart to Glenmoidart House, and on by a track to Assary at the head of the glen. Here the path ends, but the way is plain, going due north to the pass east of Roshven, called the Beallach an Fhiona, and down into Coire a Bhuiridh on the north side. Follow the Allt a Bhuiridh right down to Glen Shian House, from whence a road leads to Lochailort Hotel and Station.

4. Lochailort to Morar, by north side of Loch Morar, 13 miles. Go east for a mile and a half along the Glenfinnan road, and take a path which goes under the railway and strikes north-east towards the hills. After climbing to 1000 feet, it descends past the foot of Loch Beoraid into the glen of the Meoble River, crosses the river, and joins a road which leads to Camus Luinge on the south shore of Loch Morar. Here a boat must be obtained to cross the loch to Swordland on the north shore, from which point there is a path along the loch to Morar Station and Hotel. If no boat can be had, it is better to return to Lochailort, since there is no path along the southern shore of Loch Morar.

Note.—By crossing the peninsula from Swordland to Kylesmorar on Loch Nevis, it may be possible to get a boat across the latter to Kylesknoydart on the northern shore. From Kylesknoydart a good path leads

north-west along the coast to Inverie, where there is a temperance hotel
It is worth remembering that a launch service from Mallaig serves
Kylesknoydart on certain days in the summer months.

5. **Glenfinnan to Strathan and Kinlocharkaig, 9 miles.**
By path from Glenfinnan northwards under the viaduct
and up the western side of the glen to Corryhully. Continue
north-east and climb to the pass between Sgurr Thuilm
and Streap, descending into Glen a Chaoruinn by the
right bank of the stream. Cross the River Pean just below
its junction with the Allt a Chaoruinn and continue to
Strathan sheep farm, where there is a bridge over the
Dessary River. Kinlocharkaig is a mile to the south-east,
close to the head of the loch.

Note.—Strathan lies at a junction of several glens, and is the starting
point for a number of hill walks. Those to Kinlocheil and along Loch
Arkaig to Gairlochy are described in Route No. 4 of the Lochaber and
Locheil section, and those by Glen Dessary to Loch Nevis and by Glen
Kingie to Tomdoun in Routes Nos. 1 and 5 of the Knoydart section.
Another route goes along Glen Pean to Oban at the head of Loch
Morar. This track is very apt to be wet and boggy, and is not to be
recommended. If a through route to the head of Loch Morar is desired,
it is better to ascend Glen Dessary for 4 miles, and climb through the
pass which conducts to Kinlochmorar by way of the Glen an Lochan
Gaineamhaich. This route involves more climbing, but passes through
far finer scenery.

Ascent of Fros Bheinn (Roshven), 2887 feet

From Lochailort.—Cross the Ailort River below the hotel,
and proceed east past Glenshian House and along the
stream. Thence follow the course of the Allt a Bhuiridh
south into the corrie and ascend the pass to the east of
Roshven. This is the route described in reverse in Route
No. 3 above. From the summit of the pass, 2346 feet, climb
up a stony slope to the east summit of the mountain, 2887
feet, from which to the west top is a walk of nearly half a
mile over grass. The views obtained from Roshven are
perhaps the finest to be seen in this part of the Highlands,
extending north over the rugged hills of Morar and Knoydart to the peaks of Skye, and west to the Hebrides. The

return to Lochailort may be made as on the outward climb, or by way of Alisary. For the latter route proceed westwards from the west top of Roshven and make for the lower part of Coire na Cnamha, from whence Alisary on the shore of Loch Ailort is easily reached. From Alisary to the hotel at Lochailort is about 3 miles by path and road along the south-east shore of the loch.

CHAPTER IV

Knoydart, Glengarry and Glenelg

Maps.—*O.S. Popular Edition*, 1 inch, sheets 35 and 41.
Bartholomew's Half Inch, sheets 50 and 54.

North of Morar is Knoydart of the Goats, a wild and rugged region lying between Loch Nevis and Loch Hourn. It is a roadless land of lofty mountains, penetrated by the great sea-lochs of Hourn and Nevis, and traversed only by mountain tracks. This was the innermost fastness of the region known as the Rough Bounds, which extends from Moidart to Glenelg, a land where the Scottish king's writ did not run, and where the sword was mightier than the pen.

Communicating with the western seas through the outlets of Loch Nevis and Loch Hourn, Knoydart is cut off from the east by high mountains, traversed by narrow passes. From the head of Loch Nevis the pass of Mam Clach Ard leads over to Glen Dessary and Loch Arkaig; Kinlochhourn is joined by a steep and winding road to Glen Quoich and Glengarry. Two tracks lead from Barrisdale Bay, on Loch Hourn, to Kinlochquoich, and four tracks go north from Lochhournhead to Glen Shiel and Glenelg.

Loch Nevis, like its neighbour Loch Hourn, consists of a wide outer reach opening into the Sound of Sleat, and communicating by a narrow channel with a land-locked inner fiord. Lofty mountains rise steeply from the shores of Loch Hourn, but stand back somewhat from the beaches of the more open Loch Nevis. Each loch is about 12 miles long, and is really a drowned river valley, submerged by the sinking of the western sea-board.

The highest mountains in Knoydart cluster at the head of Loch Nevis, and in the peninsula south of Loch Hourn. Sgor na Ciche, a shapely pointed peak of 3410 feet, is the finest of the former group; its sharp summit is prominent in the eastward view from the narrows of Loch Nevis. Ladhar Bheinn and Luinne Bheinn stand further west; the former rises from the southern shore of Loch Hourn to a height of 3343 feet, and looks across the loch to Sgriol in Glenelg.

The district of Glenelg occupies the greater part of the peninsula between Loch Hourn and Loch Alsh, and is bounded on the west by the narrow waters of the Sound of Sleat and the strait of Kyle Rhea. A range of mountains separates Glenelg from Glen Shiel and Loch Duich, and over this, by the pass of Mam Ratagan, climbs the road from Fort Augustus and Glen Shiel to the bay of Glenelg, and the old ferry to Skye. Two long glens open on to the bay, that of Glen More, which carries the road, and narrow, bracken-clad, tree-shaded Glen Beg, with its Pictish towers and brawling river. Another road climbs over the western flanks of the Sgriol range, and leads to the clachans of Arnisdale and Corran, on the north shore of Loch Hourn.

From the head of Loch Hourn a steep track joins the road which leads through the hills to Loch Quoich, lying as in a cup within its ring of mountains. From this loch flows the river Garry, which flows eastwards down the 17 miles of Glengarry, and falls into Loch Oich near Invergarry Castle. On its way it passes through beautiful, wooded Loch Garry, with its silver birches. The slopes of the glen were once thickly wooded, but all this country-side was stripped during the 1914-18 War, and now, except along the shores of Loch Garry, the woods are gone. Southward beyond the loch rises Ben Tee and the mountains of the Glengarry Forest; northward, beyond a line of lower hills, is the wide, swampy valley of Glen Loyne, which opens north-eastward into Glen Moriston.

Knoydart and Glengarry were the home of the Macdonnells of Glengarry, a branch of the once mighty Clan Donald. Their chief dwelt at Invergarry Castle, on Loch Oich; his clansmen peopled the now empty glens, and his galleys rode in Loch Hourn. At one time the Macdonnells also held Dundonnell, in Ross-shire, Lochalsh, and Lochcarron, with the strong castle of Strome, but before the end of the sixteenth century these districts fell into the possession of the Mackenzies of Kintail. Between Glengarry and Kintail raged a long and bitter feud, marked by many black deeds, and culminating in the terrible Raid of Killychrist, when a church near Beauly with its Mackenzie congregation is said to have been burnt by a Macdonnell raiding party. The chief of Glengarry was old and feeble at the time; his only son had been slain in an ambush at Kyle Rhea when returning from an attack on the lost lands of Lochcarron. It was to avenge his death that the Macdonnells, under the leadership of Allan of Lundie, crossed the hills to Beauly and carried the war into the enemy's country.

Another chief of Glengarry, when threatened by the machinations of Kenneth Mackenzie of Kintail, disguised himself as Macleod of Dunvegan and attended a meeting of his foes in the hostile castle of Eileandonan. At a favourable moment he disclosed his identity, and compelled Kintail, on pain of death, to abandon his plotting against Glengarry and his clan. The fifteenth chief of Glengarry was a friend of Sir Walter Scott, and is said to have been the prototype of Fergus MacIver. He was the last of the chiefs to maintain the old ways of Highland life, going about with his " tail " of gillies and henchmen, fighting and killing his man in a duel, and causing great alarm by appearing at the coronation of King George the Fourth in full Highland dress, including pistols. He was killed in 1828 at Inverscaddle by leaping from a stranded steamer.

Glenelg was included in the territories of the Macleods of Harris, whose chiefs still hold Dunvegan Castle, in Skye. It was thus somewhat of a buffer state between Kintail and

Knoydart, and formed, through the ferry to Skye, an important link between North-west and Central Highlands. Bernera Barracks, now in ruins, were built after the 'Fifteen to control the ferry and provide a garrison to police this district. It was by the route through Glen Shiel and Glenelg that Boswell and Johnson entered Skye on their tour to the Hebrides, a route which was used, in the opposite direction, by the droves of Skye cattle going south to the annual markets at Crieff and Falkirk.

COMMUNICATIONS

Railway.—1. Train from Edinburgh and Glasgow and Fort William to Mallaig, thence by motor launch to Inverie.

2. Train from Edinburgh and Glasgow to Spean Bridge. Thence by motor-bus to Invergarry village, Tomdoun and Kinlochquoich.

Steamer.—1. Mallaig to Glenelg on certain days of the week.

2. Kyle of Lochalsh to Glenelg on certain days.

Motor Launch.—1. Mallaig to Inverie and Upper Loch Nevis.

2. Glenelg to Loch Hourn, by arrangement at hotel.

3. A motor launch can also be obtained sometimes at Arnisdale, Loch Hourn.

Road Services.—1. Fort William to Invergarry, thence motor-bus to Tomdoun and Kinlochquoich.

2. Inverness to Invergarry, thence motor-bus to Tomdoun and Kinlochquoich.

ACCOMMODATION

Hotels at Glenelg, Tomdoun and Invergarry. Other accommodation at Inverie (Loch Nevis), Arnisdale and Corran (Loch Hourn), and possibly at Kinlochquoich.

YOUTH HOSTELS

1. Glenelg. House at Bernera, 2 miles north-west of Glenelg.

2. Ratagan. On the west shore of Loch Duich.

Walks and Tramps

(a) *By Road*

1. The road up Glengarry from Invergarry to Tomdoun and Kinlochhourn is very picturesque, and Loch Quoich in particular should be visited by every stranger. To enjoy the scenery to the full it is perhaps wise to reach Tomdoun by bus, or car, or cycle, and to walk thence by way of Loch Quoich to Kinlochhourn. Leaving Invergarry village the road passes through woods to the lower end of Loch Garry, thence along the northern shore of the loch and along a wide green glen as far as Tomdoun Hotel. Just beyond the hotel a branch road goes north to Glen Loyne, and thence to Cluanie and Glen Shiel. The main road continues westward up Glengarry, passing the river-loch Poulary, and in 6 miles reaches Loch Quoich. This loch lies in a frame of splendid mountains and is about 6 miles long. It was in the Loch Quoich district that Landseer painted many of his Highland pictures. Half-way along the northern shore is Quoich Bridge, where a road goes off along the shore to Kinlochquoich. The Loch Hourn road climbs north-west for 3 miles and then drops steeply to the lodge and woods of Kinlochhourn, which stands by the Hourn River at the head of the inlet of Loch Beg, the innermost reach of Loch Hourn.

2. A short length of road connects Inverie, on Loch Nevis, with Airor, on the Sound of Sleat, and is continued along the coast by a track to Loch Hourn. It is about 16 miles from Inverie to the cottage at Li where the track ends, and another 2 miles across the water to Arnisdale.

3. From Glenelg Hotel a good road leads east up Glen More to the summit of Mam Ratagan, whence it drops 1000 feet to the shore of Loch Duich by a series of zigzags. This road commands fine views of Sgriol and of the mountains of Kintail; it leads by way of Shiel Bridge to Dornie Ferry in the west, or Cluanie and Glenmoriston and Tomdoun in the east.

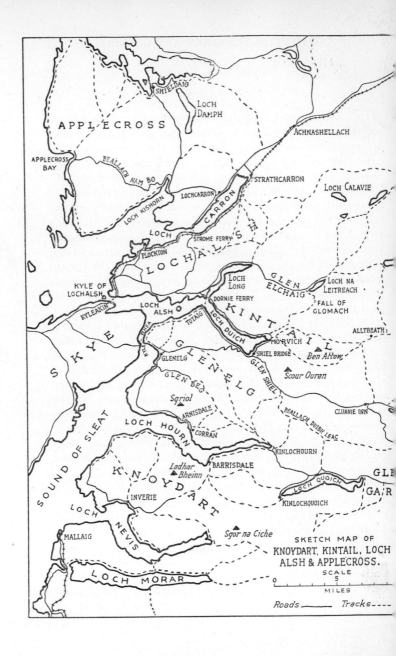

SKETCH MAP OF
KNOYDART, KINTAIL, LOCH
ALSH & APPLECROSS.

SCALE

0   5

MILES

Roads ———   Tracks ----

4. Another road from Glenelg follows the coast to the entrance of Glen Beg, crosses the river near Eileanreach House, and climbs round the seaward flank of the mountains to Outer Loch Hourn. By this route the distance to Arnisdale is 10 miles, and to Corran 11. The views across to Skye and over to Knoydart are very fine. There is also a mountain track starting near Eileanreach which keeps further inland at a higher level, and shortens the distance by some 2 miles.

(b) *By Hill-tracks*

1. Inverie to Strathan (Loch Arkaig) by the Mam Clach Ard, 16 miles. East by road from Inverie for 2 miles, then by a track which crosses the river, recrosses it, and leads up Glen Meadail toward the high pass at its head. Crossing this at a height of 1800 feet, the track descends to Carnach, with the splendid mountain Sgor na Ciche towering up across the glen to the east, and skirts the shallows at the head of Loch Nevis as far as Finiskaig. Thence it goes east through the mountains, climbing by the pass of Man na Cloich 'Airde (Mam Clach Ard), beside the mile-long Lochan a' Mhaim, and over the summit at 1000 feet. A gradual descent into Glen Dessary follows, and at Upper Glen Dessary a road is joined which leads in $2\frac{1}{2}$ miles to Strathan at the head of Loch Arkaig. The routes from Strathan to Gairlochy, to Kinlocheil, and to Glenfinnan, have already been described in Chapters I and III.

2. Inverie to Kinlochhourn and Arnisdale, 23 miles. East from Inverie by the road leading up Glen Dubh Lochan, which becomes a hill-track just beyond the lochan. Then it climbs north-east over Mam Barrisdale (1500 feet), drops steeply down a wooded gorge to Glen Barrisdale, crosses the Barrisdale River by a ford, and reaches Loch Hourn at Barrisdale Bay. From this point the track follows the south shore of Inner Loch Hourn, past the strait of Caolas Mor, to Runival and Skiary, and on to Kinlochhourn. Leave the road to Loch Quoich just before reaching a gate, and turn north across the River Hourn,

following it down to its mouth. Thence the track to Arnisdale leads north-west through a wood, crosses the Allt a Choire Reidh, and climbs round the eastern end of a long ridge ending in Carn na Caorach. Losing sight of Loch Hourn the track then descends into Glen Dubh Lochain through the woods, and leads west along the Arnisdale River to the clachan of Arnisdale on Outer Loch Hourn. (A branch track crosses the river immediately to the west of the Dubh Lochan, and leads down the south bank of the river to Corran.) Arnisdale stands on the shore of a bay at the southern base of the mountain Sgriol (Screel), and from the village a high pass leads over into Glen Beg.

3. Inverie to Kinlochquoich, by Glen Cosaidh, 18 miles. Follow Route No. 2 as far as the ford over the Barrisdale River, cross the ford, and turn back up Glen Barrisdale by a track on the right bank of the stream. Continue north-east up the glen, following the burn east and south-east to its source in the small Loch an Lagain Aintheich. Thence the track descends into Glen Cosaidh, follows the north bank of the Cosaidh River for a mile, fords it at a point one mile north of Kinlochquoich, and joins the road from Quoich Bridge at the bridge over the Gairawan River, beyond which is Kinlochquoich.

4. Inverie to Kinlochquoich, by Lochan nam Breac, 16 miles. Proceed as in Routes Nos. 2 and 3 to a point about half a mile south of the ford over the Barrisdale River, where a track comes in from the south. Take this track, crossing the stream by a bridge, and keep on through the woods up Glen Undalain, making for the high pass (2000 feet) between Luinne Bheinn to the west and Sgurr a Choirebeithe to the east. Beyond the pass the track descends to 1250 feet, and follows the southern slopes of Druim Cosaidh to Lochan nam Breac. This is a wild, rock-bound tarn lying in a gorge at the foot of Ben Aden. From its eastern end the track goes east along the hill-slopes, joining the Glen Cosaidh route at the bridge north of Kinlochquoich.

Note.—An alternative route crosses the stream at the east end of Lochan nam Breac, and proceeds to Kinlochquoich along the south side of the glen. This track fords the Allt Coire nan Gall and crosses the Allt a Choire Reidh by a bridge, from the far side of which a road leads in about a mile to Kinlochquoich.

5. Inverie to Inverguseran by Mam Uidhe, 6 miles. This is a short hill walk to Inverguseran, on the Sound of Sleat, which can be continued along the coast to Li, by the track mentioned in Road Route No. 2. Or Inverie can be regained by turning south at Inverguseran along the track to Airor, and thence by road. Leave Inverie by a track which skirts the woods and goes north along the Allt a Mhuillin, crossing the low pass of Mam Uidhe, and descending in a north-westerly direction to the Amhuinn Inbhir Ghuiserein. At a point about 3 miles from Inverie the river is crossed, the track continuing along the eastern bank down to Inverguseran at its mouth.

Note.—If, instead of keeping west to Inverguseran, one goes north east from Mam Uidhe along a diverging track and east by the south side of Glen Guseran, it is possible to reach Li by a track through the hills. This track turns north up the glen of the Amhainn Bheag and climbs to the pass of Mam Li, coming to an end at a height of 1250 feet. Keep straight on to the summit at 1500 feet, where is the lochan which feeds the Amhainn Bheag, and go east to strike the head-waters of the Allt Li, which will serve as a guide down the mountain side to the cottages of Li. The descent is rather steep, but is not at all dangerous. The distance by this route from Inverie to Li is about 8 miles.

6. Tomdoun Hotel to Strathan, by Glen Kingie, 17 miles. By road west up Glengarry to Ban Ath at the foot of Loch Quoich, where a bridge leads south across the Garry River. Take the track leading south to the Kingie River, and along its north bank to Lochan. A mile further on the track forks, one branch continuing west and the other making for a ford over the Kingie River. Cross the ford and keep on along the south bank for 2 miles to Kinbreack, at the foot of a narrow glen. Climb south up this glen and over the pass (1500 feet) between Fraoch Bheinn and Sgurr Mhurlagain, and on down the Dearg Allt (Red Burn) to Strathan.

Note.—This Glen Kingie path is often very wet, and the ford west of Lochan may be difficult to cross. In that case take the right fork and go west along the base of the 3015-foot mountain Gairich, cross the Allt a Choire Ghlais and go south to Kinbreack, crossing the Kingie River by the bridge.

7. Quoich Bridge to Cluanie, by Easter Glen Quoich, 13 miles. By path up the west bank of the River Quoich to Alltbeithe, then east along the Easter Glen Quoich Burn, with the slopes of Meall Cheann Dearg above on the north, and across the Allt Glac a Chuillin to the head of Glen Loyne. Continue along the left bank of the River Loyne and round the lower slopes of Creag Leathais to join the Tomdoun-Cluanie road east of Creag a Mhaim. North along the road over Mam Cluanie and down the long descent to Cluanie is another 4 miles. If the weather be clear a magnificent view to the north is obtained from Mam Cluanie, the grand peak of Sgurr nan Ceathreamhnan (Ceranan) in particular towering up beyond the head of Glen Affric.

8. Quoich Bridge to Shiel Bridge, by the Beallach Duibh Leac, 13 miles. By path up the west bank of the River Quoich to Alltbeithe, then north-west along the Wester Glen Quoich Burn, and over the Beallach Duibh Leac (Pass of the Black Stones), between Sgurr a' Bhac Chaolais and Creag nan Damh, down the glen of the Allt Mhalagain into Glen Shiel. This track leads through the high mountains which hem in Glen Shiel on the south, and is continued by the road down the glen at the foot of the peaks known as the Five Sisters of Kintail. Shiel Bridge is 4 miles north along the glen and Morvich 2 miles further on.

Note.—The above route can be joined from Kinlochhourn by going north up the track along Coire Sgoir adail. This was the route taken by Prince Charles Edward to reach Glen Shiel from Loch Hourn when hunted by King George's troops in July, 1746.

9. Kinlochhourn to Shiel Bridge, by the Beallach Coire Mhalagain, 12 miles. Cross the Hourn River and go north-west as if proceeding to Arnisdale (Route No. 2). At $1\frac{1}{2}$

PLATE II LADHAR BHEINN, KNOYDART, AND LOCH HOURN

Potograph by R. M. ADAM

miles from Kinlochhourn the track diverges to the north,
and in another mile forks again to the right, crosses the Allt
a Choire Reidh, and follows the lower slopes of Sgurr na
Sgine as far as the Allt Coire Mhalagain, where it ceases.
Follow that stream up to its head, and cross the Beallach
Coire Mhalagain (2300 feet) between the saddle and Sgurr
na Sgine. Then, by going north by east for a little over a
mile, one may reach a stalker's path which leads by a series
of zigzags down into Glen Shiel. Shiel Bridge is 3½ miles
north along the road.

10. Kinlochhourn to Glenelg, by Glen More, 15 miles.
Follow the previous route (No. 9) for 2½ miles, then diverge
to the west to cross the Allt a Choire Reidh, and climb
steadily to the pass between Druim na Firean and Sgurr
Leac nan Each. Go over this to the Beallach a' Chasain
and descend to the head-waters of the Glen More River,
following its right bank to the cottage known as Bealla-
chasan, where a road begins. Continue by this road
down into Glen More, joining the Ratagan-Glenelg road
at a point 3 miles east of the Glenelg Hotel. The road
continues west to the disused Kyle Rhea ferry, the branch
to Glenelg turning off to the left just before passing a church.

11. Arnisdale to Glenelg, by Glen Beg, 13 miles. East
along the north bank of the Arnisdale River, turning north
upon the glen of the Allt Utha, and north-east through
Coire Chorsalain to the junction with a track coming up
from Kinlochhourn. Turn left into this track and cross the
pass over into Glen Aoidhalain, below the shoulder of Ben
nan Caorach. Continue north down the glen to the head
of Glen Beg, turning east to cross the river, and then west
past the farm of Balvraid down to Eilanreach, where the
road turns north along the shore to Glenelg. Two miles
before reaching Eilanreach we pass the remains of two
brochs, or Pictish towers, standing one above and the other
below the road. They are believed to have been erected
by the Pictish inhabitants of the Western Highlands as
places of refuge in the time of the Viking raids.

12. Kyle Rhea to Totaig, by the coast, 7 miles. This is

a sea-board path which enjoys fine views of Kyle Rhea, Loch Alsh, and the mouth of Loch Duich. It begins at the old ferry-house on the east side of the strait of Kyle Rhea, and continues along the coast to Totaig, at the entrance to Loch Duich. Three-quarters of a mile short of Totaig are the remains of a broch, or Pictish tower, standing by the edge of a wood. It is not so high as those in Glenelg, but gives a good idea of the internal arrangements of these towers of refuge. From Totaig there is a ferry to Ardelve, opposite Dornie.

Note.—By taking a track which goes north from the road close beside the church of Glenelg it is possible to reach Totaig in shorter time through the hills.

Ascent of Ladhar Bheinn (Larven)

From Inverie go north by the Mam Uidhe and east up Glen Guseran to Folach, whence the southern slopes of An Diollaid should be climbed. By following the ridge to the south-east the summit of Ladhar Bheinn is easily reached.

CHAPTER V

Glen Moriston, Cluanie and Kintail

Maps.—*O.S. Popular Edition, 1 inch, sheets 36, 41 and 42.
Bartholomew's Half Inch, sheets 50, 51, 54 and 55.*

WESTWARD from Loch Ness runs Glen Moriston, the " Long Glen of the Grants." Narrow and wooded at Invermoriston, where the rushing River Moriston foams through a rocky channel to Loch Ness, its upper reaches are wide and level, with green meadows between the river and the hills. Lonely Loch Cluanie, where the river begins, is 19 miles from Loch Ness; Cluanie Inn is 6 miles further on the road to Glen Shiel. About Glen Cluanie the hills stand close; it is a high, bare glen of the watershed, joining Glen Moriston to Glen Shiel. At the cross-roads for Tomdoun and Glengarry stands the inn of Cluanie, now closed but at one time a hospitable oasis in a desert of dark mountains. Southward is the long range of rocky peaks which separates Knoydart from Glen Shiel and Glenelg; northward beyond a sea of rounded tops, is Glen Affric.

A hydro-electric scheme based on the catchment area of Glen Moriston is planned. Dams will be built near the outlet of Lochs Loyne and Cluanie, the combined waters being utilised at a power station to be built near Ceannacroc Bridge. Both lochs will be increased in area by several square miles. Two further dams with power stations will be constructed in Glen Moriston, one near Dundreggan and the other about two miles upstream from Invermoriston, the same water will thus be used several times. Two subsidiary stations will be built. The first will utilize the upper waters of the River Doe and the other, at

Livishie, will collect the waters of a number of streams which at present flow into Glen Moriston and Loch Ness.

Two and a half miles west of Cluanie is the water-parting, where the road begins its descent to the west coast through the narrow gorge of Upper Glen Shiel. At the foot of the gorge, where a bridge crosses the river, was fought in 1719 the action of Glen Shiel, in which a force of Highlanders and Spanish troops was defeated by the Hanoverian regiments of General Wightman. When the day was lost the Spaniards fled over the shoulder of Scour Ouran, and have left the name of the Spaniards' Corrie on the line of their flight. They were eventually captured taken to Edinburgh, and sent back to Spain. This was the occasion on which two English frigates penetrated to Loch Alsh and destroyed the castle of Eileandonan at the entrance to Loch Duich. It was also the last occasion on which hostile foreign troops landed in Scotland.

Lower Glen Shiel is a straight, level, river valley, walled in by lofty hills. The steep green slopes of the Kintail mountains rise along the eastern side: on the west are the rugged peaks of the Saddle and his mighty brethren. Below Shiel Bridge, at the head of Loch Duich, the river meets the tide; here the road divides into two, one going west to Glenelg or Totaig by the west shore of the loch, the other north to Morvich and Croe Bridge. Croe of Kintail is a wide green strath at the foot of lofty mountains; through it flows the Croe River to join an inlet of Loch Duich below the Bridge of Croe. This is the heart of Kintail (Ceann t' Sail = head of the salt water), the rugged mountainous region which extends to the east and north of Loch Duich.

Loch Duich is an offshoot of Loch Alsh, from which it extends south-east for 6 miles. At its mouth is the castle of Eileandonan on an island rock near Dornie; here also is the ferry to Totaig on the opposite shore of Loch Duich. A road runs from Totaig to Bridge of Shiel, keeping close to the sea all the way; from it goes off the Mam Ratagan road to Glenelg, with its hairpin-bends and splendid views.

The road from Dornie, on the other hand, climbs high above the loch and is steep and winding; it makes a long detour to cross Croe Bridge before turning west to Morvich and Glen Shiel.

The mountains of Kintail are part of the dorsal ridge of Scotland; from their eastern flanks flow the rivers which have carved out the long glens of Affric, Cannich, and Strathfarrar. Ben Fhada (Attow), the Long Mountain of Kintail, extends eastwards for 7 miles from Croe of Kintail, and is the source of the Affric River. South-west of it is the range of the Five Sisters, of which Sgurr Fhuaran (Scour Ouran) is chief, and to the north-east, on the border of Glen Affric, rises Sgurr nan Ceathreamhnan (Ceranan), the loftiest and most isolated summit of the district. Two wild passes lead through the mountains from Kintail to Glen Affric, that of the Beallach an Sgairne (Pass of Rumbling), north of Ben Fhada, and that of Glen Lichd and the Allt Granda, south of that mountain. North-west of Sgurr nan Ceathreamhnan, on a tributary of the Elchaig River, is the Fall of Glomach, where the river plunges 370 feet into a narrow gorge, and provides one of the most magnificent spectacles in these islands.

Glen Moriston was Grant country in the old clan days, the territory of the clan extending north into Glen Urquhart and over to Glen Affric. West of them in Glen Cluanie were the Glengarry Macdonnells, whose country extended to the head of Glen Shiel; they were often ill neighbours to the less aggressive Grants. It was in the mountains to the north of Glen Cluanie, in a cave called Tigh Mor na Seilg (Big Hunting House), that Prince Charles Edward was sheltered in 1746 by the Eight Men of Glen Moriston. In Glen Moriston, too, Roderick Mackenzie was murdered and his head sent to Cumberland as that of the Prince, whom he closely resembled. The road through Glen Moriston to Glen Shiel was constructed by English troops in the years 1770 and onwards: it was still unfinished when Dr Johnson and Boswell passed through in 1773 on their way to Glenelg.

Glen Shiel and Kintail are the homeland of the great Clan Mackenzie, whose war-cry, " Tulloch Ard," is taken from a mountain on the north shore of Loch Duich. The strong castle of Eileandonan was for centuries the centre of their power in the west; it was often besieged, but never taken until its demolition by English warships in 1719. The clan Macrae, from whose ranks were drawn some of the most loyal warriors of the Mackenzie chief, usually provided a constable for Eileandonan; these Macraes were famous archers, who did good work in Gairloch when that district was recovered from the Macleods. It was a Macrae who shot Donald Gorm from the ramparts of Eileandonan, when that chief, with a powerful fleet, was beseiging the castle in the sixteenth century. Though the garrison only counted two men at the time, the death of their leader caused the Macdonalds to raise the seige. In later centuries, when the Mackenzies had spread far and wide over Ross-shire, Kintail came to be the land of the Macraes. The present owner of Eileandonan, who resides in the restored castle, is the head of that clan.

Away back in the days of the Western Picts, Kintail must have been well populated; the brochs of Glenelg and that near Totaig, and the old fort on the shore near the clachan of Kintail were built by a numerous people to hold off the sea raiders from Norway. Here, in the seventh and eighth centuries, came the Pictish evangelists to found churches in the district. Eilean Donan was a site sanctified by St Donnan, the martyr of Eigg; Killilan, on Loch Long, was the church of St Fillan, whose mother Kentigerna has left traces of her ministry in Glen Shiel. Later still, in the eleventh century, came Dubthach, the saint of Tain, who gave his name to Loch Duich and to the ruined church which stands by its shores. In his journeys across Scotland to and from Tain he was accustomed to use the pass to the north of Ben Attow, known as the Beallach an Sgairne, which for this reason is sometimes called Cadha Dhubh-thaich (the Pass of Duthac).

The Kintail esate, covering approximately 15,000 acres,

and including Ben Attow and the Five Sisters, has been handed over to the National Trust for Scotland. Situated at the head of Loch Duich, it is bounded on the south by Glen Shiel and on the east mainly by the head waters of the Affric. The old lodge has been converted into an hotel.

Communications

Rail.—1. From Inverness to Kyle of Lochalsh, thence by motor-bus to Dornie Ferry and Glenshiel.

2. From Edinburgh and Glasgow to Spean Bridge, motor-bus to Fort Augustus, thence by private road vehicle to Invermoriston, Cluanie and Glenshiel.

Steamer.—1. From Mallaig to Kyle of Lochalsh daily, thence by motor-bus to Dornie Ferry and Glenshiel.

Road Services.—1. A mail motor runs both ways from Kyle of Lochalsh to Dornie Ferry and Glenshiel in connection with trains.

2. A mail motor runs between Glenmoriston Hotel and Cluanie, and can take a few passengers. It runs on week-days in the summer, and on Mondays, Wednesdays and Fridays in the winter.

Accommodation

Hotels at Fort Augustus, Invermoriston, Ardelve (Dornie Ferry) and Kintail Lodge. Other accommodation at Fort Augustus, Invermoriston, Shiel Bridge, Morvich, Inverinate, and Dornie. Youth Hostel at Ratagan on the west shore of Loch Duich.

Walks and Tramps
(a) *By Road*

The only road through this district is the one from Invermoriston to Cluanie and Glen Shiel, which continues in three branches to Dornie, Totaig and Glenelg. The eastern part of it, from Invermoriston to Cluanie is best traversed by the mail motor or other vehicle; it is rather too long a tramp on a high road for most walkers. From Cluanie down Glen Shiel to Shiel Bridge and Morvich is a delightful walk; the gorge of Glen Shiel with the rushing river far below, and the pointed peaks of the Saddle Range above one on the left make a picture long to be remembered. Lower Glen Shiel is also very fine; here it is the steep green slopes of the Five Sisters, rising from the eastern side of the glen, which catch the eye of the walker. Rising as they do direct from sea-level, these mountains appear to be even higher than their actual height; their sharp summits rise to 3505 feet in Scour Ouran, from which is to be had one of the finest views in the Highlands.

Even if not intending to go on to Glenelg, it is well worth while climbing the zigzags of the Mam Ratagan road as far as the summit, from which the view of Loch Duich and the Kintail mountains behind, and Sgriol, and Glen More in front, is exceedingly grand. The road to Dornie also enjoys fine views; it winds by Croe Bridge past the old church of Kintail and the clachan of Inverinate, climbs thence high above the loch, and descends by a long and winding hill to Dornie, lying at the junction of Loch Alsh and Loch Long, with Eileandonan Castle on its island rock close by. The walk by the west shore of Loch Duich to Totaig is level all the way; from it the Five Sisters are seen to great advantage.

(b) *By Hill-tracks*

The hill-tracks of this district are numerous and valuable; they give access to much of the finest scenery and take the walker through several of the wildest mountain passes in the Highlands. Most of them are rights of way, being the old routes used by the inhabitants when these glens were full of people; this is of great importance to the walker in these days of deer forests. Among the undoubted rights of way are the two passes from Glen Affric to Kintail, the hill-track from Cluanie to Alltbeath, and the track through the Beallach Dhuibh Leac from Kinlochhourn or Bridge of Quoich to Glen Shiel. The old military road from Fort Augustus to Torgyle Bridge, and its northward continuation past Loch Beinne Baine and east to Guisachan and Inver-cannich, was part of the drove road from Loch Carron to Fort Augustus and is still a right of way.

1. Fort Augustus to Cluanie, via Achlain, 21 miles. This route follows the line of the old military road across the hill into Glen Moriston. Leave Fort Augustus by the Invermoriston road, turning off westward a short distance after passing below the railway line. The track climbs west through the Inchnacardoch Forest, descends to cross the Allt Phocaichain by a sometimes difficult ford, and goes down through birch woods to join the Invermoriston-Cluanie road at Achlain. From here the route is west along the road, crossing the river at Ceannacroc Bridge, then along Loch Cluanie and past the ugly lodge at its western end, to Cluanie by the cross-roads.

Note.—From the Allt Phocaichain a branch track goes north to Torgyle Bridge, 3 miles east of Achlain. By leaving the road at the R.C. chapel at Toergyl and striking north across the hills by the east side of Loch na Beinne Baine, the walker can reach a rough road which goes north to the back of the woods above Guisachan House, and then bends north-east, eventually joining the Invercannich road at Tomich. This route forms an alternative to that described below under No. 2. It should be noted that the track between the road north of Torgyle Bridge and the north end of Loch na Beinne Baine is not marked in the Ordnance maps, but two direction posts have now been erected by the Scottish Rights of Way Society. The distance from Fort Augustus to Tomich by this route is 17 miles.

2. Cluanie to Tomich, by Ceannacroc Bridge and Glen Doe, 26 miles. East by the Invermoriston road along Loch Cluanie to Ceannacroc Bridge. Do not cross it, but take the road going north up the right bank of the River Doe. Follow this for 3 miles, at which point the track doubles back to ford the river and goes due north up into the hills. Climbing to 1650 feet the track crosses the pass west of Meallan Odhàr, and descends into the glen of the Allt Riabhach, which runs north-east towards Glen Affric. Follow the left bank of the stream downwards as far as a wood, beyond which a bridge crosses to the right bank. Cross this, and go on for a mile to Cougie, where there is

a bridge and the beginning of a road which goes through the woods past Guisachan House to Tomich, crossing the river three times and passing close to the Plodda Falls. There is an inn and other accommodation at Tomich.

3. Cluanie to Tomich by the Beallach Coire a Chait, 24 miles. East along the Invermoriston road for 2 miles to the head of Loch Cluanie, where a burn comes down from the north. This is the Allt Coire a Chait (Burn of the Cat's Corrie), which rises on the south side of the 2200-foot pass between the mountains A' Chralaig on the west and Sgurr nan Conbhairean (Peak of the Dog-men), on the east. Follow the burn to the head of the corrie (there is no marked path) and climb over into Glen na Ciche on the northern side of the pass. The descent is very steep, but a track is soon met which leads down the narrow steep-walled Glen na Ciche for 5 miles to its junction with Glen Affric at Athnamulloch. This is the name of a ford over the Affric River, where a band of Macleans from Mull were slain in bygone years. At a much later period a body of troops from Inverness, escorting the agents of the Commissioners for Forfeited Estates on their way to levy distress on the tenants of the exiled Earl of Seaforth, were attacked and routed by Mackenzies under Murchison, the Earl's factor.

Athnamulloch is close to the head of Loch Affric; a bridge now connects our track with that going west to Kintail and east by the north side of Loch Affric to Affric Lodge. A short length of road on the south side of the river leads to a jetty at the head of the loch, from which a track goes east by the south side of the latter, crosses the Allt Garbh by a bridge, and makes for Affric Lodge. Take this track as far as the bridge, turn south for a mile along the left bank of the Allt Garbh, and go east by a branch track which crosses the stream and climbs the hill-side beyond. In about 4 miles this path reaches Cougie, crosses a bridge, and joins the Allt Riabhach track described in Route No. 2. From Cougie to Tomich the route is through the woods of Guisachan.

4. Cluanie to Alltbeath through the hills, 8 miles. This is a right of way to Upper Glen Affric by the glen of Caorunn Mor, whose southern entrance opens from the road a mile east of Cluanie. Leave the road at this point and take the path along the east side of the glen, which continues over the pass (1400 feet) and down the Allt a Chomlain to the fords on the Affric River. Cross to the north bank and go east for half a mile to the keepers' houses at Alltbeath. At the south end of the glen the track is well marked, but in the middle and towards the north it may be difficult to trace. The view looking back from the pass is very extensive, as is that across Glen Affric to Sgurr nan Ceathreamhnan and Ben Attow from the northern exit. There are fine pools in the Allt a Caorunn Mor where a swim can be enjoyed in warm weather.

Note.— By going east for 3 miles from Alltbeath one can reach the bridge at Athnamulloch, whence Cluanie can be regained by way of Glen na Ciche and the Beallach Coire a'Chait (Route No. 3).

5. Cluanie to Bridge of Quoich by Easter Glen Quoich, 13 miles. This route is described in reverse under Route No. 7 of Chapter IV. The Tomdoun road should be left at the point where it turns east into Glen Loyne.

6. Shiel Bridge to Bridge of Quoich by the Beallach Duibh Leac, 13 miles.

7. Shiel Bridge to Kinlochhourn by the Beallach Coire Mhalagain, 12 miles. These two tracks are described in reverse under Routes No. 8 and 9 of Chapter IV.

8. Croe Bridge to Alltbeath and Affric Lodge, by Glen Lichd and the Allt Granda, 17½ miles. This is the more southern of the two routes from Kintail to Glen Affric. The path leaves the road a quarter of a mile south of Croe Bridge and goes east along the Croe River, turning off round the base of Sgurr na Moraich (Peak of the Sea-plain) into Glen Lichd. Then for 4 miles the river is followed up the level glen between Ben Attow and Scour Ouran, as far as the bridges near the house of Glenlicht. Here the track begins the steep and rugged ascent of the Allt

Granda, which rises along the flank of Ben Attow to a height of 1050 feet. " Allt Granda," in old Gaelic, signifies the ugly or terrible defile, and the pass is one of the wildest in Scotland. Past the now deserted cottage of Camban goes the track, and down to the fords at the junction of three streams, where the Affric River is born. Here comes in the track from Cluanie, described in Route No. 4, and from the north-west that from the Beallach an Sgairne, described in Route No. 9. Half a mile further east are the keepers' houses at Alltbeath, where milk may sometimes be had. Leaving Alltbeath the track keeps along the north bank of the Affric River as far as its junction with Loch Affric, and then along the hill-slopes north of that loch, keeping well away from the shore. Skirting the base of An Tudair Beag, an outlying spur of the mighty Mam Soul, the track gradually descends through scattered pine trees to Affric Lodge, at the east end of Loch Affric, where the road to Invercannich begins.

9. Croe Bridge to Alltbeath and Glen Affric by the Beallach an Sgairne, 17 miles. This is an alternative route to the last one, taking the north side of Ben Attow. Leave Croe Bridge as in Route No. 8, but instead of turning into Glen Lichd, cross the Croe River by a bridge near a cottage and take a path which starts behind the enclosure and goes north along the base of Ben Attow. Rounding the lower slopes of that mountain the track ascends Glen Choinneachain high above the stream, leaving the shooting lodge of Dorusduain on the left across the river, and making for the gap in the hills which can be seen ahead. Climbing the face of Meall a' Bhealaich by a series of zigzags, the path swings left into a narrow defile between steep rocky hill-sides. This is the Beallach an Sgairne (Pass of Rumbling), a wilderness of shattered stones, which was the usual route from Inverness to Kintail in pre-railway days. Just beyond the summit (1600 feet) is a shelter cairn for weather-bound travellers. From this point the track descends to skirt Loch a' Bhealaich, beyond which it reaches the stream flowing down Glen Gniomhaidh, keeps along

its left bank for 2 miles, and joins Route No. 8 half a mile west of Alltbeath.

10. Croe Bridge to the Fall of Glomach by Dorusduain, 5½ miles. This route enables the walker to reach the head of the Fall by crossing the hills. Another route, by which the Fall is approached from below, is described in Chapter VII, Route No. 1. Leave Croe Bridge by the Dornie road and after 400 yards turn right up a farm road past Lienassie and up Strath Croe to Dòrusduain Lodge, which stands above the stream at a junction of two glens. Go north behind the lodge by a good path, crossing to the east side of the glen by a wire bridge, and recrossing at a bend of the stream three-quarters of a mile beyond. Then climb east along a steep hill-side above the stream to the Beallach na Sroine, a 1900-foot pass which leads on to a plateau overlooking the wild country to the north and east. Far below is seen the deep trench of Glen Elchaig; the roar of the Fall can be heard, though the gorge is not yet visible. From the Beallach na Sroine a very indistinct path, marked by a few cairns, leads down in about a mile to the head of the Fall; be careful not to miss the junction and take a branch which goes along the flank of Meall Dubh to join Route No. 9 near Loch a' Bhealaich.

The Fall is a magnificent sight when full; it drops 370 feet into a narrow, perpendicular-sided gorge to join the Elchaig River half a mile away. A rough and precarious track leads along the western wall of the gorge to its lower end, but is essentially a path for those with steady heads, and is not to be recommended at any time. It is better to return to Croe Bridge by the outward route, or to follow the Meall Dubh track to Loch a' Bhealaich and Alltbeath. The man who does not mind heights and is anxious to get on to Dornie Ferry may do so as follows: Climb carefully along the path down the west wall of the gorge as far as the junction with the Allt na Laoidhre, which comes in from the left through a ravine of its own. Cross the Glomach River and reach the path which goes along the east side of the gorge to its mouth, go across the Elchaig River by the stepping-stones at the lower end of Loch na Leitreach and join the road which rucs down Glen Elchaig to Killilan. Go west along this road as far as the bridge, which will be found among some trees half a mile east of Coille-righ. Cross the river and continue past Camus Luinne by a path which goes west to Bundalloch on Loch Long, from which Dornie is 1½ miles further on. An alternative route from Camus Luinne would be to take the path which turns off half a mile west of the cottages and climbs by the east side of Carn Bad a' Chreamha and over into the narrow Coire Dhuinnid, from where it follows the stream right down the glen to Loch Duich, joining the Dornie road 3 miles south of that place. By this route the distance from Croe Bridge to the Fall and back is 19½ miles, and from Croe Bridge to Dornie 15 miles.

The Fall of Glomach and its catchment area, constituting a property of some 2,200 acres, and bordering on the Kintail Estate, has been acquired by the National Trust.

ASCENT OF BEN ATTOW

(Gaelic: *A' Bheinn Fhada*, The Long Mountain)

From Croe Bridge take Route No. 9 as far as the zigzags on Meall a' Bhealaich, just before turning into the Beallach an Sgairne. From the Beallach track a stalker's path turns off to the right along the west slope of Meall a' Bhealaich, and affords easy access by the ridge to the summit of Ben Attow itself. The return to Croe Bridge can be made north-west along the ridge over Sgurr a Choire Ghairbh and down the south-west slope of Ben Buidhe.

CHAPTER VI

GLEN AFFRIC, GLEN CANNICH AND GLEN STRATHFARRAR

MAPS.—*O.S. Popular Edition*, 1 inch, sheets 36 and 37.
Bartholomew's Half Inch, sheets 54 and 55.

NORTHWARD from Ben Attow, the Long Mountain of Kintail, a line of lofty peaks curves along the Inverness-shire border. This range, which terminates in the fine group of mountains at the west end of Loch Monar, forms part of the dorsal ridge of Scotland, along which runs the watershed at the North-west Highlands. High among its eastern corries are born the rivers Affric, Cannich and Farrar, which flow by loch and gorge and wooded glen to reach the sea at Beauly. The glens through which they flow are renowned for their beauty and grandeur above all Scottish glens; each has lochs and woods and rushing waters, and each is separated from its neighbour by a barrier of mountains.

Glen Affric, the southernmost of the three, stretches for 20 miles from Ben Attow to Fasnakyle, where it joins Strathglass. It is a mountain valley, containing Loch Affric and Loch Beneveian, and communicating with the low country by the defile known as the Chisholm's Pass. Below this pass, through which the river has cut for itself a deep gorge, the broad green valley of Strath Glass extends north-eastwards past Invercannich to Struy. After Glen Affric, Strath Glass appears almost tame; its wide green meadows and level roads might well be of the Lowlands, but the sparkling clearness of the river, now known as the Glass, marks it as a Highland stream. At Invercannich it receives the waters of the Cannich, and at Struy, near

Erchless Castle, those of the rushing Farrar, which have come from far Loch Monar. Beyond Struy is the wooded gorge of Aigus, where the Glass, now called the Beauly, curves north past Eilean Aigus and east to the Falls of Kilmorack, sweeps south past the lawns of Beaufort Castle, and winds by Lovat Bridge and ruined Beauly Priory to the sea.

Glen Affric falls naturally into three divisions, each taking its character from the Affric River. From its source in Ben Attow the river flows through a marshy upland glen, treeless and desolate, between high mountains. The sole signs of human occupation in this region are the keeper's house at Alltbeath, and two cottages at Athnamulloch. Then the mountains open out to form a basin, some 8 miles long, in which lie the two connected lochs of Affric and Beneveian. Woods of birch and pine clothe the shores of Loch Beneveian and the southern shores of Loch Affric; on the northern slopes above the latter are remnants of the old Caledonian Forest, which once covered the Highlands.

North-west of Loch Affric, and 3 miles distant, is the summit of Mam Soul (3862 feet) which, with its sister height of Carn Eige (3877 feet), is the highest mountain north of the Great Glen. Although of little interest to the rock climber, despite their commanding height, these two mountains provide magnificent view-points in favourable weather. Their situation near the western sea-board, with no high mountains to block the views to the east, permits one to look across Scotland from the Minch to the Moray Firth. The peaks of Skye, Harris, Mull and South Uist can be distinguished, and of the mainland giants Ben Lawers, Ben Macdhui and Ben Nevis are all visible under favourable conditions. Mam Soul, which means the Rounded Hill of Barns, was at one time famed for the excellence of its grass; this was in the old days when the black cattle of the Highlands had not been displaced by sheep and afterwards by deer. A stalker's path leads from Loch Affric, by way of the deep Corrie Leachavie, to the

PLATE III   KINTAIL PEAKS AND LOCH DUICH FROM INVERIN

summit of Mam Soul, on which stands the great cairn erected by the engineers in 1848, when the mountain was one of the triangulation stations of the Ordnance Survey. The summit of Carn Eige rises half a mile to the north and is easily reached.

The third division of Glen Affric is the country through which the road past Loch Beneveian leads to Strath Glass, through the wooded defile of the Chisholm's Pass. This is a land of low hills, covered with birch and pine, which extends southwards to the Deabhag River and the Guisachan Forest, from which most of the readily accessible wood was cut during the 1939-45 war. Through these hills the Affric River has cut its way, and roars along a narrow rocky channel, plunging over the Dog Falls and the Badger Fall, to reach the quiet levels of Strath Glass. Far above on the hill-side, the road from Affric Lodge, which leaves Loch Beneveian along the river bank, winds through the woods of the Chisholm's Pass, and swings down the long descent to Fasnakyle. This is a comparatively modern road, built to serve the shooting lodge on Loch Affric: the old pass from Strath Glass to Kintail kept further south, to the leading up the River Deabhag past Tomich to Knockfin, and thence by the south side of Loch Affric to the ford of Athnamulloch and so to Kintail.

Glen Cannich lies some 4 miles to the north of Glen Affric, to which it is roughly parallel. Its head, where two streams join to form Loch Lungard, is a swampy valley at the foot of high mountains. A low pass to the west divides it from Glen Elchaig, and on the north the sprawling bulk of An Riabhachan lies between it and Loch Monar. Lofty summits rise from its southern slopes and separate it from Glen Affric; Carn Eige, Ben Fionnlaidh and a long northern spur of Sgurr nan Ceathreamhnan are the chief of these, and all are over 3000 feet high. Loch Lungard lies at a higher level than Loch Affric and is rather smaller than that loch; east of it extends Loch Mullardoch, a long, narrow lake with wooded southern shores. From the shooting lodge at its head a road goes eastward along the north shore, and on down the glen to Invercannich; there is no road through the woods on the southern shore. From this lodge (Benula) a rough track crosses the river to Benula Old Lodge on the south side, and goes west along Loch Lungard to the shepherd's house at Lungard, and thence across the low pass to Glen Elchaig. There are also mountain tracks connecting Benula Lodge with Affric Lodge, and Lungard with Alltbeath in Glen Affric. Glen Cannich means the glen of the cotton-grass, which is plentiful along its sides; less austere than that of Glen Affric, its beauty often appeals in greater measure to lovers of softer scenery.

The North of Scotland Hydro-Electric Board has in preparation a scheme to utilise the great water-power resources of the Glen Affric—Glen Cannich area in such a way as to leave the natural beauties of these glens comparatively unspoiled.

Loch Affric is entirely unaffected by the scheme. A dam is being built at the east end of Loch Mullardoch in Glen Cannich, to raise the level of the loch by 113 feet; this raising of the level will flood up to, and beyond the western end of Loch Lungard. Another dam is being constructed in the gorge of the Affric River, to raise the level of Beneveian by almost 25 feet. A tunnel $3\frac{1}{2}$ miles long will discharge the waters of Loch Mullardoch into Loch Beneveian, and a similar tunnel will convey the combined waters of both lochs to the power station at Fasnakyle in Strath Glass. Arrangements are being made to ensure a good flow of water in the Rivers Cannich and Affric below the points where they are affected by the scheme. An improvement in the roads of the two glens, due to the constructional requirements of the scheme, should make certain areas more readily accessible to the motorist and cyclist, for example, it is expected that a good road will be available to the west end of Loch Beneveian.

Glen Strathfarrar is the longest and most northerly of the three glens: from the Beallach an Sgoltaidh, at the head of Loch Monar, to Struy Bridge its length is 22 miles.

Like Glen Affric it consists of three divisions of mountain-valley, loch and wooded glen. It is to the last section, which extends from Loch Monar to Struy Bridge, that the name Glen Strathfarrar is usually confined.

Loch Monar, some 4 miles long, lies in a remote position among the mountains. To the west and north are the peaks of the West Monar Forest, of which Sgurr a Chaora-chain (3452 feet) and Bidean an Eoin Deirg (3430 feet) are the chief summits. The Peak of the Boiling Torrent and the Little Peak of the Red Bird are the English renderings of the names of these mountains. South of these heights is the upland glen of Strathmore, extending from the high pass called the Beallach an Sgoltaidh (Pass of Splitting) to the western end of Loch Monar. Down this glen flows the Strathmore River, which is the true source of the Farrar.

Except for some plantations at the outlet of the loch, the shores of Loch Monar are bare of trees; a shooting lodge stands at either end of the loch, and there is a ruined shepherd's house at Lub an Inbhir on the north shore. To the north a tract of high ground divides the loch from Glen Fhiodaig and Strathconon ; north-east rises a group of mountains culminating in Sgurr Fhuar Thuill (Peak of the Cold Hollow) and Sgurr a Coire Ghlais (Peak of the Green Corrie), behind which lies desolate Glen Orrin. Below the southern slopes of this range runs the River Farrar, which has left Loch Monar as the Garbh Uisge (Rough Water), and flows past Monar Lodge and the woods of Inchvuilt to Loch a' Mhuillidh and the larger Loch Beannacharan. Then for 6 miles it winds through woods of birch and pine, plunges over the Culligran Falls, and sweeps by Struy Bridge to join the Glass.

There is no road along Loch Monar side : a path connects Monar Lodge with Strathmore Lodge at the west end. A private road leads up Glen Strathfarrar to Monar Lodge and is closed to motor cars ; it is, however, a right of way for pedestrians and droves.

Glen Affric and Glen Cannich are the country of the

Chisholms, an ancient clan whose chief had his seat at Erchless Castle in Strath Glass, and was known as The Chisholm. In this he was unique among Highland chiefs, and it was his proud boast that there were only three persons thus distinguished, these being the King, the Pope and the Chisholm. Clan Chisholm was too small in numbers to have played a distinguished part in history ; it is probable that they took part with the neighbouring Clan Fraser in the wars and conflicts of the district, of which few records have come down to us.

Between Inverness and Beauly and southward to Strath Glass lies the district known as the Aird. This region, together with Glen Strathfarrar, Monar and Lower Strath Glass was the country of the Frasers, a numerous clan which rose to power on the ruins of the Bissets. Their chief, who takes his title of Lord Lovat from a former castle which stood near Beauly, traces his descent from Norman forebears, who carved out for themselves wide estates in the rude north; his seat is at Beaufort Castle, which stands beside the Beauly not far from the Falls of Kilmorack. The Frasers in Inverness-shire, like their neighbours the Mackenzies in Ross-shire, were bitter foes of Clan Donald, of which clan they had once been vassals. At the disastrous Battle of the Shirts, in 1544, the chief, his eldest son, and almost every gentlemen bearing the name of Fraser fell before the Macdonald broadswords, and the clan was nearly annihilated. Two hundred years later Simon Fraser, Lord Lovat, played an ignoble part in the drama of the 'Forty Five, and lost his head on the block. Another Lord Lovat, at the close of the nineteenth century, raised a corps of mounted men for service in South Africa, and Lovat's Scouts served in both World Wars. The present Lord Lovat served with distinction in the 1939-45 war with the rank of Brigadier in the Commandos. The Frasers, like the Ross-shire clans, did not join Montrose or Dundee in their campaigns; they were Covenant men rather than Royalists, as were the neighbouring clans of Ross and Munro.

COMMUNICATIONS

Rail.—There are no railways in the district, the nearest station being Beauly, on the L.M.S. line from Inverness to Dingwall.

Road Services.—A mail motor runs daily from Tomich to Struy and Beauly and back.

Temporary mail-passenger services are being run between Cannich and Benula Lodge on Wednesdays and Saturdays, and between Cannich and Affric Lodge on Mondays and Thursdays.

Roads.—1. A road leads from Beauly by Lovat Bridge up the left bank of the river to Struy and Invercannich, and thence by way of the Chisholm's Pass to Affric Lodge at the eastern end of Loch Affric. Branch roads lead from Struy by Glen Strathfarrar to Monar Lodge, and from Invercannich by Glen Cannich to Benula Lodge.

2. A second road goes up the right bank of the Beauly, and up Strath Glass to Tomich, where it is continued as a forest road to Guisachan, Hilton Cottage and Cougie. At Struy, Invercannich and Fasnakyle, bridges connect with the road along the other side of the glen.

3. At the bridge near Invercannich a road comes in from the east from Glen Urquhart and Loch Ness, dropping into Strath Glass down a long hill. This affords an alternative route from Inverness to Glen Affric and Glen Cannich, and is particularly useful to cyclists coming from Fort Augustus and Fort William.

ACCOMMODATION

This district is wide and sparsely populated, and hotels are scarce. There are only three actually within the district, these being at Struy, Invercannich (the Glen Affric Hotel) and Tomich, but others are available in the surrounding districts, from which Glen Affric and its neighbours can be reached. Beauly to the north-east, Drumnadrochit to the east, Invermoriston to the south, Loch Duich, Strathcarron and Achnasheen to the west, have all hotels:

there is accommodation to be had at Croe Bridge, Bridge of Shiel and Inverinate on Loch Duich, and a Youth Hostel is open in the summer months at Buntait, at the western end of Glen Urquhart. Tomich, in Glen Affric, can also offer accommodation in private houses, and it is sometimes possible to secure a night's lodging with keepers and shepherds at the head of the three glens.

WALKS AND TRAMPS
(a) *By Road*

1. Lovat Bridge to Invercannich, 16 miles. This is the main road up Strath Glass to Glen Affric, which at times carries heavy motor traffic. For this reason walkers will probably prefer the road along the opposite bank of the river, which is described below. The main road leaves the Inverness-Beauly road at Lovat Bridge, comes down to the river at Kilmorack Church and climbs through the woods over the hill known as the Crask of Aigas, descends past Aigas Ferry and westward along the level to Erchless Castle and the entrance to Glen Strathfarrar. Turning south in the castle woods, it crosses the Farrar at Struy Bridge, and leads past Struy Church and village by wooded slopes to Invercannich, where there is a hotel and a post-office. From this place, where a road comes in from Glen Urquhart on the east, a branch road climbs over the hill into Glen Cannich.

2. Lovat Bridge to Tomich by Kiltarlity and Eskadale, 19 miles. This road leaves the main road at Ballacrask, before reaching Kilmorack, crosses the Beauly to Kiltarlity, turns to the right and climbs over Fanellan Hill, coming down to the river again at Eskdale. Thence it continues along the south side of the valley, passes the branch road to Struy, and leads south-west up Strath Glass till opposite Invercannich. Here it is joined by a road from Glen Urquhart, and the branch road to Invercannich. Keeping up the valley along the edge of the Balnahoun Woods, it passes the junction of the Affric and the Deabhag, and follows along the latter stream to Tomich, with its hotel.

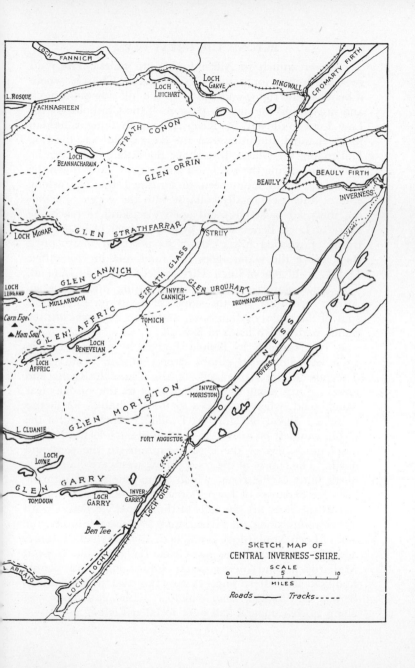

SKETCH MAP OF
CENTRAL INVERNESS-SHIRE.

SCALE

0   5   10

MILES

Roads ———   Tracks- - - - -

LOCH FANNICH

L. ROSQUE

ACHNASHEEN

LOCH LUICHART

LOCH GARVE

DINGWALL

CROMARTY FIRTH

STRATH CONON

LOCH BEANNACHARAIN

GLEN ORRIN

BEAULY FIRTH

BEAULY

INVERNESS

LOCH MONAR

GLEN STRATHFARRAR

STRUY

GLEN CANNICH

STRATH GLASS

GLEN URQUHART

INVER-CANNICH

DRUMNADROCHIT

LOCH LUNGARD

L. MULLARDOCH

Carn Eige

Mam Soul

GLEN AFFRIC

LOCH BENEVELAN

TOMICH

LOCH AFFRIC

GLEN MORISTON

INVER-MORISTON

LOCH NESS

FOYERS

L. CLUANIE

FORT AUGUSTUS

CANAL

LOCH LOYNE

GLEN GARRY

LOCH GARRY

INVER-GARRY

LOCH OICH

TOMDOUN

Ben Tee

L. ARKAIG

LOCH LOCHY

CANAL

3. Invercannich to Affric Lodge, 12 miles. The road goes south-west for 2 miles to Fasnakyle Church, where it bends to the right, and winds up the hill-side amid birch and bracken to the narrow passage of the Chisholm's Pass. Low down to the left, the River Affric rolls along its hidden rocky channel, tumbling over the Badger Fall and the Dog Fall to join the Glass. Just above the latter, which can be visited by leaving the road and going a few yards down the slope, the rocks have been undermined by the rushing waters, and occasionally collapse into the gorge. Further on, the road passes through open woodland to reach the shore of Loch Beneveian, a beautiful sheet of water in a frame of wooded hills. Along its northern shore, on a shelf above the water, goes the road, making for Affric Lodge, at the foot of Loch Affric, where it comes to an end. The lodge stands on a peninsula jutting out into Loch Affric; behind it rise the slopes of Sgurr na Lapaich, a spur of the mighty Mam Soul, and from its gates runs the public path which leads to Kintail.

4. Invercannich to Benula Lodge, by Glen Cannich, 13 miles. This road climbs steeply out of Strath Glass, descends to the right bank of the Cannich River, and follows it up along the birch woods to the bridge near Muchrachd, where it crosses to the left bank. From this point the ascent of Sgurr na Diollaid, which rises on the north, can best be made. It is a hill of 2676 feet, affording a splendid view of the high mountains to the west and north. The course of the road is now westwards, along the north bank of the river, which soon widens out into the loch-like expanses of Loch Corrie and Loch Sealbhanach. Across the river are the hills of the Fasnakyle Forest, with birch woods along the river banks. After some miles, the foot of Loch Mullardoch is reached, and the road continues along its northern shore, past Cozac Lodge to the bridge at Mullardoch, and on to Cozac Old Lodge and Benula Lodge at its western end. Across the river to the south is Benula Old Lodge, from which a public path goes west along Loch Lungard and over to Glen Elchaig.

5. Struy to Monar Lodge, by Glen Strathfarrar, 15 miles. The road leaves Strath Glass on the north side of Struy Bridge, and leads up the left bank of the River Farrar, which is well wooded for some 4 miles as far as Deanie Lodge. Two miles from Struy are the Culligran Falls, below which a bridge crosses the river and leads back to Struy. Beyond Deanie Lodge, which lies back from the road on the north, the glen is bare of trees, and soon the route lies along Loch Bennacharan, climbing to its neighbour, Loch a' Mhuillidh, and along the steep slopes beneath An Carnais to Inchvuilt, near Broulin Lodge. At this point, some 60 yards west of the bridge, was the crossing place of the old drove road which led from Loch Monar to Glen Cannich, Fasnakyle Bridge, and on to Fort Augustus. From Inchvuilt westwards the road keeps near the river, with the mountains close above, then turns to the north through woodland to reach Monar Lodge. The road continues round the back of the lodge towards the outlet of Loch Monar, where it becomes a track which runs along the loch to Strathmore Lodge at its western end.

(b) *By Hill-tracks*

1. Tomich to Torgyle Bridge and Fort Augustus, 17 miles. This route, which leads past Guisachan House and over the moors to Glen Moriston, has been described in reverse in Route No. 1 of Chapter V.

2. Tomich to Claunie by Glen Doe, 26 miles. This route, which leads up the Allt Riabhach to Glen Moriston and Cluanie, is described in Route No. 2 of Chapter V.

3. Tomich to Cluanie by Athnamulloch, Glen Allt na Ciche, and the Beallach Coire a' Chait, 24 miles. This route, which goes through the wooded hills on the south of Glen Affric, is described in Route No. 3 of Chapter V.

4. Affric Lodge to Croe Bridge by the Beallach an Sgairne, 17 miles. This route, by the northern side of Ben Attow, is described in Route No. 9 of Chapter V.

5. Affric Lodge to Croe Bridge by the Allt Granda, 17½ miles. This route is described in Route No. 8 of Chapter V.

6. Affric Lodge to Cluanie, by Alltbeath and the Allt a' Chaoruinn Mor, 16 miles. This path is described in Route No. 4 of Chapter V.

7. Affric Lodge to Lungard, by the Beallach Coire Ghaidheil, 12½ miles. From the gates of the lodge this path goes west along the lower slopes of the mountains, passing through groups of magnificent Scottish pines. It keeps well above Loch Affric, passes a bothy at the entrance to Coire Leachavie, where a stalker's path to the summit of Mam Soul goes off to the north, and bends southwards, past two small lochs, to join the track from Athnamulloch half a mile west of the head of Loch Affric. Keeping west for a mile the path reaches the Allt Coire Ghaidheil, and turns north along the eastern bank of the stream, climbing steadily and steeply to the head of the glen, to cross the pass at a height of 2350 feet, and descend into Gleann a' Choilich on the northern side. This is a narrow, sombre, steep-walled glen, down which the Amhuinn a' Choilich flows north to join Loch Lungard. Along its western side rises the long ridge of Creag a' Choir' Ard, a northern spur of lofty Sgurr nan Ceathreamhnan; on the east are the slopes of Mam Soul, Carn Eige and Ben Fhionnlaidh, the two former rising to nearly 3900 feet. Near the foot of the glen the path divides, one branch crossing the river and going west. Our way lies north-east round the base of Ben Fhionnlaidh to the shore of Loch Lungard, where another path leads north across the river to the keeper's house at Lungard.

8. Affric Lodge to Benula Lodge by the Allt Toll Easa, 6 miles. This is the shortest route from Glen Affric to the head of Glen Cannich. It makes use of a high pass across the long range of mountains which extends eastward from Carn Eige. Immediately to the north of Affric Lodge a stalker's path climbs up the hill-side, turns west at a height of 1500 feet and continues for half a mile, where it bends back east and then north, crosses the western foot of Am Meallan, and descends to the bridge across the river in Glen nam Fiadh. Here it joins another track which leaves

the road near the western end of Loch Beneveian and leads up the left bank of the Amhuinn Gleann nam Fiadh. At the bridge the path goes east for a quarter of a mile, then climbs north along the Allt Toll Easa to the pass below the eastern slopes of Tom a' Choinich (3646 feet). Crossing this pass at a level of 2750 feet, the path descends the northern slopes of the mountain by a series of zigzags, crosses the Allt a Choire Domhain by a bridge, and continues above a waterfall down to the bridge at Benula Old Lodge, at the west end of Loch Mullardoch. Benula Lodge stands among trees across the river to the north (see page 58).

9. Benula Lodge to Glen Elchaig and Aird Ferry, 22 miles. This route is described in Route No. 2 of Chapter VII (see page 58).

10. Lungard to Patt Lodge, by Loch an Droma, 13 miles. This track goes west from Lungard along the north side of the valley, past the little Loch Droma, and down to Iron Lodge, where it crosses the Allt Doire Ghairbh, turns north along that stream, and crosses its tributary the Crom Allt. Continuing to climb along the west bank of the Allt Doire Ghairbh, the path leads past Loch Moichean, and descends into a northward-going glen, where it crosses to the eastern side of the valley, and follows the Allt Coire nan Each downwards. Keeping north and then north-east round the lower slopes of An Cruachan, the track passes between Ben Beag and a long, double loch called Loch an Tachdaidh and An Gead Loch, and continues down the river bank to Patt Lodge.

11. Patt Lodge to Strathcarron Station, 13 miles.

12. Strathmore Lodge, Loch Monar, to Achnashellach, 14 miles.

These two routes are described in the reverse direction in Routes Nos. 7 and 8 of Chapter VII.

13. Strathmore Lodge to Milltown, Strathconon, 15 miles. This route leads from Loch Monar through the mountains into desolate Glen Orrin, and thence by Glen Chaorainn to Strathconon. From Strathmore Lodge a

path goes east along Loch Monar to Lub an Inbhir. Half a mile east of this a mountain track goes north and then west, making for the pass which leads to Glen Orrin. After crossing this pass it descends north-east along the River Orrin, passes along the north-west shore of lonely Loch na Caoidhe, and climbs over a second pass into Glen Chorainn. Continuing down the latter to Inverchorainn, the track reaches Strathconon, and leads north-east by the wooded eastern bank of the River Meig, past Balnacraig and Crannich to Dalbreac Lodge. Here it becomes a road, which presently crosses the river and reaches Milltown.

14. Strathmore Lodge to Scardroy Lodge in Glen Fhiodhaig, 13 miles. This is a more direct route to Strath-conon, joining the road at Scardroy Lodge. The track as far as Lub an Inbhir is the same as in Route No. 13, but at that point it turns north along the left bank of the river, and continues up to the head of Coire Fionnarach, and thence north-eastwards along the Allt an Amise down into Glen Fhiodhaig. Here the River Meig is crossed, and the track continues down its left bank for 4 miles to the lodge at Scardroy, which stands near the head of Loch Beannacharain at the end of the road leading to Strath-conon.

CHAPTER VII

LOCHALSH AND LOCHCARRON

MAPS.—*O.S. Popular Edition, 1 inch, sheets 35 and 36.*
Bartholomew's Half Inch, sheets 54 and 55.

FROM the narrow strait of Kyleakin, where Ross-shire is only half a mile from Skye, Loch Alsh stretches eastward to Eileandonan and Totaig. To the north is the district known as Lochalsh, a broad, blunt-nosed peninsula bounded by Loch Carron, Loch Alsh and Loch Long. Unlike a Kintail or Knoydart, it is land of low, rocky hills, with few prominent mountains; its villages stand along the coast, and through it runs the railway to Strome Ferry and Kyle of Lochalsh, the latter being now the ferry-port for Skye. Until 1940 is was only by crossing a ferry that a road traveller could reach Lochalsh. A good road bridge has now replaced Dornie ferry across the entrance to Loch Long, although the other two ferries of Kyle, to the west, and Strome, to the north, still exist.

Strome Ferry, at the narrows of Loch Carron, was once the railway terminus, and the most important centre in the district; it was a port of call for steamers from Glasgow, Oban and Stornoway, and the starting point for Skye. From Strome Ferry a road goes south to Loch Alsh, Ardelve and Aird Ferry, opposite Dornie, with a branch to Balmacara and Kyle of Lochalsh. When the railway was extended to Kyle at the end of last century, Strome Ferry lost its importance; it is still the ferry over which all road traffic for the north must pass, but Kyle is now the terminus and the steamer port. The latter is an ugly little town in a beautiful situation, huddled among the rocks beside the railway sidings and looking across Loch Alsh to Kyleakin in Skye. A hydro-electric scheme to provide power for the district is in course of construction. It comprises a dam and reservoir in Allt Gleann Udalain, and a pipe line leading the water to a generating station near Nostie Bridge.

Between Kyle and Strome Ferry, on a peninsula projecting into Loch Carron, is the village of Plockton, which is becoming a resort for summer visitors and affords good sea-fishing. Close by, in a setting of wood and water, is the modern castle of Duncraig, through the grounds of which goes the private road to Strome Ferry. Curiously enough, there is no road along the southern shore of Loch Carron from Strome Ferry to Strathcarron Station, and no public road direct from Strome Ferry to Kyle, the public road making a long detour by way of Balmacara. In the early summer of 1946, the beautiful estate of Balmacara was bequeathed by the late Lady Hamilton to the National Trust for Scotland. This estate of some 8000 acres extends from Loch Carron on the north, round by Plockton and Kyle to Kirkton, on Loch Alsh.

Loch Carron is a long sea-loch extending south-west from the foot of Glen Carron, and opening on to the Inner Sound. Though less imposing than those of Loch Duich or Loch Hourn the blue mountains at its head combine with its wooded bays to form a lovely picture. On its northern shore is the village of Lochcarron, also known as Jeantown, the chief centre of population in the district of Lochcarron. Here, in pre-railway days, travellers to and from Skye used to stay overnight, as the coach to Dingwall only ran by day. Coming from North Strome the road follows the northern shore of the loch, passing through Strath Carron and up the narrowing Glen Carron to Achnashellach and on to Achnasheen. At the west end of Lochcarron village the road to Shieldaig and Applecross goes off to the west, climbing a long hill before it swings down the descent of the pass to Kishorn.

Lochalsh was once the land of the Mathesons, an

ancient clan which, like the Macraes, was allied to the Mackenzies. A Matheson was constable of Eileandonan Castle in 1539, when it was beseiged by Donald Gorm of Sleat; an arrow shot by a Macrae mortally wounded the latter, while Matheson was killed by a Macdonald bowman.

The Macdonalds were lords of Lochalsh in the fourteenth and fifteenth centuries; they held the strong castle of Strome, which watched the ferry across Loch Carron. During the sixteenth century, when the power of the Lords of the Isles had been broken, the Macdonalds came into collision with the rising strength of the Mackenzies, with whom they were soon at feud. Strome Castle was taken and blown up in 1602 by Kenneth Mackenzie of Kintail and Lochcarron and Lochalsh became Mackenzie territory.

The narrow, tide-swept strait of Kyleakin was guarded by Castle Maol, on the Skye shore; there is a legend of a Norse wife of an island chief who barred the strait with an iron chain and levied toll on passing ships.

Communications

Rail.—L.M.S. from Inverness to Kyle of Lochalsh. Stations at Achnashellach, Strathcarron, Attadale, Strome Ferry, Plockton and Duirinish.

Steamer.—1. Mallaig to Kyle of Lochalsh daily.

2. Kyle of Lochalsh to Applecross and Stornoway daily.

3. Kyle of Lochalsh to Broadford and Portree daily.

4. A motor-boat service, carrying mails and a few passengers, runs daily to Glenelg and back.

Road Services.—1. Motor-bus runs daily from Kyle to Glenshiel via Balmacara, Ardelve, Dornie and Inverinate.

2. Motor-bus from Strathcarron Station to Lochcarron, Kishorn and Shieldaig.

Ferries.—1. North Strome to Strome Ferry.

2. Kyle of Lochalsh to Kyleakin.

3. Ardelve to Totaig.

Accommodation

1. Hotels at Aird Ferry (Loch Duich Hotel), Balmacara,

Kyle of Lochalsh, Strome Ferry, North Strome, Lochcarron, and Strathcarron Station.

2. Other accommodation at Ardelve, Auchtertyre, Kyle of Lochalsh, Plockton and Lochcarron.

3. Youth hostels at North Strome and Kyle of Lochalsh.

WALKS AND TRAMPS
By Road and Path

1. Aird Ferry to Fall of Glomach, via Glen Elchaig, 13 miles. This is the route by which the Fall can best be reached by road, from which it is about 1 mile distant. The approach is up the gorge towards the Fall, and involves considerable scrambling, and the crossing of at least one stream. If there has been heavy rain in the hills, this crossing may not be practicable, and the route to the top of the Fall from Dorusduain should be chosen. Leave Aird Ferry by road, turning east at Ardelve, past the church and north along the shore of Loch Long. Continue past Salachy and along the shallow muddy upper end of the loch, cross the River Ling and turn south at Killilan into Glen Elchaig. The road beyond Killilan is private and permission should be obtained to take vehicles along it. It is a right of way for pedestraians and droves. At Faddoch, below the slopes of Sguman Coinntich, the glen turns east and becomes narrower, the road rising steadily along the slopes above the Elchaig River. Presently the junction of the Glomach with the Elchaig is reached, and half a mile beyond, at the foot of Loch na Leitreach, are the stepping-stones by which the Elchaig is crossed. Beyond the stepping-stones a path makes for the bank of the Glomach; it is best to keep up the right bank of the stream, by a narrow and precipitous track, until opposite the point where the Allt na Laoidhre ravine joins the Glomach from the south. Here the Glomach must be crossed, and the path along the left wall of the gorge reached. This is a steep and narrow track, which eventually leads up a rocky slope to a headland which juts out opposite the Fall. From this point, which is marked by a lone tree, the spectacle

PLATE IV   PLOCKTON AND LOCH CARRON

The village of Plockton on a peninsula in
running into the mountains. The peaks
in the far centre are the hills around Loch To

Photograph by R. M. ADAM

In the distance can be seen Loch Kishorn
ng to the Applecross Forest group, those

is most impressive; the Fall is seen at close quarters and its great height can be appreciated. The river plunges 370 feet sheer into the gorge, and although the highest part of the cataract is not visible, this does not detract from the grandeur and majesty of the scene, which has no rival in these islands.

It is best to return by the outward route to Killilan and Aird Ferry, but an alternative is available for the clear-headed. From the headland of the lone tree it is possible, by continuing upwards along the wall of the gorge, to reach the lip of the Fall and thence to make for Dorusduainn and Croe Bridge by way of the Beallach na Sroine. This track is described in Route No. 10 of Chapter V.

2. Aird Ferry to Glen Cannich (Benula Lodge), 22 miles. This is one of the old routes through the mountains from Kintail to the eastern districts of Ross and Inverness; it follows the glen of the Elchaig and crosses a low pass to reach the head of Glen Cannich. A made road extends as far as Iron Lodge, leaving 9 miles of hill-track to connect with the road head at Benula Old Lodge, whence the road leads along Loch Mullardoch and on to Invercannich (see page 58).

Leave Aird Ferry as in Route No. 1, following that route along Loch Long and up Glen Elchaig to the foot of Loch na Leitreach. Thence the road continues north-east along the loch to Carnach, and up Strath Duilleach to Iron Lodge, where it crosses the river just above its junction with a stream from the east. Take the track up the right bank of this stream and climb through a wooded glen to the summit of the pass near Loch an Droma (Loch of the Ridge). Thence the route is along the north side of a widening upland glen, which descends gradually to the shepherd's cottage near the west end of Loch Lungard (see page 58). At this point the track turns south to ford the river, and joins another track coming up from Glen Affric to the south. The united tracks then turn eastward along the base of Ben Finlay (Bheinn Fhionnlaidh), hugging the south shore of Loch Lungard for $2\frac{1}{2}$ miles as far as Benula Old Lodge. The lodge stands by the river between the foot of Loch Lungard and the head of Loch Mullardoch; a bridge connects it with Benula Lodge on the north bank, whence there is a road along Loch Mullardoch and down Glen Cannich to Invercannich and Beauly. (see page 58).

3. Killilan to Attadale and Strathcarron Station, 9½ miles. This hill-track from the head of Loch Long to the head of Loch Carron avoids the long detour by Strome Ferry and Lochcarron village. The track leaves the main road close by Killilan school, on the east side of the bridge over the River Ling, and goes north along the river bank. In less than a mile the river is crossed to join a path coming from Nonach Lodge, which then continues up the western bank of the River Ling as far as its junction with another stream coming in from the west. Cross this latter and keep on to a junction of paths, where the left fork is taken. Now the track climbs northwards to a height of 1000 feet, passes Loch an Iasaich to the west, and descends towards the Attadale River.

Presently the track joins a rough shooting road from Attadale to Bendronaig Lodge; this leads north-west to a bridge over the Attadale River, and then west along the river to Attadale House. From thence to Achintee and Strathcarron Hotel is a walk of 2 miles, the road running between the hill-side and the railway line. On the left are the sandy flats at the head of Loch Carron; across the water is the village of Lochcarron on the western shore. The mountains to the north are those separating Strathcarron from Glen Torridon.

Note.—The road past Attadale House is a private one and may not always be available. It can be avoided by following the alternative route now described. Instead of crossing the bridge over the Attadale River, take a path which diverges to the east along the southern bank, crosses the river, and climbs north-east up the hill-side along the edge of a wood. Just beyond the wood it meets a track coming from the east, over the Beallach Attan Ruaridh, turns west with this track and reaches Achintee and Strathcarron in another 3 miles.

4. Aird Ferry to Strome Ferry, by road, 8 miles. Take the road past Ardelve as far as Nostie Bridge (2 miles), just beyond which a track goes north up the hill-side, rejoining the main road near the top of a steep hill. From here the road continues north, descends into and climbs out of Glen Udalain, and reaches its highest point at the third milestone from Strome Ferry. The next 2 miles are downhill into Strath Ascaig, then comes another rise with a steep winding descent into Strome Ferry.

5. Balmacara Hotel to Kyle of Lochalsh, by the coast, 3½ miles. This is a fine coast walk along a good path, with splendid views of Lochalsh and the coast of Skye. Balmacara Hotel stands on the eastern curve of a fine bay 5 miles west of Aird Ferry and looks south across Loch Alsh to the narrow strait of Kyle Rhea. Half a mile along the Kyle road a minor road goes off towards the beach, and curves round the bay to Balmacara House, behind which begins the coast track to Kyle. At first this goes through the woods on the hill-side in a westerly direction, making for Scalpaidh, and leaves to the left the monument erected to the memory of Donald Murchison, standing on its rocky point above Loch Alsh. Murchison was factor to the Earl of Seaforth in the years following the Rising of 1719. Despite all the efforts of the English commissioners he continued to collect and to remit to his exiled master the rents of his forfeited estates. The path follows the windings of the coast, keeping well up the hill-slopes, descends to the shore by Scalpaidh to cross the burn, and rising again to a shelf between the cliff and the rocky shore soon reaches Kyle of Lochalsh. From this latter portion of the route there are delightful views of Kyleakin with its guardian mountain, Ben na Caillich, and of the Kyle with its islands and lighthouse.

6. Kyle to Strome Ferry, by Loch Achadh na h'Inich, 11 miles. This is a variation of the usual road route by Duncraig Castle, taking the cyclist or walker along the shores of the beautiful and little-known Loch Achadh na h'Inich. Leave Kyle by the north road which skirts the

coast past Badicaul and Erbusaig, forking shortly after passing a school 2½ miles out. Take the left fork and continue over the hill to Drumbuie, keep right to Duirinish, up through the village, and turn left across a bridge. Just beyond the bridge a road goes off to the right and climbs for nearly a mile to three cross-roads. Take this road and turn right at the cross-roads, past a farm and through a gate and by delightfully wooded country to the shore of Loch Achadh na h'Inich, lying in a setting of low wooded hills at a height of 349 feet. The loch is triangular in shape, with hills to the south and east; along its northern shore runs the narrow, tree-shaded road, with a tiny islet, where in the spring the gulls nest, not far from the shore. On a summer evening, with the westering sun lighting up the slopes of Torr Fhionn, Loch Achadh na h'Inich is indeed lovely. The road continues to the farmhouse at the east end of the loch, climbs north over a hill, and descends towards Loch Carron.

Just where the roads bends sharply round a wood to the west, a track strikes off to the north-east, and in half a mile joins the road along Loch Carron side to Fernaig and Strome Ferry. Steep, wooded slopes rise above the road on the south; through the trees one catches glimpses of the rocky islets and brown sea-wrack along the shore. At the mouth of Strath Ascaig the road turns inland, past Fernaig with its picturesque ford, to join the main road at the first milestone from Strome Ferry. A long ascent and a steep, winding descent to the ferry bring the walker to the railway station and hotel of Strome.

7. Achintee (Strathcarron Station) to Loch Monar by the Beallach Attan Ruaridh, 13 miles. This is one of the old cross-country routes from the west coast to Central Ross-shire, leading to Patt Lodge at the west end of remote and beautiful Loch Monar. It traverses a wild and lonely country and affords a through route to Glen Strathfarrar, Struy and Beauly.

Go south from Strathcarron Station to the village of Achintee and take the path leading south-east into the hills. In 3 miles this is joined by a track from the south-west (see Route No. 3), and turns east past two lochans to cross the Beallach Attan Ruaridh (1250 feet), and descend to the glen of the Allt Feithe Chaillich. This stream is crossed and shortly afterwards re-crossed to the south, the path making for a bridge across the larger Black Water, where it joins a road to Bendronaig Lodge. Beyond the lodge a track goes east for half a mile, crosses a tributary of the Black Water, and at once divides into a northern and an eastern branch. The former leads up the Black Water to Loch an Laoigh, to slant north-eastwards up the mountain-slopes and comes to an end on the side of Ben Tharsuinn. By quitting this track to the east of Loch an Laoigh and climbing east by way of Coire Sheasgaich the walker can reach the fine pass known as the Beallach an Sgoltaidh (Pass of Splitting), which leads between Ben Tharsuinn (2597 feet) and Bidean a Coire Sheasgaich (3102 feet) to Strathmore Lodge at the head of Loch Monar. From the lodge a path leads along the north shore of Loch Monar joining the road to Struy at Monar Lodge.

The eastern branch leads by way of Loch Calavie along the southern slopes of Lurg Mhor, 3234 feet, past a large double loch in the valley, towards the head of Loch Monar. It turns sharply south to cross the river by a bridge leading to Patt Lodge. As there is no track between Patt Lodge and Strathmore Lodge it is advisable to arrange to be ferried across the head of Loch Monar, thus avoiding the boggy tract to the west. The mountains at the west end of Loch Monar form a splendid and little-known group, of which Bidean an Eoin Deirg is the most striking. The Little Peak of the Red Bird (grouse?), which is its name in English, rises to a height of 3430 feet behind Strathmore Lodge; its peak can be seen from many miles distant.

8. Achnashellach Station to Loch Monar, by Craig, 14 miles. This route, which really begins at Craig, 2½ miles east of Achnashellach Station, formed part of the old drove road from Glen Carron to Strath Glass, Fort Augustus and Dalwhinnie. Until the mid-nineteenth century there was

an inn at Craig and there is still a road from Craig to
Glenuaig Lodge. Leave Achnashellach by the road for
Achnasheen, and at Craig go south across the railway by a
road which turns east parallel with the line, crosses the
river by a bridge, and goes east through the woods up the
glen of the Allt a Chonais. At a point about 2½ miles from
Craig a track diverges to the south, by taking which it is
possible to climb to the Beallach Bhearnais (1900 feet),
and to reach Strathmore by way of the steep glen of the
Allt Beallach Crudhain. The drove road, however, continues east to near Glenuaig Lodge, where it crosses the
stream and turns south-west up the glen of An Crom Allt
(the Crooked Burn), and climbs south-east along the slopes
of Bidean an Eoin Deirg and over into Strath Mhuilich,
at the foot of which is Strathmore Lodge and the head of
the path to Glen Strathfarrar.

Ascent of Sguman Coinntich (2881 feet)

Although this mountain, which rises east of Killilan, is
under 3000 feet high, its position constitutes it one of the
finest view-points on the west coast. It is easily ascended
from Killilan, to which point a vehicle can be taken. A
good path leaves the road at Killilan, and goes up the glen
of the Allt a Choire Mhoir to within a few hundred yards
of the summit. As the mountain is in a deer forest, it
should not be climbed during the stalking season. The
view comprehends the main range of the Ross-shire mountains, with those of Inverness, as well as Skye, Applecross,
and the Outer Hebrides. Sgurr nan Ceathreamnhan is
very well seen from this point, as well as Scour Ouran and
Ben Attow.

CHAPTER VIII

SKYE

MAPS.—*O.S. Popular Edition, 1 inch, sheets* 24, 25, 34 *and* 35
Bartholomew's Half Inch, sheet 54.

THE island of Skye is the largest of the Inner Hebrides; it is situated off the west coast of Ross- and Inverness-shires, and forms part of the latter county. Its Gaelic name of the Winged Isle is said to be derived from its appearance on the map, where the long promontories of Trotternish, Vaternish, Duirinish and Minginish resemble great wings. It is these four promontories, with the districts of Sleat and Strathaird, which constitute the island, and have given their names to the districts into which it is divided.

Although Skye may be described as a mountainous island, the great peaks are almost entirely confined to a region in the south. Here are the Black Coolins, a volcanic range of jagged rock peaks, which cluster round the head of Loch Scavaig, and the strange looking Red Hills, which line the eastern side of Glen Sligachan. In the north of the island the long ridge which forms the backbone of Trotternish culminates in the lofty summit of the Storr, and breaks off beyond Staffin in the extraordinary crags and pinnacles of Quiraing. Westward, in Duirinish, are the two flat-topped hills known as MacLeod's Tables and the lofty cliffs of Waterstein Head.

The coast-line of the island is much indented and broken up by numerous lochs and bays. In the north are the great sea-lochs of Snizort and Dunvegan, each with smaller inlets at its head. Opening to the west is Loch Bracadale and the narrower inlets of Loch Harport, Loch Eynort,

Loch Brittle and Loch Pooltiel. Southward lies the deep
Loch Scavaig, and the twin lochs of Slapin and Eishort.
The far-extending eastern coast is less broken up and has
only five inlets—the sea-lochs of Sligachan and Ainort
opening towards Raasay and Scalpay, and the bays of
Staffin, Portree and Broadford.

The Sound of Sleat separates Skye from the mainland
of Inverness-shire, and is connected with Loch Alsh by
the tide-swept passage of Kyle Rhea. Further west the
narrows of Kyleakin lead to the Inner Sound, which
separates Rassay from Applecross. This is the largest of
the islands off the coast of Skye; it is long and narrow,
and contains the flat-topped mountain known as Duncaan.
To the north of Raasay is the rocky island of Rona, with
its lighthouse; southward is Scalpay, with its satellites
Longay and Pabbay. The island of Soay lies to the south-
west of Skye, off the entrance to Loch Scavaig, and is the
largest island along the west coast.

The glories of Skye are her mountains and sea-coast:
she has few inland lochs and hardly any woodlands. Much
of the interior of the island is desolate moorland, where
habitations are far to seek and peat is the only product.
The Isle of Mist is an apt name, for mist and rain are
frequent, but this has its compensations. Under a summer
sun the colouring of hills and rocks and sea is often astonish-
ingly vivid, and has been compared to that of Italy. Only
in Connemara can similar effects be found in these islands.

As the centres of population are by the shore, the main
roads follow the coast-line. From Kyleakin in the east of
the island a road leads by Broadford and Sligachan to
Portree, with branches to Ardvasar in Sleat, and to Elgol
in Strathaird. From Sligichan another road strikes westward to Drynoch, Loch Bracadale and Dunvegan, with
branches to Carbost on Loch Harport, and to Glendale at
the head of Loch Pooltiel. Portree is connected with
Dunvegan by a road which runs north-west to Skeabost
and Edinbain, and cuts across the base of the Vaternish
peninsula to the head of Loch Follart, sending off a

northerly branch to Trumpan at the mouth of Loch Dunvegan. Trotternish is served by two coast roads which join at Uig, the one going north from Portree by the sparsely peopled east coast, to Staffin, and thence by Flodigarry and Duntulm Castle round the north of the peninsula, the other crossing from Portree to the head of Loch Snizort and following the east shore of that loch to Uig. A short transverse road runs through the hills, connecting Uig with Staffin, and passing immediately below Quiraing; another, of indifferent surface, crosses the island from Portree to Struan, in Bracadale.

Skye is renowned in song and legend: it was the kingdom of the warrior Queen Sgathach, who ruled from Dunscaith with her Amazon guard. Here came the young Cuchullin, afterwards the paladin of Ulster, to learn the art of war, and to lose his heart to the white-bosomed Bragela. It was at Dunscaith, on the shores of Loch Eishort, that she awaited his return, when he sailed to Ulster to his death. Centuries later came Columba, another man of Ulster, bringing the gospel message to the Picts of Skye. A Columban monastery stood for many years on an island in a loch in Trotternish; the loch was drained in the eighteenth century, when the monastery boat was brought to light.

Skye was occupied by the Norsemen at an early date, and shows many traces of their influence. Even to-day a majority of the place-names is of Norse origin. Trotternish, Bracadale, Staffin, Uig and Scavaig come from the Norse, as do the terminations -ster, -stadr, -shader, and -bost. The great clan of the Macleods, which rose to power when the Norse sovereignty was on the wane, is of Norse descent, and the Mackinnons of Strath were allied by marriage with the strangers from the north. The Macleods held the west of the island; their chiefs have resided in the castle of Dunvegan for many centuries, and still treasure the Fairy Flag and the drinking horn of Rory Mor. The flag was given to the chief by a fairy wife in bygone years; it was to bring victory to the clan if waved in time of need. Twice it was used, and with success; the third time it was waved without cause, and dire results followed.

In Sleat and Trotternish lived the Macdonalds, a branch of the great clan whose head was once Lord of the Isles, and the peer of the Scottish kings. Their ancient castles of Dunscaith and Duntulm have long been in ruins, and have been succeeded by the modern castle of Armadale, standing in its sheltering woods by the shore of the Sound of Sleat, which is still the seat of Lord Macdonald. The history of Skye is largely made up of conflicts between the Macleods and the Macdonalds; for generations there was enmity between them, and the claymores were never long idle. From the year 1490, when the two clans met at Glendale, right into the seventeenth century, the red tartan and the yellow could never agree. At the Bloody Stone in Hart a' Corrie, at Trumpan in Vaternish, in Glen Brittle, and even in North Uist there was fierce fighting, sometimes marked by acts of savage cruelty. Such was the terrible massacre in the island of Eigg, when the entire population, with one exception, was suffocated in a cave by the Macleods. In revenge the Macdonalds crossed from North Uist to Skye, and burnt the church of Trumpan with all its congregation. But retribution came swiftly, for the tide was ebbing, and time was needed to launch their boats. Warned of the raid by a survivor, the Macleod fighting men were quickly on the spot, and made short work of their enemies, whose bodies were buried under a turf dyke, which was overturned for the purpose.

The Mackinnons, known as Clan Fingon, occupied the districts of Strathaird and Strath Suardal, behind Broadford, and the coast as far as Kyleakin and Kyle Rhea. Their burial-ground in Strath Suardal is still to be seen close to the ruined church of Kilchriosd. When Prince Charles Edward was being pursued through Skye in 1746, the Mackinnon chief was instrumental in effecting his escape to the mainland.

Of Flora Macdonald there is little that can now be said, for her story is familiar to all. Her monument stands near the road on the way to Duntulm, in the burying-place of Kilmuir, and her memory is still green in Skye.

COMMUNICATIONS

Steamers.—1. Daily from Mallaig and Kyle of Lochalsh to Portree, returning early next morning.

2. There is a motor-boat service between Mallaig and Armadale daily.

3. The Outer Isles steamer from Mallaig or Kyle serves certain ports on the west of Skye; *e.g.* Dunvegan.

4. The steamers *Hebrides* and *Dunara Castle* sail every ten days from Glasgow on a round voyage which includes places on the western side of Skye.

Ferries.—From Kyle of Lochalsh to Kyleakin at frequent intervals during each week-day. A motor launch runs daily between Glenelg and Kyle of Lochalsh, and will call at Kyle Rhea if required. There is also a ferry from Glenelg to Kyle Rhea.

Road Services.—There are mail motor services between Kyleakin and Ardvasar, between Broadford and Elgol, and from Portree to Uig and Staffin, to Dunvegan and to Sligachan. During the summer a full service of passenger motor-buses is in operation from Kyleakin, Portree and Broadford, by means of which almost any part of the island can be reached.

ACCOMMODATION

Hotels or inns at Ardvasar, Isleornsay, Kyleakin, Broadford, Sligachan, Portree, Uig, Flodigarry, Edinbain, Dunvegan, Orbost, Carbost and Struan. Other accommodation at Kyleakin, Broadford, Portree, Brogaig (Staffin), Uig, Dunvegan, Glendale, Struan, Harlosh, Glen Brittle, Elgol and Armadale.

Youth Hostels at Rha, near Uig, at Harlosh, near Dunvegan, at Staffin, and at Glen Brittle.

WALKS

Except between Broadford and Sligachan, and Sligachan

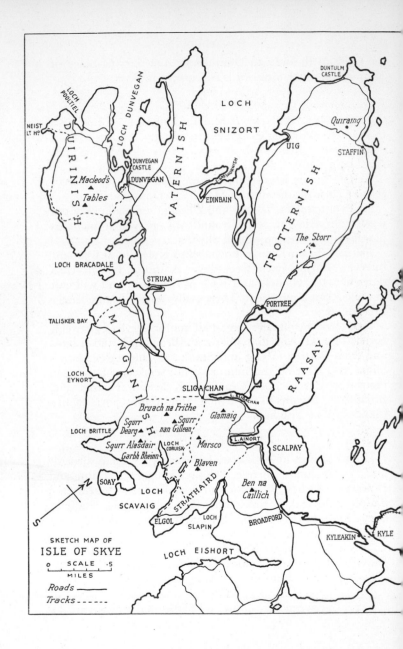

SKETCH MAP OF
ISLE OF SKYE

0   SCALE   .5
MILES

Roads ———
Tracks - - - - -

to Loch Bracadale, the main roads of Skye do not command the finest scenery in the island, which must be sought along byroads and hill-tracks. For this reason the walker is recommended to make use of the motor services along the main roads, and thus gain more time to devote to the Coolins, Trotternish, Dunvegan, and the fine scenery of the west coast.

(a) *Main Roads*

1. Kyleakin-Sligachan-Portree, 35 miles. Leaving the ferry pier at Kyleakin the road passes along the green strip above the beach, bends inland to cross a burn, and continues over featureless moorland to Broadford. At Lusa Bridge the old road from Kyle Rhea Ferry comes in on the left, and nearing Broadford the important road from Ardvasar in Sleat comes in from the south. Passing round the head of Broadford Bay, with its pier and hotels, where the road to Elgol diverges along Strath Suardal, the Portree road bends north round the base of Ben na Caillich, and hugs the shore-line all the way to the head of Loch Sligachan.

This part of the route is very fine, commanding ever-changing views of sea, islands and mountains. To seaward, across a narrow channel, lies the island of Scalpay, then the road bends round the promontory of Ard Dorch, opening up the south end of Raasay to view, and swings south to circle the shores of Loch Ainort. (Walkers can take the old road, which cuts across the base of the promontory from Strollamus.) The mountains rise close about the head of Loch Ainort; from Luib, on its eastern shore, the trough of Strath Mor leads across the island to the head of Loch Slapin. Through that glen went Prince Charles Edward and his guide Malcolm Macleod, in July 1746, when making for Elgol and the mainland.

Just beyond the head of Loch Ainort a disused road climbs steeply along the base of Ben Dearg and over the pass to Loch Sligachan, rejoining the main road at the foot of Glamaig. This was the route taken by the main road until the present shore road was made some few years ago.

Walkers should certainly follow this old road for the sake of the mountain views. The main road keeps close above the sea, rounding the peninsula to Loch Sligachan, and passes along the base of Glamaig to the head of the loch. The seaward views are very effective, the islands of Raasay and Scalpay and the Storr Rock standing out in the distance.

Sligachan Hotel stands inland from the head of Loch Sligachan on the west bank of the river, with the peaks of Sgurr nan Gillean towering beyond: to the south stretches the mountain-walled valley of Glen Sligachan. The road going straight past the hotel leads to Drynoch and Loch Bracadale. The Portree road turns off at right angles to the north, ascends to a low watershed, and leads down Glen Varragill towards Portree. This part of the route has little interest, except for the views of the Storr seen in the distance beyond the bay of Portree. Near the foot of Glen Varragill the road crosses to the west side of the river, and continues along the west side of the shallow inlet known as Loch Portree, to join the road from Uig and enter the town from the west. The town of Portree is the capital of Skye; it stands on the north-west shore of a fine bay, which opens on to the Sound of Raasay. From the pier, where the mail steamer arrives each evening, a road ascends to the upper part of the town, from which there are road connections to all parts of the island.

2. Portree to Uig, Staffin and back by the east side of Trotternish, 46 miles. This road goes west from Portree, and soon turns north and later north-west towards Loch Snizort. At Borve the Dunvegan road diverges to the west, and the Uig road begins its descent to Loch Snizort Beag, a narrow arm of the wide Loch Snizort. Passing the school and church at the head of the loch, the road goes north past Kingsburgh House, keeping at a distance from the shore, crosses Glen Hinnisdal, and comes down to Outer Loch Snizort at the bay of Uig. The houses of the populous township of Uig are situated on the hill-slopes at the head of a sheltered bay; there is a hotel, schoolhouse, church and pier, at which a steamer calls regularly.

From Uig a secondary road goes east up the glen of the River Rha, climbs to 853 feet, and descends to Brogaig, at the eastern foot of the Quiraing, where it rejoins the main road on its way back to Portree. The pass by which it reaches Brogaig is steep and winding; above it on the north rise the cliffs and pinnacles of Quiraing.

The main road from Uig continues north up the west coast of the peninsula, passing Monkstadt and Kilmuir; it runs at some height above the sea and commands wide views across Loch Snizort to the Ascrib Islands and the promontory of Vaternish. Beyond Kilmuir, on a byroad going off to the east, is the burying ground where Flora Macdonald sleeps. Close by is Peingown, where dwelt the Macarthurs, hereditary pipers to the Macdonald chiefs. Like the MacCrimmons at Boreraig, they held their lands in virtue of their office, and maintained a pipers' college for the instruction of aspiring musicians. Two miles further on, where a high rock overhangs the sea, stands the ruined castle of Duntulm, where the Macdonalds once ruled. Beside it is the Hill of Justice; below it, in a rocky creek of the bay of Duntulm, are the grooves worn by the keels of the Macdonald birlinns when being hauled up or launched.

Turning east at Duntulm the road passes through Kilmaluag, leaving on the left the headland of Rudha Hunish and the extreme north point of Skye, crosses to the east coast, and passes the mansion of Flodigarry, recently opened as a hotel. Continuing southwards below the dark crags of Quiraing, it reaches Brogaig, and the long straggling township of Staffin. Climbing out of Staffin to the cliffs beyond, it passes above the Kilt rock, a tall precipice with transverse markings which is best seen from the sea, and goes south across an elevated plateau which extends from the cliff edge to the base of the western hills. Across the sea are Rona and Raasay, with Applecross and the great peaks of Ross-shire beyond; to the right runs the line of inland cliffs which forms the backbone of Trotternish and culminates in the high Storr Rock. Below the Storr, road and hills bend towards each other, the former bending to the west to round the head of Loch Leathan, and pass down its western shore. Loch Leathan and the smaller and more southerly Loch Fada, from which a faint track leads up to the Beallach Mor and on to the Storr, are being incorporated in a hydro-electric scheme. A dam, 170 feet long and 36 feet high is to be constructed at the North end of Loch Leathan, whose level will be raised to the same as Loch Fada. The generating station will be on the shore at the mouth of the Bearreraig River. From Loch Fada another 3 miles of rise and fall brings us to Portree.

3. Portree to Dunvegan, 22 miles. This road diverges from the Uig road near Borve, descends past Carbost to cross the Snizort River at Skeabost and turns north along the estuary to Bernisdale. From here it describes a great semicircle to Edinbain at the head of Loch Greshornish, where it passes the hotel and goes west to Fairy Bridge, cutting across the base of the Vaternish promontory. At Fairy Bridge the road divides, one branch going north to Stein and Trumpan in Vaternish, the other south to Horneval and Dunvegan. At Horneval the Dunvegan road turns off to the west, reaching the shore of Loch Follart about a mile south of the castle, which stands on its rock above the sea. A short-cut for walkers leaves the main road a mile south of Fairy Bridge, and reaches the castle from the landward side.

4. Dunvegan to Bracadale, Drynoch and Sligachan, 24 miles. From Dunvegan the road leads south-east to Fairfield Cottage, where it turns south to Roskhill, at the head of Loch Vatten, an inlet of the island-studded Loch Bracadale. Thence it swings south-east to the head of Loch Caroy, skirts that inlet, and climbs inland across a peninsula to Struan on Loch Beag. Struan has two churches, a school and a hotel; beyond it the road winds round the head of Loch Beag and begins its five-mile switch-back coarse along the length of Loch Harport. This is a long narrow loch which penetrates inland towards the distant Coolins, which are well seen from the road. After

PLATE V CUILLIN RANGE—SOUTHERN END

The peak in the centre is Garsbheinn, tha
Da Bheinn. Beyond lie Loch Scavaig, th

Photograph by HUBERT J. WALKER

...gurr nan Eag, and on the left Sgurr Dubh na
...at, and in the distance the mainland hills.

ascending the last of its many hills, the road drops for nearly 400 feet to Drynoch, by the shore at the head of the loch, where it turns east up Glen Drynoch. This is a depression which extends across the island to the head of Loch Sligachan, from which it is divided by a narrow strip of higher ground just west of the hotel. To the south are the foothills of the Coolins, with Sgurr nan Gillean and Bruach na Frithe soaring into the sky beyond. The road descends from the head of Glen Drynoch to join the Portree-Broadford road beside the hotel at Sligachan.

5. Broadford to Ardvasar, 16 miles. This route leaves the Kyleakin road near the south-east corner of Broadford Bay, and crosses the peninsula to Loch na Dal on the Sound of Sleat. It passes through Isleornsay, with its inn, harbour and lighthouse, bends inland, and again reaches the sea at Knock Bay, to continue along the well-populated coast of Sleat to Armadale. The castle stands among its woods above the shore, looking across to the entrance to Loch Nevis; the road continues along the shore of the bay, passes the pier and reaches the hotel at Ardvasar, which stands not far from the church.

(b) *Byroads and Hill-tracks*

1. Kyle Rhea to Lusa Bridge, 6 miles. This is the old road from the Glenelg Ferry, now no longer used. It climbs very steeply from the pier at Kyle Rhea to the pass (911 feet), between Sgurr na Coinnich and Ben Aslak, and makes a more gradual descent of Glen Arroch to Lusa Bridge. At one place in the descent there is a broken bridge across a burn, which will cause little trouble to walkers, but would stop motor cyclists. The northward views across the sea from the summit of the pass are very fine.

2. Broadford to Elgol, via Torrin and Strathaird, 14 miles. This route goes up Strath Suardal, with Ben na Caillich overshadowing it on the north-west, passes the loch and ruined church of Kilchriosd, where the Mackinnons rest, and bends northwards to Torrin, above Loch

Slapin. From the road at this point there is an excellent view of Blaven, whose channelled sides and splintered crest tower up beyond the loch in all their majesty. The road descends to the level of Loch Slapin, rounds its head, and goes south along the shore at the base of Blaven. Then it climbs a long hill and bends inland, passes Strathaird House and the church of Kirkibost, skirts the eastern foot of Ben Meabost, and slants across the peninsula to Elgol. This is a populous village standing on the slopes above Loch Scavaig and enjoying a magnificent view of the peaks of the Coolins. It is a good centre from which to visit Loch Coruisk.

3. Elgol to Coruisk, Drumhain and Sligachan, 13 miles. For good walkers this is perhaps the finest excursion in Skye, embracing as it does the magnificent Loch Scavaig and dark Coruisk, and passing along the eastern skirts of the Black Coolins. Since the path in Glen Sligachan is easily lost, and is in any case rough and wet, care should be taken to begin the descent from Drumhain in ample time to arrive at Sligachan before dusk. The path leaves Elgol near the centre of the township, passes between Ben Cleat and the shore, and follows the eastern shore of Loch Scavaig as far as the Bay of Camasunary at its head. Turning west past the cottages by the bay, the track crosses the river by the stepping-stones, and goes south along the base of Sgurr na Stri, across a rocky plateau above Loch Scavaig. The going is very rough, but the views of the Coolins across the loch and southwards to Rhum and Eigg are very fine. At one point on the way to the head of Loch Scavaig it is necessary to cross the Bad Step, a smooth slab of rock sloping towards the sea far below, along which one must move with care by the aid of a transverse ridge. It is, however, possible to avoid this traverse by climbing higher up the hill-side.

At the innermost part of the loch a narrow barrier of rock separates it from Loch Coruisk, a fresh-water loch surrounded on three sides by steep mountain walls. Crossing this barrier the way lies along the eastern shore of

Coruisk, from which it turns north-east and makes for the ridge of Drumhain, over which goes the path to Sligachan. The path descends into Strath na Creitheach, joins at the foot of Rudha Stac another path coming up from Camasunary, and leads down Glen Sligachan to the hotel. The Sligachan River flows out of the recesses of Hart a' Corrie, turning into the main glen at the base of Marsco, where it is met by the path which accompanies it down the glen. Above on the left rises Sgurr nan Gillean, and on the right the Red Hills, Marsco, Glamaig and Ben Dearg. The main road is reached at a point just east of the bridge at Sligachan.

4. Sligachan to Glen Brittle, 8 miles. Leave the Drynoch road about half a mile west of the hotel, and take the path which leads up the glen of the Allt Dearg Mor and over the Beallach a Mhaim down to the road at the head of Glen Brittle. This pass leads round the north-west spurs of Bruach na Frithe and across the mouth of Coire na Creiche, where the Macleods were defeated by the Macdonalds. Glen Brittle is a wide glen lying at the back of the Coolins, whose main range rises on its eastern side. A road runs down it to the village at its foot, near the head of Loch Brittle. This road begins at Drynoch, goes west along the south shore of Loch Harport to Merkadale, and turns up the Vikisgill Burn to cross the hills and descend into Glen Brittle. The mountains which rise from the eastern side of Glen Brittle can conveniently be described as the Western Coolins; they consist of a main ridge extending from Sgurr nan Gobhar in the north-west to Gars Bheinn in the south-east above Loch Scavaig. This ridge contains the peaks of Sgurr na Banachdich, Sgurr Alasdair (3309 feet), Sgurr nan Eag and Sgurr Dearg, and sends out several spurs to east and west. A second ridge runs north-east to Sgurr a' Ghreadaidh and forms a link with Bidein Druim nan Ramh and the northern Coolins. By crossing the river near the schoolhouse at the head of Loch Brittle and going east along the base of the mountains it is possible to reach Coruisk and the track to Sligachan or the path to Elgol.

5. Drynoch to Talisker and Loch Eynort, 18 miles.

The north-west region of Minginish, which lies between Loch Harport, Loch Eynort and the sea, is well away from the beaten track and possesses striking coast scenery. From Drynoch Lodge, on the main road from Sligachan, a road goes west along Loch Harport to Carbost, near which is the Talisker distillery. From Carbost this road continues along the south-west side of the loch to Rudha Ban at its mouth, sending off a branch at Port nan Long by which it is possible to reach Talisker from the north. It is better, however, to take the hill road south from Carbost, climbing up the glen of the Carbost Burn to cross the pass at 610 feet and descend into narrow Glen Oraid, down which the Talisker River flows to the sea. This is a sheltered valley, containing the woods and gardens of Talisker House, above which rise the steep slopes of Preshal Mor, an abrupt rocky hill to the south. A little to the west is the bay of Talisker, shut in to north and south by high cliffs, and looking westward to the Outer Isles. Southward extends a line of cliffs, culminating in the 937-foot precipice near Biodh Ruadh, inland from which rises the hill of Preshal Beg, another of the abrupt rocks peculiar to this district. By going south along the cliffs and making his way between Ben Scaalan and the sea the walker can reach Glen Caladale and Husdale on Loch Eynort, which lies at the mouth of the fine glen known as Clachan Gorma. From Husdale, which the Ordnance map spells as Tusdale, there is a track across the hill to Borline at the head of Loch Eynort, where the road begins. This goes up Glen Eynort and climbs over a pass to join the Drynoch Road at Carbost.

6. Round the Duirinish peninsula, from Dunvegan, 24 miles. The coast scenery of Moonen Bay and along the south-western shores of Duirinish is very fine indeed, and cannot be viewed from a main road. The following route will take the walker round the peninsula by rough roads and paths, and will enable him to see the best of the coast scenery and to climb Healaval Beg (Macleod's Table South) if he is so inclined. Leaving Dunvegan for the south and crossing the Horneval River where it joins the sea near

the school at Kilmuir, the walker goes south to the head of Loch Follart, fords a burn and joins the road to Glendale. This road skirts the shore of Loch Dunvegan, passes the houses of Colbost and shortly afterwards, near a school, turns off to the west, climbs over a saddle of higher ground and descends into Glendale. By keeping north from Colbost the walker can reach Galtrigill and Dunvegan Head, south-west of which is the place where the cliffs drop from a height of 1025 feet towards the sea. From that point to Glendale it is possible to make one's way along the coast, but there are no paths.

Glendale is a populous valley which extends inland from the head of Loch Pooltiel. It was the scene of a battle between Macleods and Macdonalds in 1490, when the waving of the Fairy Flag brought victory to the former clan. There is a pier on Loch Pooltiel to which a steamer comes regularly from Glasgow. From Glendale the road goes west, dividing into three branches. One of these serves Milovaig and the pier, a second leads to the shore of Oisgill Bay and to the lighthouse on Eist Point, and the third goes south parallel to the coast. Moonen Bay lies open to the south, a crescent curving round from the Eist promontory to the high cliffs of Waterstein Head. The Head may be climbed from the landward side by going west from the road about a mile south of Borodale. This road climbs southwards to a height of 702 feet between Ben Vratabreck and the cliffs and descends to Ramasaig, where it comes to an end. From this point a rough track is the only foot-way; it leads south at the landward side of the high sea-cliff of the Hoe, crosses the Lorgill River and comes down to the lower shelf along the coast. The coast is then followed for some 3 miles past the mouth of Glen Dibidal to the fork just beyond, where a path cuts across the hill shoulder to Glen Ollisdal and ascends to the Beallach Varkasaig south of Healaval Beg. This is the flat-topped mountain known as Macleod's Table (South), and is the smaller of the two " Tables." From its flat summit in clear weather an extensive view is to be obtained;

Loch Bracadale and all Western Skye are spread out below, with the Coolins rising in the south-east; northward are Vaternish and Trotternish and to the south the jagged peaks of Rhum. Leaving Healaval behind, the path descends Glen Varkasaig to the head of the sea-loch of that name, turns north to Orbost and joins the road close to the head of Loch Follart, from which it is some 2 miles further to Dunvegan.

7. Portree to Struan by the hill road, 10 miles. Take the Uig road from Portree, turning off to the left at about a mile from the pier. The road leads west round the foot of Ben Grasco, crosses the Snizort River and is joined by a track coming from Skeabost. At Glengrasco, before descending to the Snizort River, it has crossed another track leading from Carbost on the Dunvegan road, up to Glen More and Mugeary, which stand isolated in the centre of the island. After crossing the river, the road climbs north, crosses the Lon Dubh Burn, and ascends to 500 feet a little to the south of Loch Connan. At this point, from which there is a splendid view to the west, begins the long descent along the course of the Allt Mor and through the glen to Struan.

8. Portree to Quiraing, by the Storr, 20 miles. This is certainly one of the finest high-level tramps in the whole of Scotland, traversing as it does the long ridge which extends along the axis of Trotternish, and commands magnificent views of the mainland hills. Leave Portree by the Staffin road, and at the north end of the small Loch Fada turn off to the left by a path which goes northwest towards the cliffs above. This path may be difficult to trace, but if one makes for the gap in the cliffs it should not be difficult to climb up to the Beallach Mor, as the pass is called. Once on the level of the cliff top, there is little difficulty in following the path along to the Storr, passing on the way the other pass of Beallach Beag, with its path coming up from Loch Leathan. The view from the summit of the Storr is probably the most extensive to be had in the Highlands, its wonderful array of mainland mountains, islands and sea-

lochs being rendered far more impressive by the moderate height of the rock and the absence of neighbouring hills. The grassy platform of the summit forms a restful couch on a warm day and would be an excellent camping place on a warm June night.

Northward from the Storr the ridge runs by Creag a' Lain (1995 feet) to Beinn Edra (2003 feet), and on to Bioda Buidhe above the Uig-Staffin road. It is broken by several gaps, such as the Beallach a' Chuirn, below the Storr, and the Beallach Harteval a little to the north. There is no defined path, but the way lies clear to anyone, so long as the hills are clear of mist. In descending to the road to reach Quiraing, or to find a night's shelter at Brogaig, it is well to go down the western side of the ridge, which is far less abrupt than the eastern. Quiraing can be reached from the road at the top of the pass to Brogaig by taking a track which leads along the lip of the cliff to the north, and brings the walker into the green hollow at the foot of the western crags. Another route leads up from the road at the eastern end of the bend which it makes in descending the pass, and works up to the Prison and the base of the Needle.

Quiraing is an extraordinary freak of Nature, a green, rock-encircled hollow in the heart of a mountain. As at the Storr and all along the ridge of Trotternish, the eastern face of the mountain breaks off in sheer precipices of black rock, which rise from a wide terrace or plateau. On the outer side of this terrace is another wall of cliffs, incomplete and broken away in places, which slope down to the moorlands of the east coast, and form the true outer wall of the mountain. In the considerable space between the two cliffs is a green hollow, and further on a table-like plateau of rock, covered with green turf, which is known as the Table. The narrow space between the two lines of cliffs towards the south is known as the Prison, and from it a rocky path leads out past the base of the Needle and round to the Table. The Needle is a tall column of rock which rises from a base of screes close to the main wall of cliffs.

Like the somewhat similar Old Man of Storr, it must once have formed part of the cliff behind it.

To visit Quiraing to best advantage it is well to climb from below into the Prison, pass along the foot of the cliffs and below the Needle to the Table, and make one's way out on to the cliff top near Loch Hasco, returning by way of the mountain summits to the road, and rejoining it above the top of the pass. Or one can descend from the north end of the mountain to the road near Flodigarry Hotel.

9. Broadford to Sligachan, by Strath Mor and the Red Hills, 18 miles. This is a circuitous route which affords an opportunity of traversing Strath Mor, the straight glen which connects Loch Ainort with the head of Loch Slapin, and of seeing something of the corries of the Red Hills. The section of the route which lies between Loch Slapin and Sligachan was traversed by Prince Charles Edward and his guide Malcolm Macleod on their way to Elgol in July 1746. From Broadford the route lies up Strath Suardal to Torrin, along the road already described in Route No. (b) 2. Torrin will always be celebrated for the magnificent view of Blaven, which many consider to be the finest mountain in Scotland. The road descends to the level of Loch Slapin and rounds the head of the loch, where the path leaves it on the east side of the bridge over the Strathmore River. This path goes north along the east shore of the river, passes haunted Loch na Sguabaidh, and continues along the base of steep-sided Glas Bheinn Mhor to Luib on Loch Ainort. Then the route goes southwest, along Loch Ainort, by the main road, turning off at the head of the loch after crossing the bridge, and climbing towards Marsco by way of Coire nam Bruadaran. At the head of this corrie, which ascends along the flank of Ben Dearg Mheadhonach, is the pass to Glen Sligachan, crossing the col between Marsco and Ben Dearg and descending into the steep and narrow Coire Dubh Measarroch. This corrie opens to the north-west into the glen, where the path from Camasunary to Sligachan is joined at a point 2 miles south of the hotel.

CHAPTER IX

APPLECROSS AND TORRIDON

MAPS.—*O.S. Popular Edition*, 1 *inch, sheets* 25 *and* 26.
Bartholomew's Half Inch, sheet 54.

APPLECROSS is a broad peninsula in Wester Ross, separated from Loch Carron by the inlet of Loch Kishorn. In the west it presents a long straight coast-line to the Inner Sound: to the north the great sea-loch of Torridon penetrates deep into the land. It is a wide plateau of brown moorland, shining with scores of lochs, and rising in the south to the rocky summits of Bheinn Bhan, which drops in sheer, black precipices towards Loch Kishorn. All its villages are on the coast, the interior being given over to deer and grouse. Applecross, on the Inner Sound, and Shieldaig, on an inlet of Loch Torridon, are the chief centres of population; both are linked by road with Lochcarron and with Strathcarron Station.

This road descends to Courthill, on Loch Kishorn, by way of the Kishorn Pass, goes north past Couldoran and the corries of Bheinn Bhan, to cross the low watershed and continue down Glen Shieldaig to the sea. Near the bridge of Tornapress the Applecross road goes off to the left around the head of Loch Kishorn, turns north into a deep glen flanked by black cliffs, and climbs by zigzags and hairpin-bends to a height of 2054 feet. This is the famous Beallach nam Bo (Pass of the Cattle), the second highest road in Britain; from the summit, on a clear day, the panorama of mountain, sea and islands is unequalled. A long rough descent of 5 miles leads to the bay of Applecross and the clachans of Milton, Camusterach and Toscaig, which look across the sea to Raasay and Skye. Off this southern corner of Applecross are the Crowlin Islands, with their curious mile-long fiord forming a natural harbour.

Bheinn Bhan, whose flat summit rises to 2936 feet, is the monarch of the Applecross hills: a series of deep corries, flanked by sheer cliffs, forms the eastern face of the mountain. Buttresses of black rock separate corrie from corrie, and project eastwards into the glen. Coire na Poite, in whose depths lie two green lochans, is the most striking of the corries; it lies immediately below the summit of Bheinn Bhan, and is reached by climbing from Loch Coire na Poite over the natural rock-dam behind which it lies. Coire nan Each, Coire na Feola and Coire an Fhamhair are other notable mountain hollows, while Coire nan Arr, with its loch and burn, penetrates deep into the range to the south of Bheinn Bhan, and gives access to the summit of that mountain.

Loch Torridon is one of the larger inlets on the west coast, ranking with Loch Hourn and Loch Nevis; like these it consists of a broad outer reach, communicating by a narrow straight with a land-locked inner loch. Outer Loch Torridon, which separates Applecross from Gairloch, sends out an offshoot to the south, which is known as Loch Shieldaig; on its east shore is the village of that name. The road from Lochcarron continues past Shieldaig to Balgy, on Upper Loch Torridon; there is no public road from Balgy to the head of the loch. Lofty mountains rise from the shores of Upper Loch Torridon, and make navigation difficult by reason of sudden squalls. Ben Alligin, on the north shore, rises to a height of 3232 feet; from its summit one may on occasion see the mainland mountains from Sutherland to Ardnamurchan. Liathach, a grand, white-capped giant of 3358 feet, towers above the village of Torridon at the head of the loch; his steep, terraced sides form the north wall of Glen Torridon, extending for 3 miles as far as the Black Corrie which separates this mountain from Ben Eighe. On the south shore, with Loch Damph at his feet, stands bulky Ben Damph; further to the west the long ridge of Ben Shieldaig shuts in the glen of that name.

Diabaig, on the northern shore of Outer Loch Torridon, Inveralligin, at the foot of Ben Alligin, and Torridon village, at the head of the loch, are, with Shieldaig, the centres of population in the district. The main road is that from Kinlochewe by way of Glen Torridon, which connects Loch Torridon with the head of Loch Maree. It rises gradually from Kinlochewe to a height of 343 feet, reaching the low summit of the watershed in 5 miles, and descends in another 6 miles to Torridon village, and the mansion house at Torridon. A steep and narrow road, with acute bends and indifferent surface, leads along the north shore to Diabaig, and is continued by a coast path to Craig, Red Point and Gairloch. On the opposite shore of the loch a right-of-way track leads to Balgy, passing along the hill-side at the back of the Ben Damph woodlands. The road which leads to the lodge along the shore, and thence to Balgy, is not open to the public.

Glen Torridon is a sombre, wind-swept glen, walled by high mountains, of which Ben Eay and Liathach are the most striking. On the south, above the entrance to Glen Coulin, towers the pyramid of Sgurr Dubh, its base washed by the waters of beautiful Loch Clair. Through Glen Coulin comes the road from Achnashellach, by way of the lovely Coulin Pass; northward, through the Black Corrie below Ben Eay, goes an old track by which the sturdy walker can reach Gairloch. Opposite the mouth of the Black Corrie, in the main glen, is the moraine deposit known as the Corrie of a Hundred Hills.

Applecross is notable as the site of one of the earliest religious foundations in the Highlands, or indeed, in all Scotland, for this was the spot chosen by Saint Maelrubha as the headquarters of his mission to the Western Picts. Maelrubha was an Irish cleric, trained at the great monastery of Bangor, in Ulster; he settled at Applecross in 673, and from there evangelised the districts now known as Ross and Sutherland. The tall, burly, red-haired priest, striding tirelessly through the glens and preaching by the loch-sides, soon endeared himself to the rude inhabitants, and spread the gospel amongst them. Even to-day, after twelve hundred years, men still speak of the Red Priest (An t' Sagairt Ruadh), and many a well and ancient church bears his name. Stately Loch Maree is the loch of Mael-rubha (or Maruve), for there, in the little island now known as Isle of Maree, was the well where he preached and the site of his wattle church. The loch was formerly known as Loch Ewe, for in the old days the sea-loch of that name extended inland as far as the foot of Glen Dochartie, where now stands Kinlochewe.

Saint Maelrubha's missionary journeys extended far into the North; he was slain by Vikings in Strathnaver in the year 722, and buried at Skail. His monastery at Applecross also suffered at the hands of the Norse and Danish sea rovers, but flourished anew after their raids ceased. It became a sanctuary where the homicide could find shelter; the lay abbots of mediæval times, who succeeded the Pictish clerics, were known as Fer na Comaraich (Lords of the Sanctuary). Even as late as the early nineteenth century the Mackenzie lairds of Applecross retained that title, but with the passing of the estate to English owners it is unlikely that the appellation is still in use. One of the stone crosses marking the boundary of the sanctuary still stands at Camusterach (the Boat Cove), by the old churchyard.

Applecross and Torridon, like other parts of Wester Ross, must have felt the Norse influence during the period of Norse rule in the Hebrides, for Diabaig, Toscaig and Shieldaig are Norse names. In later centuries the districts were included in the territories of the Earls of Ross, passing to the Mackenzies when that clan rose to power on the ruins of the Macdonald Lords of the Isles. During the conflicts between the Macleods and the Mackenzies to decide the ownership of the lands of Gairloch, a fierce battle was fought in 1610 on the south side of Glen Torridon, ending in the rout of the Macleods and the capture of their leader. Loch Torridon was at one time noted for its herring fishery, but of late years the fish seem to have deserted its waters.

COMMUNICATIONS

Rail.—There are no railways in the district, Strathcarron (L.M.S.) being the nearest station.

Steamer.—Kyle of Lochalsh to Applecross every week-day. The south-going service from Applecross to Kyle only operates during the summer. (May to September.)

Road Services.—1. Motor-bus from Strathcarron Station to Lochcarron, Courthill and Shieldaig daily. Also in reverse direction.

2. Motor-bus from Kinlochewe to Torridon, in connection with mails from Achnasheen daily. Also in reverse direction.

3. Mail motor-bus from Diabaig to Torridon and return daily.

ACCOMMODATION

Temperance hotels at Applecross and Shieldaig. Other accommodation in private houses at Inveralligin, Torridon and Annat (head of Loch Torridon).

Youth Hostels at Craig, Opinan and Inveralligin, also at Achnashellach in Glencarron.

HILL WALKS

(a) *By Road*

1. Lochcarron (Jeantown) to Applecross, 16 miles. Although the entire distance is along a road, this is a very fine walk indeed, provided that the hills are clear of mist. A full day should be allowed. The road begins at the west end of Lochcarron village, climbing west, north and again west to a height of 452 feet. Then comes a long descent through the Kishorn Pass, with the river in its gorge below, to the shore of Loch Kishorn, where the road turns north past Courthill House and goes on towards Shieldaig. Two miles beyond Courthill, the Applecross road diverges to the left, crosses the Kishorn River at Tornapress Bridge,

and begins its long climb to the Beallach nam Bo (Cattle Pass), curving round the lower slopes of Bheinn Bhan. The Russel Burn, which drains the deep Coire nan Arr to the north, is crossed, and the road swings away southwards to round the base of Sgurr a' Chaorachain and climb along its side towards the pass. Between this mountain and the opposing height of Meall Gorm is a deep hollow, walled by black crags, below which, on a ledge of rock, runs the road, making for the high saddle at the head of the glen. It climbs up to the summit by a series of zigzags and hair-pin-bends, with a mile of straight road to reach the highest point at 2054 feet. The finest views are obtained from the top of the zigzags, looking back down the glen. Below one's feet is the winding road, wavering downwards along the slopes between frowning bastions of black rock. High in the sky, beyond the shining waters of Loch Kishorn, tower the great peaks of Central Ross and Inverness-shire. To the south-west the black mass of Meall Gorm shuts out the view of Skye and Loch Alsh; these are seen to advantage from a point close to the summit of the road.

Continuing in a north-westerly direction the road begins to fall, curls round the flanks of Meall Gorm down a steep and twisting hill, and opens up an extensive view to the north and west. The brown moors of Applecross roll northwards to Loch Torridon, with Longa and the low lands of Gairloch beyond in the blue distance: Raasay, Rona and Skye lie west across the sea. A long, rough descent to the bridge over the Allt Beag is followed by a short rise, then with a westward sweep of 3 miles the road swings down to Applecross village, on the south side of Applecross Bay.

2. Applecross to Toscaig, 4 miles. This is a continuation of the previous route. It leads south along the coast to the clachan of Camusterach (Boat Cove), with its school, manse and churches, standing by the side of a long, reef-guarded bay. Before reaching Camusterach, a branch road goes off to Camusteel, which stands on an inlet near the mouth of the same bay. The main road passes along the eastern

shore, goes inland to cross the base of the peninsula, and finishes at Toscaig, near the head of the sea-loch of that name. A path leads from Toscaig round the coast to Tornapress, at the head of Loch Kishorn.

3. Lochcarron to Shieldaig and Balgy, Loch Torridon, 17 miles. As far as the turn to Tornapress Bridge this route is the same as that described in Route No. 1. The Shieldaig road keeps on up the glen to the north, passes the white house of Couldoran which stands below the towering cliffs of Bheinn Bhan, and climbs above the west shore of the long and narrow Loch an Loin. Avoiding the head of Loch Damph, which stretches northwards in its own long glen, the road ascends to the watershed at a height of 422 feet, and crosses over into Glen Shieldaig. Descending this glen past the fresh-water Loch Dughaill, with its wooded eastern shore, it reaches the sea at the head of Loch Shieldaig, and runs by the shore through the village of that name. The shores of the inlet to the west, and the hill-sides above Loch Dughaill were well wooded, but many trees have been felled for timber, leaving the hill-sides bare. Shieldaig Island, which lies off the village, is covered with trees. At the school the road bends to the east, crosses the peninsula, and rounds the head of Ob Mheallaidh, an inlet of Loch Torridon. Thence it continues along the coast to the farm of Balgy, where it comes to an end. There is, however, a bridge across the river, from which a path leads east to Annat at the head of Loch Torridon, keeping outside the boundary fence of the Ben Damph Woods. This path later on leads down a lane with the woods on each side, climbs out along the open hill-side, dropping once more to the woods behind Ben Damph House, crosses a stream and joins the road just east of the lodge gates. (This road leads to Torridon village, or eastward through Glen Torridon to Kinlochewe.) The path runs for part of the way high on the hill-side, and affords magnificent views of Ben Alligin and of Liathach seen across Loch Torridon.

4. Torridon to Diabaig, 8 miles. This is a narrow and winding road, with steep hills and acute corners, from which

there are fine views south and west over Loch Torridon. From Fasag, the proper name for the village of Torridon, the road from Kinlochewe continues west along the north shore of the loch as far as the gates of Torridon House. A branch road diverges to the right to climb the hill-side, skirts the woods behind Torridon House, crosses a bridge over the Amhuinn Coire Mhic Nobuil, and goes west along the base of Ben Alligin to the bridge over the Alligin River. Beyond the bridge is a steep and winding ascent to the Beallach na Gaoithe (Windy Pass), and an equally steep descent to Loch Diabaig's Airde, a long sheet of water beside which the road runs for more than a mile. Lower Diabaig stands by the shore half a mile to the south-west of the end of this loch: the road, however, has to go west and make a sharp turn before descending to the village. From Diabaig a path goes north along the coast to Craig, Red Point and Gairloch.

(b) *By Hill-tracks*

1. Strathcarron to Couldoran, by the Beallach a' Glas Cnoic, 8½ miles. This is a hill-track which will be of use to walkers making for Shieldaig. Leave Strathcarron Station for the main road to Lochcarron, and go south along it for nearly a mile. Take a cart track which leads to the farm of Tullich, where a path begins. Follow this path, which slants north along the hill-side and round the eastern and northern slopes of Glas Bheinn, crossing the pass at 1350 feet, and descending past a wood and along the Allt a' Ghiubhais to Loch an Loin. Here the Shieldaig road is joined, some three-quarters of a mile north of the house of Couldoran.

2. Strathcarron to Torridon, by Coulags, 12 miles. This is a fine path through the mountains, which materially shortens the journey from Loch Carron to Loch Torridon. Coulags is on the Achnasheen road, 2¼ miles north of the turn to Strathcarron Hotel. From it a path goes north up the glen along the Fionn Amhuinn, leading to Loch Coire Fhionnaraich, which lies at a height of 800 feet between

Sgurr Ruadh (3142 feet) and Maol Cheann Dearg (3060 feet). Skirting this loch the track climbs to the Beallach na Lice (1250 feet) and goes west along Loch an Eoin, then between two smaller lochs, and down the northern slopes of Beinn na h' Eaglaise to Annat, at the head of Loch Torridon.

3. Achnashellach to Torridon, by Glen Lair, 10 miles. This path begins by Achnashellach Station, and goes north through the woods up the east bank of the River Lair, climbing steeply out of Glen Carron. Glen Lair, with its rushing river and steep mountain walls, is particularly impressive, and the Coulin mountains are seen to great advantage from this route. Turning west the track climbs steadily up between Ben Liath Mhor (3034 feet) and Sgurr Ruadh (3142 feet), crosses the high pass at the head of the glen, and circles round a nothern spur of Sgurr Ruadh to the Beallach Ban. Crossing this pass it proceeds along the southern flank of Meall Ban, and joins Route No. 2 at the Beallach na Lice. This route is a little shorter than that by Coulags, reckoned from Achnashellach Station; it penetrates deeper into the mountains and crosses the pass at a higher level.

4. Tornapress to Toscaig by the coast, 12 miles. This route leaves the road at the foot of Bheinn Bhan, 1 mile south of Tornapress Bridge, and goes south along the shore. Fording the Russel Burn it continues along the coast for 3 miles, and then climbs to a height of 500 feet along the hill-side above the cliffs of Outer Loch Carron. Rudha na h' Uamha (Cave Point), forms the southern corner of Applecross; here is a wood and the cottages of Uags, where the track bends to the north. In the offing are the Crowlin Islands, with their curious narrow fiord-like harbour, opening to the north. Toscaig is 2 miles north of Uags: the path leads along the hill-side, with the inlet of Loch Toscaig below to the left, crosses the Toscaig River and joins the Applecross road a short distance beyond the village.

5. Applecross to Shieldaig by the coast, 21 miles. This track follows the west coast of the peninsula and keeps well

up on the hill-side above the cliffs, commanding fine views of Raasay, Rona, Skye, Lewis and Loch Torridon. It leaves Applecross at the bridge near the manse and church at the mouth of the Applecross River, and at once climbs the hill-side above the bay. Six miles further on it passes the clachan of Lonbain, and then a school. A mile beyond is Kalnakill, with its natural arch of rock below the cliffs. At Cuaig, where a river is crossed, a short-cut may be taken by going east across the hills to Arinacrinachd. The coast track, however, leads north-east to Fearnmore, a village and church at the mouth of Loch Torridon, opposite Red Point in Gairloch. Thence the route runs south to Arina-crinachd, passing through woods by Kenmore and Loch a' Chracaich, and thence by a track which turns inland, and down to Ardheslaig at the head of Loch Beag. Crossing the neck of the peninsula which shelters Loch Shieldaig, the track follows the shore through the trees to Inverbain and Rhuroin, turning inland from thence to the head of the loch. The Shieldaig River is forded close to its mouth, and the road joined three-quarters of a mile south of the inn.

6. Applecross to Shieldaig, by Strath Maol Chaluim, 9 miles. This route leads up the glen of the Applecross River, and thence over the hills to Shieldaig. The road goes from the village past Applecross House, crosses the river and continues as a cart track along the right bank. Another way is to follow the public road along the shore, cross the bridge near the church, and turn to the right along the road until the cart track is reached. Two miles up the glen it becomes a path, which shortly afterwards divides into two, the right-hand one crossing the river just above its junction with a tributary, and heading north-east to a pass below the southern shoulder of Croic-bheinn (1618 feet). At the summit (1213 feet) the path again divides, that to Shieldaig going north-east to cross the Amhuinn Dubh, and join the sea-board path from Ardhes-laig in the woods 1 mile from the head of Loch Shieldaig.

7. From Torridon round the base of Liathach, by Coire Mhic Nobuil and the Black Corrie, 14 miles. This route

leads through the heart of the Torridon range, and passes close to Liathach, Ben Alligin, Ben Dearg and Ben Eighe. By extending the time allowed it is possible to visit also Coire Mhic Fhearchair at the back of Sail Mhor, and Loch a' Ghlas Tuill at the foot of the northern precipices of Liathach. Take the Diabaig road from Fasag (Torridon village), turning off by the path which goes north along the Amhuinn Coire Mhic Nobuil. This track follows the river for a mile, crosses to the north bank, and continues along it below the slopes of Ben Dearg, where it ceases. From here, with the stream as guide, we go east, past Loch Grobaig to the smaller Lochan a' Coire Dhuibh, which lies below the steep slopes of Sail Mhor, at the mouth of the Black Corrie. To the south towers Liathach, his black splintered pinnacles culminating in the 3456 feet of Spidean a' Choire Leith, which rises above Loch a' Ghlas Tuill. A stream flows from this loch and joins the river west of Loch Grobaig: by following its course up into the mountain it is possible to reach the high, cliff-encircled corrie in which Loch a' Ghlas Tuill, with three smaller lochs, lies hidden.

Loch Coire Mhic Fhearchair is a larger sheet of water, lying at a height of 1900 feet among the precipices of Ben Eay. It is reached by rounding the north-west flank of Sail Mhor, and working up the course of the stream which issues from the loch. Ruadh Stac Mor and Sail Mhor rise from the shore of the loch, which is hemmed in on the south by the great rock buttresses of Ben Eighe. The stream which issues from the loch flows down to Loch Maree, and is the head stream of the Grudie River.

Beside Lochan a' Choire Dhuibh is the head of the path which leads through the Black Corrie, between Liathach and Ben Eighe, into Glen Torridon. After crossing the watershed it follows the course of the burn, known as the Burn of the Great Black Corrie, first along its left bank and later down the opposite one, down to the Kinlochewe road in Glen Torridon. The end peak of Liathach rises abruptly to the west, and across the glen is the black pyramid of Sgurr Dubh. To the east the loose screes and jagged summit-ridge of Ben Eighe curve away towards Loch Maree. It is 4 miles down Glen Torridon to Fasag, at the head of the loch.

Note.—If this walk is taken in the reverse direction, it may be possible to make use of the morning mail motor service as far as the mouth of the Black Corrie, where a bridge carries the road across the Burn of the Great Black Corrie.

8. The old drove road from Torridon to Achnashellach, 14 miles. Instead of crossing to Achnashellach by way of the high passes of Beallach na Lice and Beallach Ban, walkers may prefer to use the old drove road which runs by Coulin to Achnashellach. This old track, which is sometimes used even to-day, followed the line of the present road from Torridon as far as Lochan an Iasgaich, where it forded the stream which flows from the Black Corrie, and went north of the loch, along the good going on the hill-side, parallel to and to the south of the present road. Passing to the south of Loch Bharranach, it curved to the south along the west side of Loch Clair, forded the Allt na Luib, and went on along the western shore of Loch Coulin. The present shooting path from Loch Bharranach to Coulin Lodge runs along the line of the old road, which followed the present private road along its course from the lodge southward.

At the south end of Loch Coulin this old road was joined by the track coming along the hill-side from Kinlochewe, and from that point to Achnashellach its course is followed by the modern road. This is one of the old and necessary drove roads; it would be a great pity if its course ceased to be used. Walkers can do much to maintain the right to use these roads by traversing them whenever possible.

CHAPTER X

KINLOCHEWE AND LOCH MAREE

MAPS.—*O.S. Popular One Inch, sheet* 26.
Bartholomew's Half Inch, sheets 54 *and* 58.

THE village of Kinlochewe stands where three glens meet, at the head of the long trough in which lies Loch Maree. The loch was once known as Loch Ewe, a name now applied to the big sea-loch into which, along the River Ewe, Loch Maree pours its waters. At one time the sea penetrated as far as Kinlochewe, and covered the flats where the village now stands; but this was before the days of human occupation, and has nothing to do with its present name. Glen Torridon from the south, Glen Dochartie from the south-east, and Glen Cruaidh Choillie from the north-east converge on the head of the level strath through which the Kinlochewe River flows. The last-named glen is sometimes called Glen Logan, but its correct name is Cruaidh Choillie.

Kinlochewe of to-day centres on its hotel, church and post-office; it has a few shops, a shooting-lodge, and numerous houses, at some of which travellers can often find accommodation. The road from Achnasheen, after descending the long, steep slopes of Glen Dochartie, passes the plantations of Kinlochewe Lodge, crosses the stream flowing from Glen Torridon, and arrives at the hotel and the post-office. A few yards further on it is joined by the road from Torridon, and then continues for 2 miles to the head of Loch Maree on its way to Talladale and Gairloch. Behind the village towers Ben Eighe, whose long slopes of unstable screes lead up to a narrow summit ridge of splintered rock. The whitish quartzite of which the mountain is composed gives it the appearance of having a permanent snow-cap. North of Ben Eighe the lesser hill of Meall Ghuibhais (Fir Tree Hill) overlooks the end of Loch Maree, across which rise the steep sides of Slioch, the monarch of the Loch Maree hills.

Loch Maree lies in a frame of splendid mountains: it is 12 miles long, and extends in a north-westerly direction to the outflow of the River Ewe. The southern end of the loch is long and narrow; further north is broadens out and is studded with numerous wooded islands. Three centuries ago its shores were densely wooded, but the iron smelting works which were established at Furnace and in other places on the east shore required great quantities of fuel, and the hill-sides were stripped of their trees. To-day there are fine woodlands along certain portions of the loch shore, notably near Rhu Nohar, at the head of the loch, and near the hotel at Talladale. The trees are mostly pines and silver birches, growing among the rocks and soft green mosses above the shore; they are the remnants of the forests which once covered all the Highlands. There are also beautiful woods along the eastern shore, at Ardlair and Letterewe, and in all the islands, while on the slopes above Slattadale are the ordered plantations of a Government Forestry estate. It is the trees which lend such charm to the loch-side road between Loch Maree Hotel and Kinlochewe, and along the road to Gairloch.

Along the north-east shore of the loch extends a line of mountains, whose slopes rise directly from the shore. Nearest to Loch Ewe is Ben Airidh Charr (Hill of the Rough Shieling), whose long gradual western slopes break off in mighty precipices to the east. Meall Mheinnidh (the Middle Hill) stands further to the south, and is separated by a pass, the Beallach Mheinnidh, from the long range of cliffs which forms the eastern face of Ben Lair. Ben Lair, with its outlying buttress of Sgurr Dubh, extends to the south-east, and drops to the depression in which lies Loch Garbhaig, a high mountain loch situated between

Loch Maree and lonely Lochan Fada. Beyond the loch are the western slopes of Slioch, the dominating height of Loch Maree, whose lofty summit rises from a broad and rugged base to a height of 3217 feet above the sea.

On the opposite side of Loch Maree the mountains stand further back from the shore and are less regular in their arrangement. Meall Ghuibhais, close to the head of the loch, is somewhat of an exception; its flanks descend to the shore at Glas Leitire (the Grey Slope), and hardly leave room for the passage of the road to Talladale and Gairloch. Behind this mountain, at the head of Glen Grudie, stand Ruadh Stac Beag, Ruadh Stac Mor and Sail Mhor, all three spurs of the long Ben Eighe, and Ben a' Chearcaill (Mountain of the Hoops), which forms the western side of the same glen. Further to the west is Ben an Eoin (Bird Mountain), which lies back behind Loch Maree Hotel, and is hardly seen from the road. Most of these mountains are composed of a dark brown sandstone, known as the "Torridon Red," but north of Ben an Eoin this formation gives place to the Archæan Gneiss, sometimes termed Lewisian Gneiss, which is the oldest rock in Scotland. The low, rounded, rocky hills which separate Loch Maree from Gairloch and extend northwards towards Poolewe, are all of this gneiss formation; their grey rock surfaces have been smoothed and ground by glacier action, which has also deposited great boulders along the high ridges and upon the plateaux. Worn down and eroded through countless winters the gneiss hills are rarely of great height; the highest summits in this Gairloch-Loch Maree-Poolewe area are the twin heights of Meall an Dorein and Meall an Spardain, of 1381 and 1356 feet respectively.

In the broad lower reach of Loch Maree is an archipelago of wooded islands, divided from each other by narrow channels. Eilean Suthainn, Garbh Eilean and Eilean Ruaridh Mor are the largest of these; in the first are two small lochans, beside one of which ospreys used to nest. Between Eileen Suthainn and the east shore of Loch Maree is the little Isle Maree, with its ancient burial ground, holy well and wishing tree. Here also is the site of a church founded by Saint Maelrubha of Applecross, after whom the island and the loch are now named. Isle Maree is very small, but within the compass of its pebbly beaches are trees of oak, ash, alder, holly, larch, beech and rowan. Seen from miles away on the shores of the loch it is sharply distinguished from its neighbour islands by the lighter shade of its foliage. The Wishing Well is now dry, and the ancient oak tree, on whose branches offerings were once tied, now leans, a mere dead stump, beside it. It was the custom during the nineteenth century to drive copper coins edgewise into the bark of the tree, which probably killed it. Even now the bare grey trunk bristles with coins, and many lie at its foot.

Only one road runs along the shore of Loch Maree, that from Achnasheen and Kinlochewe to Gairloch. Reaching the head of the loch opposite the farm of Taagan, it runs for 3 miles through the woods of Glas Leitire, hugging the windings of the shore and affording glorious vistas of tree and rock and mountain. On the right, near the head of the loch, is the little pier of Rhu Nohar (the Giant's Point), where passengers once used to embark in the steamer *Mabel* for the sail up the loch to Talladale and Tollie. Once clear of the woods, the road turns inland to cross the Grudie River, beyond which is an impressive view up Glen Grudie to the peak of Ruadh Stac Mor. Then comes 4 miles of open country, over which the road rises and falls, keeping at a distance from the shore and at a considerable height above it. Two and a half miles from Loch Maree Hotel is Bankes Bay, from which a ferry goes across to Letterewe, then the road cuts across the base of a broad peninsula, swings down a hill to Talladale Bridge, and arrives at Loch Maree Hotel. The hotel stands in a well-wooded hollow on the shore of a wide bay to the west of the Talladale River, which flows down the long straight Strath Lungard from its source under Ben Dearg.

Beyond the hotel the lochside is shaded with woods of silver birch, through which the road leads west to Garavaig

Bridge, and turns inland up the hill-side to climb through
the plantations of the Slatterdale Forestry Centre and over
the pass to Gairloch. The old house of Slattadale can be
seen down by the loch shore. It is a long climb to the road
summit, with glorious rearward views of Slioch, the loch
and the islands. Then comes a short descent to the shore
of Loch Bad an Sgalaig, across which the majestic mountain
of Baeish Bheinn heaves his great bulk into the sky. Baeish
Bheinn is actually a long ridgy hill, with three summits,
but only the northern end of the mountain is seen from
this point. Half a mile beyond the loch is the head of the
Pass of Kerrysdale, down which goes the road to Gairloch.
A hydro-electric scheme to unite both Loch Bad an Sgalaig
and the more southerly Dubh Loch is planned. A dam
across the River Kerry will raise the water of the first loch
30 feet. This raising will cause the two lochs to merge and
will submerge the line of the present road between Gairloch
and Loch Maree. The generating station will be on the
north bank of the River Kerry about $1\frac{1}{4}$ miles downstream
from the outlet of Loch Bad an Sgalaig.

The north-east shore of Loch Maree has no roads and
few houses. Ardlair, at the foot of Ben Airidh Charr, is a
mansion built in the mid-nineteenth century; at Letterewe, among trees and gardens is the shooting-box of the
Marquis of Zetland, which is connected by a ferry with the
opposite shore. From Letterewe a path goes east through
the hills past Loch Garbhaig to the shore of lonely Lochan
Fada, which stretches for 4 miles in a deep trough to the
north of Slioch. Another path crosses a pass, the Beallach
Mhcinnidh, to the west of Ben Lair, and descends to the
head of the Fionn Loch and the keeper's house of Carn
Mor. Fionn Loch is an extensive sheet of water which
occupies the depression to the north of Ben Airidh Charr,
and drains by the Little Gruinard River into Gruinard
Bay. At its head is the mountain-walled Dubh Loch,
separated from the larger loch by a narrow causeway.
From the head of Lochan Fada towards the Dubh Loch
runs Glen Tulacha, a narrow gash at the foot of the cliffs

of Ben Lair. At its upper end is the Beallach a' Chuirn, a green pass leading west to join the Letterewe path at the top of the Beallach Mheinnidh.

Many competent judges consider Loch Maree to be the finest of the Highland lochs; it is certainly the most majestic in the North-West Highlands. Its mountain screen is unequalled, even by Loch Lomond; its silver birches and Scots pines can compare with any in the North, and its islands and bays still preserve their quiet beauty, remote from the clamour of modern mechanical civilisation.

Long ago, when the Picts lived by Loch Maree, Saint Maelrubha of Applecross made his way to the isle of the Holy Well, where his wattle church soon became a centre of Christianity in the district. It is probable that the island had been a centre of pagan worship, perhaps of a water-god, for even as late as the seventeenth century bulls were still sacrificed at this spot, nominally in honour of " Mourie" (Maelrubha or Maruve). How soon after the saint's death it was called Isle Maree we do not know; it is said that a hermit's cell stood in the centre of the island, and that a Norse chief and his bride lie buried under two slabs nearby. Their story has been told of other lovers in other lands; it is that of the Black Flag and the White.

The princess, who lived in Isle Maree while her lover was absent on a Viking cruise, was to hoist a white flag when he returned, to indicate that all was well. Wishing to test his love, she feigned death, stretched herself on a bier, and had the black flag hoisted in her barge. The sea-rover, landing in Loch Ewe, hastened to Loch Maree and sailed to meet his bride.

> " But when the black flag he afar descried,
>   In heedless sport displayed, sank shuddering down and died."

When the vessels met, and the princess learnt the truth, she stabbed herself and died with her lover.

The Norsemen ruled in Gairloch for several centuries, and were followed by MacBeaths from the north, a clan of Gaelic blood. They were succeeded by Macleods from

Lewis, belonging to the Siol Torquil; they held Gairloch for many years, and occupied several of the islands in Loch Maree. The Macleods are thought to have expelled their predecessors by force of arms; they lost Gairloch to the Mackenzies in the same way. Kinlochewe saw much fighting in those days, for it took almost a century to clear the Macleods out of Gairloch. The name of the farm of Anacan, a corruption of Ath nan Ceann (Ford of the Heads), is a reminder of one such battle, when the heads of slain men choked a ford on the Kinlochewe River. When the Mackenzies had secured a footing in Gairloch, several of their chiefs resided in the islands of Loch Maree: the famous Ruaridh Mor (Big Rory) has given his name to one of the larger ones.

Roads in Gairloch and by Loch Maree are of comparatively recent introduction, for there were no wheeled vehicles in the district at the beginning of the nineteenth century. The road from Loch Maree to Gairloch was constructed at the end of the 'Forties as part of a scheme for employing the hungry people at the time of the potato famine. Prior to its construction it was necessary to cross the hills by a rough track from Slattadale to Flowerdale, which can still be followed for some 4 miles from near Loch Bad an Sgalaig. Another old track went over the hills from Slattadale to Poolewe, going through the pass below Craig Tollie to join the modern road at the top of Poolewe Brae. The mails used to be carried by post-runners along the roadless eastern shore of Loch Maree to Poolewe, from which a mail packet sailed at intervals to Stornoway.

COMMUNICATIONS

Rail.—Achnasheen, on the L.M.S. line from Inverness to Kyle of Lochalsh, is the nearest station.

Road Services.—A mail and passenger motor-bus runs daily between Achnasheen and Laide, calling at Kinlochewe, Loch Maree Hotel, Gairloch, Poolewe and Aultbea. Additional passenger services are in operation from

May to November, which terminate at Strath, in Gairloch, and also serve Badachro and Port Henderson on the south shore of the sea-loch.

There is a daily motor-bus service between Torridon and Kinlochewe, connecting with Achnasheen.

An additional mail and passenger service runs daily in both directions between Poolewe and Inverasdale.

Accommodation

Hotels at Kinlochewe, Loch Maree (Talladale) and Achnasheen. Other accommodation at Kinlochewe.

Youth Hostel at Alligin, Loch Torridon.

Walks

(a) *By Road*

1. Achnasheen to Kinlochewe, 10 miles. Leaving the station at Achnasheen the road joins that from Achanalt, and soon passes into the woods which fringe Loch a' Chroisg (Loch Rosque). Passing the entrance to Loch Rosque Lodge, where in former years a pair of golden eagles were caged near the road, the highway continues for 3 miles along the shore, and then climbs for 2 miles towards the head of Glen Dochartie. The view from the summit on a clear day is very fine: the long straight glen runs north-west down to the head of Loch Maree, whose whole length of 12 miles is visible in the distance. The road winds steeply down between the river and the hill-side, turns west at the glen foot to cross the stream, and runs past the lodge and over the bridge to Kinlochewe Hotel.

2. Kinlochewe to Achnashellach, 10 miles. This route follows the right-of-way path to the head of Loch Coulin, and then goes along the road and over the pass to Achnashellach. There is also a private road connecting Glen Torridon with Loch Coulin; this passes Loch Clair and Coulin Lodge and is closed to motor traffic. Leave the Achnasheen road at the east side of the bridge near the Kinlochewe Hotel, and take the path which leads south

SKETCH MAP OF
GAIRLOCH, LOCH MAREE,
AND LOCH BROOM.

SCALE
0   5   10
MILES

Roads ——— Tracks - - - - -

SUMMER
ISLES

Cul Mor
KNOCKAN
Stack Polly
Cul Beag
ACHILTIBUIE
Ben More
Coigeach

LOCH BROOM

LOCH Achall

GRUINARD
BAY
LITTLE LOCH BROOM
GRUINARD
Ben Ghobhlach
ULLAPOOL

RUDHA
REIDH
COVE
AULTBEA
DUNDONNELL
An Teallach

MELVAIG
LOCH EWE
LOCH NA SHEALLAG

FIONN LOCH
Ben Dearg Mhor

NORTH ERRADALE
POOLEWE

STRATH
GAIRLOCH HOTEL
FLOWERDALE
Ben Aridh Charr
A'Mhaighdean
Mullach Coire Mhic Fhearchair

LONGA ISLAND
GAIRLOCH
Meall an Doirein
Meall Mheinnidh
Ben Lair
LOCH BHRAOIN

LOCHAN FADA
LETTEREWE

LOCH BAD AN SGALAG
LOCH MAREE HOTEL
Slioch

RED POINT

LOCH MAREE

Baeish Bheinn
Ben an Eoin
Ben a' Chearcaill
Meall a Ghiubhais

LOCH TORRIDON
DIABAIG
Ben Dearg
Ben Alligin
Ben Eay
KINLOCHEWE

Liathach
TORRIDON
L. CLAIR

SHIELDAIG

along the river side. Soon the path begins to ascend along the hill-side, diverging from the course of the river, which flows out of Loch Clair. Steadily climbing, and command-ing fine views of Ben Eighe across the glen, the track reaches a height of 950 feet on the flank of the mountain called Carn Domhnuill Mhic a' Ghobha (Hill of Donald the Smith's Son), and forthwith drops swiftly down to the head of Loch Coulin. Four burns are now forded in succession, and the Coulin River is crossed by a bridge before the path joins the road from Coulin Lodge.

This road goes up the left bank of the river, crosses a bridge over the Easan Dorcha, and climbs steadily up to the Coulin Pass, which is crossed at a height of 950 feet. All the way up the ascent there are fine views of the Grey Heads, the mountains of the Coulin Forest which rise to the west, and of the crest of Ben Eighe towering above Loch Clair to the north. From the summit of the pass one looks down into deep Glen Carron, and across at the mountains beyond; there is a magnificent view-point close to the gate which marks the limits of Coulin Forest. Passing through this gate the road turns west and descends the side of the glen through the woods to Achnashellach, where it crosses the railway line close to the station, and joins the road to Lochcarron.

3. Kinlochewe to Torridon, 11 miles. This road turns south past the post-office, and ascends very gradually along the west bank of the river, with the slopes of Ben Eighe on the right and the dark peak of Sgurr Dubh in front. Presently the road bends to the south-west, and the private road to Coulin and Achnashellach diverges to the south; Loch Clair is passed on the left, and the summit of the low watershed is reached opposite the northern cliffs of Sgurr Dubh. Thence the road descends gradually to Loch Torridon, crossing the Burn of the Black Corrie, which foams down from the rocky defile to the north, and curving along the base of Liathach, the giant mountain of Torridon. The village of Torridon stands at the head of the loch, 11 miles from Kinlochewe. It has a school and post-office

and can accommodate walkers in at least one private house.

4. Kinlochewe to Loch Maree Hotel and Gairloch, 19½ miles. This route has already been described as far as the head of the Kerrysdale Pass. It reaches the head of Loch Maree in 2 miles, runs for 3 miles along the shore through the woods of the Grey Slope, turns inland to cross the Grudie River, and reaches Loch Maree Hotel after 4 miles of up and down going across open country. Slioch is well seen for the greater part of the way, and there is a fine glimpse up Glen Grudie to the peak of Ruadh Stac Mor. Before reaching Talladale Bridge another peep up into the hills enables the walker to catch a glimpse of Ben an Eoin, whose broad and lofty southern summit somewhat resembles that of the more distant Baeish Bheinn. Leaving the Loch Maree Hotel, the road passes through the woods for some 2 miles, turns inland to cross the Garavaig Bridge and climbs the long ascent above Slattadale, with its Forestry Centre and Youth Hostel. Then comes a short descent, a level stretch past the beautiful Loch Bad an Sgalaig, above which towers Baeish Bheinn, and we are at the top of the steep descent to Gairloch. The road winds along high above the rushing Kerry River, on a shelf cut in the hill-side; the opposite banks are clad with splendid woods, and far in front is the sea. Reaching the level of the river banks in 2 miles, the road passes the bridge of Kerrysdale, where a branch road goes off to Badachro and Red Point, climbs through thick woods and below rocky slopes of gneiss, and swings down a hill to the post-office and bay of Flowerdale. Here is the pier of Gairloch; the hotel is a mile further on.

(b) *By Hill-tracks*

1. Kinlochewe to Lochan Fada by Glen Bianasdail and back by Glen na Muice, 14 miles. Leave the Kinlochewe Hotel as if for Achnasheen, and take the road which goes off to the north opposite the lodge. In about 250 yards turn left at the cross-roads. Half a mile further on the road becomes a track, which eventually reaches the

Kinlochewe River and follows its course for another mile before reaching the eastern end of Loch Maree. The path skirts the loch for half a mile, passes a small pier, and shortly afterwards crosses a bridge over the Fasagh River. Here we turn north-east into Glen Bianasdail by a track which keeps high above the river, flowing far below in deep brown pools. Soon we are well into the glen, and can look across the stream to the grey perpendicular cliffs of the eastern side. By looking back across Loch Maree we obtain a striking view of the Ben Eighe summits framed in the mouth of the glen. It is 3 miles through the glen to the shore of Lochan Fada, and the path climbs to 1300 feet before descending to the end of the loch. Here it is necessary to cross the Fasagh River, and make one's way round the foot of the loch to reach the head of the path from Glen na Muice. This will be found just to the north of Loch an Sgeireach, at the extreme east corner of Lochan Fada. The view from this point along the length of the loch with the slopes of Slioch and Ben Lair on the one side, and those of Ben Tarsuinn on the other is very grand.

From Loch an Sgeireach the path goes south past another loch and down Glen na Muice to the cottages known as the Heights of Kinlochewe, crossing the river by a bridge a mile before reaching them. From the Heights a road leads south-west down the Bruachaig River, joining the main road by the lodge of Kinlochewe.

2. Kinlochewe to Letterewe, by the shore, 9 miles. This is a pleasant walk along the unvisited side of Loch Maree, along which the mails once used to be carried by a runner. Leave Kinlochewe as in Route No. (b) 1, and follow the same route as far as the bridge over the Fasagh River. Thence the path keeps north-west along the base of Slioch, at some distance above the loch, passing the old burial ground called Cladh nan Sasunnaich (The Lowlandmen's Grave), and the site of the old "bloomery" at Fasagh. Iron ore was mined and smelted on Loch Maree side early in the seventeenth century, and some of the workmen from the South rest in Cladh nan Sasunnaich.

Beyond Fasagh the path goes on past the deserted clachans of Smiorsair, Regoilachy and Coppachy, crosses the Furnace River, and reaches the woods and gardens of Letterewe. This is indeed a lovely spot in early summer. There is a private ferry from Letterewe to the opposite shore of the loch at Bankes Bay, by which walkers can often cross to reach the Loch Maree Hotel.

3. Letterewe to Lochan Fada by the Beallach a' Chuirn, and back by Loch Garbhaig, 10 miles. This walk is most conveniently begun at Loch Maree Hotel, from which a boat should be taken to Letterewe. (The *ferry-boat* crosses from Bankes Bay, about 2 miles south-east of the hotel.) On landing at Letterewe take the path which goes through a gate behind the mansion, and leads north up the hill-side, following the course of a stream. In about a mile the stream is crossed and the path bears north-eastwards: half a mile further on it turns north and makes for the pass between Meall Mheinnidh and Ben Lair, known as the Beallach Mheinnidh (Middle Pass). The northern face of Ben Lair (the Mare's Mountain) is one long range of precipices, extending for 3 miles above Glen Tulacha; across the face of these, where they bend round to the Beallach Mheinnidh, is cut a narrow track which leads to a second pass called the Beallach a' Chuirn (Pass of the Cairns). This path leaves the main track just where the latter has begun to descend to the Fionn Loch and the Dubh Loch causeway, by which it is possible to reach Strath na Sheallag and Dundonnell. The Beallach a' Chuirn is actually a green platform set between two glens; it looks away across the Dubh Loch towards Ben Dearg Mor and the jagged Teallach mountains. To the south-east is a fine vista down Glen Tulacha to Lochan Fada, with the great cliffs of Ben Lair towering up on the right. In the centre of the pass is a great grey boulder; this is often the rendezvous for the ponies when deer-stalking is in progress in these hills.

The path comes to an end at the Beallach a' Chuirn, and the way lies along the base of the cliffs, with the stream on the left, as far as Lochan Fada. The loch is skirted for half a mile along its south-western shore, until, after crossing a small burn, the end of the path from Furnace is reached. This path climbs straight up the hill-side, passes on the right a small tarn lying beneath the slopes of Sgurr Dubh, and descends to the end of Loch Garbhaig. This is a mile-long loch lying between Lochan Fada and Loch Maree, at a height of 1000 feet above the sea; beyond it to the south rises the northern face of Slioch. Leaving Loch Garbhaig the path descends along the right bank of the Furnace River, bends north at the back of the Letterewe Woods, and arrives at the pier from which we set out.

4. Loch Maree Hotel to Coire Mhic Fhearchair, via Glen Grudie, 16½ miles. The mountain-walled loch of Coire Mhic Fhearchair, which lies at a height of 1900 feet between the spurs of Ben Eighe, is perhaps the most striking example of wild mountain scenery near Loch Maree. It is not unlike Toll an Lochain in the Teallach group, but is even more shut in than that remote and high-lying sheet of water. It is best reached by way of Bridge of Grudie, 4 miles along the road to Kinlochewe. About 400 yards before reaching the bridge a track goes off to the right, past a deserted building, and soon begins to ascend the slopes on the west side of Glen Grudie. In about 2 miles, at a height of 750 feet, it crosses a tributary of the Grudie River, flowing from Coire Briste in the west. From about here there are fine views of Slioch to the north, and to the south, where the great mass of Ruadh Stac Mor (the Great Red Mountain) rises at the head of the glen. For the next mile and a half the track runs below the eastern flank of Ben a' Chearcaill (Mountain of the Hoops), and comes to an end on the bank of the stream south-east of that hill.

From this point the simplest way is to follow the northern and western banks of the Allt Coire Mhic Fhearchair to its source in the loch of the same name, lying in the deep hollow between Ruadh Stac Mor and Sail Mhor. A more direct route is to cross the stream and climb the north-west slopes of Ruadh Stac Mor until a point is reached from which the loch can be seen. Its surface is 1900 feet above the sea, and from its shores the cliffs go up for another 1200 feet. The black buttresses rising from the south-east shore are part of the main *massif* of Ben Eighe.

Instead of returning by the outward route, the walker can descend into the glen and continue round the base of Ben a' Chearcaill into Strath Lungard, and down it to Loch Maree. There is no defined path down this glen, but by following the right bank of the Talladale River down to Talladale Bridge the main road will be reached not far from the hotel. This route takes the wayfarer along the foot of the steep western cliffs of Ben a' Chearcaill, with Ben an Eoin rising from the opposite side of the glen. The total distance by this route is $15\frac{1}{2}$ miles.

5. Loch Maree Hotel to Poolewe by the old road, 8 miles. This route is the way by which, about the middle of the nineteenth century, traffic used to reach Poolewe. It leaves the Gairloch road at a gate situated where the road leaves the loch-side to reach the bridge of Garavaig, and makes for the farm-house of Slattadale, now the head-quarters of a Forestry Centre. The path goes north through the trees near the shore, then along the open hill-side past a tiny lochan and close to an inlet of Loch Maree. The big island nearest to the land is Eilean Ruaridh Mor, named after a celebrated Mackenzie chief who resided there. Then the path turns inland, and begins to climb towards the pass, crossing a burn, and ascending to 750 feet. Close to the track, on the left, rises a small hill with a sharp peak; a little beyond it two small lochans are passed in succession, and the track begins its descent, through the narrow gap below the grey rocks of Craig Tollie, towards Poolewe. Two burns are crossed, then the path ascends to the Poolewe road, which is joined at the head of the long hill which leads down to the village. It is $1\frac{1}{2}$ miles to the bridge at Poolewe, where the river meets the tide. The view of Loch Maree from the road above Tollie Farm is world-renowned for its beauty.

CHAPTER XI

GAIRLOCH, LOCH EWE AND GRUINARD

MAPS.—*O.S. Popular Edition, 1 inch, sheets* 19 *and* 25.
Bartholomew's Half Inch, sheets 54 *and* 58.

GAIRLOCH is a sea-board parish in Wester Ross lying between Loch Torridon to the south and Gruinard Bay to the northward. It comprises the long glen in which lies Loch Maree, with the mountain ranges bordering it to east and west, together with the moorland tract surrounding the sea-lochs of Gairloch and Ewe. Traversed only by one main road and having no railway within its bounds, it is still unspoiled by the machine-made civilisation of the cities, and is one of the most delightful districts in which to spend a holiday.

Unlike its southern neighbours, Loch Torridon and Loch Carron, the inlet of Gairloch is short and lies open to the Minch. At its mouth is the large island of Longa, now uninhabited; the smaller Isle Horisdale shelters the bay of Badachro, on the south shore of the loch. The shores of Gairloch are comparatively low; only at the head of the loch does the land rise abruptly in low hills of gneiss which extend to Loch Maree. The higher mountains of the Flowerdale Forest lie well back from the coast: even Baeish Bheinn, which dominates Gairloch, is 5 miles from the sea. South of the Gairloch is the broad peninsula terminating in Red Point, a wide expanse of loch-studded moorland sloping up to the mountains of Torridon. Along its coast are the townships of South Erradale, Opinan, Port Henderson, Badantionail and Badachro, with the clachan of Shieldaig on its bay in the south-east corner of the loch.

At the head of the sea-loch are the beautiful wooded bays of Kerrymouth and Flowerdale, and the curve of yellow sands below the old church. The Kerry River comes from an upland loch on the way to Loch Maree: it plunges down a rocky gorge and through the wooded Pass of Kerrysdale to the sea. The large hotel stands by the shore near the Free Church; further on is the clachan of Achtercairn, where the Poolewe road goes off to the north. Strath is the largest village in Gairloch: it stands on the north shore of the loch and straggles for a mile along the slopes towards the west.

Northwards extends the big rectangular promontory which divides Gairloch from Loch Ewe: its villages lie along the coast, from Strath to Melvaig, and at its north-west point is the lighthouse of Rudha Reidh. Loch Ewe is a broad and deep sea-loch opening northward to the Minch: at its head is the large village of Poolewe, standing above the deep pool where the River Ewe meets the tide. Aultbea, with its hotel and pier, clusters round a fine bay on the eastern shore in the shelter of Isle Ewe. Another peninsula, known as the Greenstone Point, separates Loch Ewe from Gruinard Bay: it contains a number of villages, of which Mellon Charles, Laide and Mellon Udrigill are the chief, and the once well-known Loch na Beiste. In this loch lived a monster whose presence was so terrifying to the neighbouring crofters that they prevailed on the proprietor to take action. An attempt to drain the loch proved unsuccessful, so barrels of lime were deposited in a deep hole in the middle. Nothing was found, but the monster was not seen again. These incidents took place about ninety years ago.

The bay of Gruinard, with its islands, sandy coves and clear green waters, is one of the most beautiful inlets on the West Coast. Here is no austere grandeur as of Loch Hourn; the mountains are a distant background, and the beaches lie open to the sun and the salt sea winds. At Mellon Udrigill on the west, at Little Gruinard at the head of the loch, and near Gruinard House on the east shore, are glorious stretches of yellow sand, backed by grey hills of gneiss. Out in the bay lies Gruinard Island, with the Summer Isles beyond.

Three rivers flow into Gruinard Bay, one coming from the high-lying Fionn Loch, one from Loch Toll a' Mhadaidh (Loch of the Fox's Hole), and the third from Loch na Sheallag, at the foot of the Teallach mountains. This last is the Gruinard River, which drains the long basin of Strath na Sheallag and rattles down a wooded defile past Gruinard House into the sea.

Gairloch looks west to the blue hills of Skye and the Long Island; the finest view, however, is that of the Torridon mountains seen across the loch from the cliffs at Carn Dearg. Baeish Bheinn and Ben Alligin, with their neighbours, form a magnificent group whose effectiveness is enhanced by the apparent plateau from which they rise. Loch Ewe enjoys fine views of the mountains around Loch Maree, which are well seen from the Aultbea-Poolewe road. Further east, from above Gruinard Bay, the distant Sutherland mountains come into view, with Ben More Coigach and Ben Gobhlach standing above the two Loch Brooms, and the jagged Teallach peaks peering over the hills behind Gruinard.

The early inhabitants of Gairloch were the Picts, who have left singularly few traces in the district. The place-names are almost all of Norse or Gaelic origin, for the coast lands were occupied by the Norsemen for some centuries. Erradale, Horisdale, Shieldaig and Longa are Norse names, and all are on the coast; the Gaelic-speaking Scots who succeeded the Picts never relaxed their hold on the inland mountains and glens, which all bear Gaelic names. By the thirteenth century Norse rule in Gairloch had given place to that of the MacBeaths, a clan which is said to have come from the north. Their chiefs lived on an island in Loch Tollie, from which one of them was expelled by two archers from Kintail, shooting from the loch-side at dawn. These men were Macraes, allied to the Macken-zies of Kintail, the powerful clan which was later to wrest the lands of Gairloch from the Macleods. The Macleods had obtained a grant of Gairloch from the Earls of Ross, and had then expelled the MacBeaths by force of arms. They held Gairloch for many years, and one of their chiefs, Allan Macleod, married a daughter of Alexander the Upright, chief of the Mackenzies. The marriage was displeasing to Allan's brothers, who hated the idea of a future chief being of Mackenzie blood. Two of them surprised Allan asleep on a sunny bank above the Ewe, slew him and crossed to the crannog in Loch Tollie where his wife and two boys were. Carrying off the boys, their uncles killed them and buried them at a spot still known as the Rock of the Burial Place. The widow fled to her father, produced the blood-stained shirts of her sons, and demanded vengeance on the murderers. Clan Kenneth was roused; armed with a royal warrant they proceeded to make war on the Macleods and to drive them out of Gairloch. Under the leadership of a cadet of the House of Kintail, the Mackenzies made their way into Gairloch, gradually secured the points of vantage, and waged unremitting war on the men of Clan Leod. The Macleods were bonnie fighters, and it was many years before they were finally expelled from Gairloch and from the islands of Loch Maree. At one time, while Hector Roy, the Mackenzie chief, was living on the site of the present Flowerdale House, a Macleod garrison occupied the Dun above the present golf-links. There are many stories of this period, in most of which the Macrae archers play a prominent part.

The Macraes were a clan resident in Kintail, from whom the Mackenzie chiefs drew their best fighting men. " Mackenzie's Shirt of Mail " was his Macrae bodyguard, many of whom were skilled archers. When Hector Roy led his men into Gairloch, many Macraes went with him; two of these are still famous for their skill with the bow. They were the brothers Donald Odhar and Iain Odhar, who slew most of the crew of a Macleod birlinn by shooting from a rock on the shore. This was after the expulsion of the Macleods, when the survivors were living in Skye.

A band of young men, roused by the taunts of an old woman, sailed in a black birlinn to reconquer Gairloch. Arriving at night, they moored their vessel inside the little Fraoch Eilean, not far from Shieldaig. But Donald Odhar and his brother, warned of the arrival of a strange vessel, hastened round the head of the loch and took up their position behind a rock on the shore. When dawn came they picked off the Macleods one by one, until the few survivors cut the cable and sailed back to Skye. The rock-trench where the Macraes stood is known to-day as Leac na Saighead (Slab of the Arrows).

Another famous archer was Fionnlaidh Dubh na Saighead (Black Finlay of the Arrows), who flourished in the sixteenth century. He lived near Melvaig, on the northern peninsula of Gairloch, and was walking by the shore one day when a chief's birlinn rowed past. In it was young Macleod of Assynt, returning crestfallen from Gairloch after soliciting the hand of the daughter of Mackenzie of Gairloch. Finlay was tactless enough to jeer at the unsuccessful wooer, who returned in due course with a crew of hard-bitten fighters, eager to deal with the unmannerly longshoreman. But Finlay, too, was ready; he and a brother archer took up a position under cover by the shore, and created such havoc with their arrows that the men from Assynt turned tail and made off.

When Hector Roy and his sons were firmly established in Gairloch, the chief of Kintail grew jealous of his success and planned to murder him. At the invitation of Kintail, Hector Roy spent the night with him at the head of Loch Torridon, and only the presence of his bodyguard of tall sons saved the laird of Gairloch from assassination.

As the sixteenth century drew to its close and Clan Kenneth increased in territory and power, the Gairloch branch flourished exceedingly. The next century saw the end of clan warfare, and since then Gairloch has seen no fighting. In the Great War, Gairloch men served on many fronts and suffered heavily; the proportion of serving sailors and soldiers was as great as in any parish in Scotland.

Gairloch of to-day is still a Mackenzie district, but the residents are not confined to members of that clan. There are Grants from Rothiemurchus, descendants of a gillie who accompanied a Grant bride to her new home in the west; Frasers from the Aird, Chisholms from Strathglass, Macintyres, Macleans, Macraes and Camerons. There are still Macleods in Gairloch, and it is said that they are pre-eminent in stature and good looks among their neighbours. A Mackay came from Sutherland many years ago and the Gairloch Mackays have been famous as pipers ever since. The ironworkers of Loch Maree have left descendants in Gairloch with Lowland names: there are even Taylors, who owe their origin to an English sailor shipwrecked on the coast.

COMMUNICATIONS

Rail.—Achnasheen, on the L.M.S. line between Inverness and Kyle of Lochalsh, is the nearest station.

Steamer.—A steamer from Glasgow calls at Gairloch every ten days.

Road Services.—A mail motor, carrying passengers, runs daily in both directions between Laide, Aultbea, Poolewe, Gairloch, Loch Maree, Kinlochewe and Achnasheen. From May to November an additional passenger service is maintained from Port Henderson and Badachro via Strath and Flowerdale, to Loch Maree, Kinlochewe and Achnasheen. Motor-buses also run, daily in both directions, to North Erradale and Melvaig.

ACCOMMODATION

Hotels at Gairloch, Poolewe and Aultbea. Other accommodation at Kerrysdale, Flowerdale, Achtercairn, Badachro and Poolewe.

Youth Hostels at Carn Dearg and Opinan.

WALKS

(a) *By Road*

1. Gairloch Hotel to Badachro and Red Point, 11 miles.

This excursion is best made on a summer evening when the distant views of Skye, Rona and the Torridon hills are at their best. It can also be made the opportunity for a bathing picnic at the splendid sands of Red Point.

Leaving Gairloch Hotel, the road passes the Free Kirk, the Established Kirk, the golf-links and the bank. A deep green circular hollow in the grassy level opposite the Established Kirk is known as the White Cow's Bed, in which at Sacrament time religious services used to be held. Beyond the bank is a steep brae down which the road descends to the Bridge of Flowerdale, at the head of the bay of the same name. On the left is the entrance to the policies of Flowerdale House, the west-coast mansion of Sir Hector Mackenzie of Gairloch. Beyond the bridge is the post-office of Gairloch and the clachan of Charlestown, after which the road climbs a long gradual ascent through the woods, to descend again beside the Kerry River to Kerrysdale House. Just before it leaves the woods we obtain a fine view of Baeish Bheinn, seen directly ahead.

The Kerry River is now on the right hand, flowing along the open strath of Lower Kerrysdale. It is crossed by a stone bridge which carries the road to Shieldaig and Badachro on the south side of the Gairloch. It was by this bridge that Queen Victoria met a gathering of her subjects from Skye and Lewis on the occasion of Her Majesty's visit to Loch Maree in September 1877.

Crossing the bridge, the road traverses a wooded defile to Shieldaig, where Shieldaig House stands beside its pleasant bay. On the left will be noticed the beginning of a track which leads to Loch a' Bhealaich and Torridon. Just beyond Shieldaig are the few houses of Leac na Saighead, with a rough track leading north-west to the shore. By following this track through a gate, past a cottage and over a ridge down to the sea we may reach the rocky trench from which the Macrae archers slew the Macleods.

The Macleods had sailed from Skye to raid Gairloch and had moored their black birlinn close to Fraoch Eilean, the little island lying not far to seaward. But their arrival had been seen, and Donald Odhar and his brother were behind the rock at dawn. Only a remnant of the raiders lived to reach Skye; the rest lie buried on the island. The rock is known to this day as Leac na Saighead (Slab of the Arrows).

Ascending a hill, the road descends to skirt Loch Bad a' Chrotha, from which flows the picturesque Badachro River. Further on, to the right, is the land-locked harbour of Badachro, with its inn, shops and post-office. Some twenty-five years ago this was a busy fishing port, with three curing stations and a fleet of herring boats. Beyond Badachro is Loch Bad na h'Achlaise, a rather featureless sheet of water, then comes Port Henderson, where we again reach the sea.

Looking back from this point, there are magnificent views of the mountains inland, Slioch in particular coming into sight. It is one of the charms of this road that it commands a view of the whole semicircle of mountains about Loch Maree and Loch Torridon, from Ben Airidh Charr, past Slioch, Ben an Eoin, Baeish Bheinn and Ben Dearg to Ben Alligin on Loch Torridon.

Leaving Port Henderson, the road turns south, climbs an incline, and then descends to the sandy bay of Opinan, with its school and post-office. Looking back we see Longa and Sand, and the red roof of Carn Dearg House. The next village is South Erradale, beyond which comes a steep ascent. From the summit opens up a magnificent view over Rona to Skye and Lewis, with the Torridon hills on the left. Two miles beyond Erradale is a lonely letter-box set in a rock by the road-side, and 200 yards further the road ends at Red Point. From here we look south into Outer Loch Torridon, with Ben Bhan of Applecross rising beyond Shieldaig. A splendid curving beach of red sand lies 300 yards from the road.

A mile further on, by a rough track, pedestrians can reach a fine sandy beach, where there is a fishing station. Another 6 miles' walk along the coast will take one to

Diabaig on Loch Torridon. This track is not suitable for cyclists.

2. Gairloch Hotel to Strath, Melvaig and Rudha Reidh, 15 miles. Turn right on leaving Gairloch Hotel and take the Poolewe road as far as the first fork at the clachan of Achtercairn. Then to the left past the police station and schoolhouse down the brae to the seashore. The road now passes a church on the right and soon crosses the Achter-cairn River before arriving at the village of Strath with its shops and post-office. Boats may be had here for fishing or rowing.

Beyond the village the road climbs a short steep brae and continues for three-quarters of a mile through the scattered crofts of Lon Mor before reaching a gate, which marks the ceasing of cultivation. Beyond it lies a moorland tract of stones, heather and bog, through which the road winds along above the rocky bays on the left. Soon the prominent chimneys of Carn Dearg House come in sight, and at 2 miles from Strath we reach the plateau where it stands above red cliffs. Here it is well to halt and look back towards the head of the loch, for the view is certainly the finest in Gairloch.

To the south-east the mountain mass rising from the lower slopes of the coast forms a magnificent background to the wide expanse of the sea-loch. The prominent mountains from east to west are named Ben an Eoin, Baeish Bheinn and Ben Alligin, the latter rising from the north shore of Loch Torridon. Further to the south is the entrance to Badachro, then comes Badantionail with its chequer of green and yellow crofts, and Port Henderson lying within the shelter of its headland. Beyond the Minch are the blue hills of Skye, with the Quiraing showing as a double-hummocked mountain at the north end; further south is the Storr Rock standing up over the island of Rona, whose white lighthouse can be seen in clear weather.

The wild island of Longa seems to be close at hand to the westward; it is about $1\frac{1}{2}$ miles away. By ascending the hill behind Carn Dearg it is possible to see beyond

Longa to the Shiant Isles and the long blue outline of Lewis; in clear weather the jagged peaks of the Coolins can be seen over the Applecross plateau in the far south, and even the summit of Ben na Caillich which rises behind Kyleakin.

Half a mile beyond Carn Dearg is the bay of Ceann a Chreagán (Head of the Rock), where good bathing is to be had. An expanse of smooth sands separates this bay from the Sand River, which comes down from the moorlands to the north and flows through sand-dunes into the sea. Above the bay the road turns inland past the farm of Little Sand, crosses the Sand River above a fine pool and follows its course past Sand schoolhouse to North Erradale. Beyond this straggling township the road again nears the sea and continues above the cliffs to Altgreshan and Melvaig, affording magnificent views of the Minch and its islands. Melvaig, which is 11 miles from the Gairloch Hotel, is a fishing village built on low cliffs, with a stretch of sandy shore below. Motor-cars should be left here, but it is well worth while following on foot the path along the cliffs which leads to Rudha Reidh, the north-western point of Gairloch. The lighthouse on this rocky point was built before the Great War, when Loch Ewe was for a time an important naval base. By climbing the slopes to the east of the lighthouse, a fine view of the Sutherland mountains is obtained in clear weather.

3. Gairloch Hotel to Poolewe, Aultbea and Dundonnell, 32 miles. Leave by the Poolewe road, turning up the Achtercairn brac (fine view from summit), past Loch Tollie, beyond which a magnificent view of Loch Maree opens up on the right. The prominent mountain on the east shore of Loch Maree is Ben Airidh Charr (Mountain of the Rough Shieling). Descending the steep Poolewe brae, the River Ewe is crossed just above a deep pool, leaving the village of Poolewe with its comfortable hotel behind on the left. A mile further on are the ruins of Inverewe House, occupied for many years by Mr Osgood Mackenzie, the author of *A Hundred Years in the Highlands*. Thence

through pine woods and past a little loch, the road leaves Tournaig House to the right and climbs to 225 feet, crossing a tract of open moorland before descending to Aultbea with its hotel and steamer pier. Loch Ewe, with the large green Isle Ewe, has been in view on the left since leaving Tournaig, but at Aultbea the road turns inland to cross the peninsula to Gruinard Bay. Before reaching Laide, the first village, a magnificent view opens up to the northward, and includes the Summer Isles of Loch Broom and the distant mountains of Sutherland. Passing the scattered hamlets of Sand, First Coast and Second Coast, the road climbs a long slope, then drops abruptly to sea-level down the steep and winding hill of Little Gruinard. Here, beyond the Little Gruinard River, which comes from the Fionn Loch, is a beautiful sandy bay, which seems made for a picnic and bathe. Two miles further on, in a wooded nook by the shore, stands Gruinard House, beyond which the road turns inland to reach Dundonnell on Little Loch Broom.

This is a long narrow fiord, opening to the north-west, and is separated from Loch Broom by a mountainous peninsula; the dark mass of Ben Gobhlach stands out prominently as we reach the summit of the road. In front, on the right, rise the rocky Teallach mountains, which rank with the Coolins of Skye as the wildest range in Britain; only the end peak of the range, known as Sail Mhor, is visible from the road at this point. Just beyond the head of Little Loch Broom is the Dundonnell Hotel, 32 miles from Gairloch: here the road leaves the coast and turns southwards up the wooded Strath Beg.

4. Poolewe to Cove by west side of Loch Ewe, 7 miles. Leaving the hotel at Poolewe the road goes west above the shore of Loch Ewe, passes Boor and the township of Naast and reaches the pier at Inverasdale. (A short way north of the pier a path diverges to the north-west, following a clearly marked escarpment which the moors of the west present to the north-east. This path permits of a fine walk to the lighthouse at Rudha Reidh, which is 7 miles

from Inverasdale.) The road continues northwards along the coast, with pleasant views across Loch Ewe, crosses a river, and passes the bays of Smoo and of Allt Eoin Thomais. Here by the shore is a Preaching Cave, one of those used for worship in bygone years. The road ends at Cove, a rough road continuing northwards towards Rudha nan Sasan, the promontory at the entrance to Loch Ewe.

(b) *By Hill-tracks*

1. Shieldaig to Torridon by Loch a' Bhealaich, 16¼ miles. Take a boat or motor-bus to Shieldaig, landing at the jetty below Shieldaig House. About 250 yards along the road to Gairloch a path strikes off to the south-west. In a mile it turns to the south, and passes on the right Loch Braigh Horisdale, from which flows the Bada-chro River. Thence for 3 miles it follows the course of the river which flows into the south end of the loch, coming down from the high-lying Loch Gaineamhach (the Sandy Loch) and tumbling over a waterfall on the way. Just before reaching the Sandy Loch, by a stone stable, the remains of a bridge mark where an old track diverges to Diabaig.

Leaving the Sandy Loch behind, the path climbs for 2 miles, attaining a height of 1100 feet before reaching Loch a' Ghobhainn and its extension Loch a' Bhealaich (Loch of the Pass). These two lochs extend for 3 miles in the hollow below the south-western face of Baeish Bheinn. They lie at an elevation of 1000 feet, and belong to the Shieldaig Estate. The track comes to an end on the shore of Loch a' Bhealaich, and it is necessary to take to the hill-side, keeping parallel to the south shore until level with the eastern end of the loch. Here we turn southwards, and make for the pass known as the Beallach a' Chomla, between the flank of Ben Alligin, to the west, and a spur of Ben Dearg on the east. At the summit of the pass is a cluster of tiny lochans, from which two streams run north and south. Follow the latter for about a mile, cross it to the west, and join a track which leads to a bridge over the good-sized stream which runs down the glen to Loch Torridon. This glen is known as Coire Mhic Nobuil, in the Torridon Forest. From the bridge the views are exceedingly grand; Ben Alligin, with his numerous peaks to the west, Ben Dearg to the north, eastward the long glen terminating in the cliffs of Sail Mhor, a spur of the mighty file-topped Ben Eighe. Southward Loch Torridon has come into view, with Ben Damph prominent above its farther shore. Leaving the bridge and heading southward the path keeps close above the river, with its deep brown pools, joining the Diabaig-Torridon road in the woods above Torridon House. From this point it is 1½ miles west to Inveralligin (where accommodation may often be obtained), and rather more than 2 miles east to Torridon village.

2. Flowerdale to Meall an Dorein, and back by Poolewe road, 12 miles. Leave the main road by Flowerdale Bridge, and take the road on the left past Flowerdale House. Keeping the river on the right, continue up the glen as far as the waterfall, where we turn south-east along the valley between the crags of An Groban and Sithean Mhor. Working round the far end of the former, we climb out of the corrie by the side of a waterfall and reach a second broad corrie among the hills. Still keeping the little stream on the right, follow it in an easterly direction over a gap in the hills to its source in Loch na Feithe Mugaig, which lies at a height of nearly 1000 feet. By climbing Meall an Dorein (1381 feet), which rises from the north shore of the loch, a very extensive view to all points of the compass can be obtained, the hill being the highest point between Gairloch and Loch Maree. A little to the west rises the sister hill of Meall an Spardain, which is worth climbing on account of the uninterrupted view to the west. From either of these hills the way lies down their northern face to join the track leading from Slattadale to the Poolewe road, which is described in Route No. (b) 5 of Chapter X. This track descends through a rocky pass at the base of Craig Tollie, crosses two streams and reaches the Poolewe road at the top of the Poolewe brae. The road back to

PLATE VI   THE FLOWERDALE FOREST HILLS, GAIRLOCH

The peak in the left centre is Baeish Bheinr
other Torridon giant, Liathach, just visi

Photograph by R. M. ADAM

nd lying further back is Ben Alligin, with the
rth shoulder of Baeish Bheinn.

Gairloch Hotel and Flowerdale goes along the side of Loch Tollie, descends through broken country to the west, and arrives in Gairloch by way of the Achtercairn brae, from the top of which a splendid view over Gairloch to Skye is obtained.

3. Flowerdale to Loch Bad an Sgalaig by old road and on to Poca Buidhe and back, 20 miles. Cross Flowerdale Bridge and take the track opposite the post-office leading up the south bank of the river. At cross-roads, in about a third of a mile, turn right and keep on through the woods south-by-east until Kerrysdale House is passed below on the right. Here the track bears away across the open hill-side towards the east and up a narrow glen, crosses a swampy valley and curves round the base of Meall Aundrary to join the main road at a point just short of Loch Bad an Sgalaig. Continue along the Loch Maree road past Loch Bad an Sgalaig as far as the red-painted iron building which stands by the road. Opposite this a line of stepping-stones crosses the river flowing to Loch Bad an Sgalaig, and from them a track goes south into the hills. It ascends along the eastern side of Meall a' Ghlas Leothaid (Hill of the Grey Slope), and in 1½ miles reaches the stream which is the main feeder of Loch Bad an Sgalaig. Keeping the stream on the right for nearly 2 miles, Loch na h'Oidhche (Loch of the Night: i.e. Loch which fishes best by night) lies close at hand in the wide trough ahead; it is not, however, seen from the path at this point. On the right rises Baeish Bheinn, showing the entire length of his eastern side; ahead is the northern end of Beinn an Eoin (Bird Mountain). Loch na h'Oidhche lies in the trough between the two mountains at a height of 1250 feet: the track ascends to its northern end, passes a boat-house and follows the eastern shore for 1½ miles, where it slants uphill and finishes at the shooting-bothy of Poca Buidhe. This is a small building standing among rocks at the foot of Ben an Eoin, above the south end of the loch. It looks south to Ben Dearg and north-west to Baeish Bheinn, and is the stalking rendezvous of the Flowerdale Forest.

To the south lie a number of small lochs, which are said to provide good fishing; beyond them is a curious plateau of bare white rock, sloping down to a stream, around which rises a tremendous circle of dark mountains.

Note.—Instead of returning to Gairloch, the good walker has three alternatives. He may walk round the southern flanks of Ben an Eoin and go down Strath Lungard to Talladale and Loch Maree Hotel, making 18 miles in all. Or by striking south-east, passing round Carn na Feola, and by Loch nan Cabar, and making for the Black Corrie, he may reach Glen Torridon and Kinlochewe, which is 24 miles from Flowerdale.

If instead of entering the Black Corrie near Lochan a' Coire Dhuibh, he turns west past Loch Grobaig and takes the path down Coire Mhic Nobuil, he may reach Inveralligin, or Torridon village, making a day's walk of 19 miles.

4. Red Point to Diabaig, 7 miles. This path links up the road end at Diabaig with the Gairloch roads at Red Point, and is thus particularly useful for walkers who wish to keep to the coast on their way to or from Torridon. The road from Gairloch ends 2 miles south of South Erradale, where a path goes on across the levels past Redpoint Farm to a fishing station on the coast, reaching the shore of Outer Loch Torridon opposite Tioram Island. Then for 3 miles it skirts the shore, turning inland to cross the Craig River, and keeps up on the hill-side for 2 miles, descending to join the road at Lower Diabaig on the inlet of Loch Diabaig. This route commands splendid sea views across to Rona and Skye, and of the Torridon mountains to the east.

5. Gairloch Hotel to North Erradale and the Gold Cave, 14 miles. Take the road past Achtercairn and Strath to Carn Dearg House and Sand. This road is described in Route No. (*a*) 2. Turning inland past the farm of Little Sand the road crosses the Sand River, and ascends past Sand schoolhouse to the scattered township of North Erradale. Here a track diverges from the main road to the left and leads towards the coast. By following this to its termination and thence taking a path along the banks of a little burn, the walker will reach the shore at the bay

of Port Erradale, where the rocky cliffs give place to a stony beach. To visit the Gold Cave a guide is necessary, for there are several caves along the coast, and the right one is difficult to find. A boy or man can usually be engaged at North Erradale, but candles, or flash-lamps, should be brought by the visitors.

The cave lies among the rocks to the north of the bay; it is not accessible during the two hours before and the two hours after high water. At other times a rough scramble will take one to its mouth, and it is possible to penetrate some way into its dark passages. A short distance within the cave, and well above high-water mark, are the traces of a rude hearth, where an illicit still was probably worked in former years. A low opening further in leads to an inner cave, which does not appear to have been explored.

The name of the cave refers to a tradition of hidden treasure; it is said that ages ago eleven men, headed by a piper, entered the cave to seek for gold. The pipes were heard underground as far away as Strath, but the twelve stout fellows never returned.

Instead of retracing one's steps to the main road, it is pleasanter to return by the track which runs south-east from Erradale over a low hill and passes through the scattered crofts of Big Sand. This route gives fine views over Longa to Skye and Applecross. It crosses the Sand River by a wooden bridge and continues along the landward slope of the dunes, joining the road to Strath half a mile west of Carn Dearg House. From thence to the hotel is $3\frac{1}{2}$ miles.

6. Poolewe to Kernsary and the Fionn Loch, 6 miles. For this walk permission should be sought from the proprietor of the Inverewe Estate, or the shooting tenant, the road beyond Inveran being a private one. When this is obtained, cycles can be taken to the shore of the Fionn Loch, but no further, and the return must be by the same route. Cars are not permitted to use the road. The walker is not tied down in this way, and can make a circuit

by way of the Dubh Loch, returning to Kernsary by a hill-track. An alternative way is via Letterewe and thence by boat to Loch Maree Hotel. In this case a boat should be arranged for to meet the walkers at Letterewe.

Leave the Poolewe Hotel by the Gairloch road, cross Poolewe Bridge, and take the road along the east side of the River Ewe as far as Inveran House. Continue past the policies of Inveran, crossing a small bridge, until Loch Kernsary is seen on the left, and the farm of the same name is reached. Just beyond the farm a track goes off to the right, which would take us in some 7 miles to the far end of the Fionn Loch; but our road continues in a north-easterly direction for 2 miles, climbing gradually to 700 feet and commanding fine views of the Fionn Loch and the mountains beyond. Then comes a slight descent, and in another mile the shore of the loch is reached at a point opposite a small island.

The Fionn Loch lies at a height of 559 feet in a depression between the mountains which border Loch Maree and those of the parallel range to the north. Ben Airidh Charr (Mountain of the Rough Shieling), Ben Lair (the Mare's Mountain) and Meall Mheinnidh (the Middle Hill), belong to the former group; of the latter the two Ben a' Chaisgeans and the rocky peak called the Maiden are the most prominent. The loch is termed " fair " (Fionn), in contrast to the dark aspect of its upper reach, the Dubh (Black) Loch, which lies in gloomy stillness among the mountains at its head. A stone causeway separates the two lochs and carries the old hill-track from Letterewe to Loch na Sheallag, Dundonnell and Ullapool.

7. Poolewe to Kernsary and Dubh Loch Causeway, 10 miles. This route as far as Kernsary Farm is the same as the previous one. Just beyond the farm a track goes off to the right, leading up the valley of the Allt Caol Doire towards the eastern end of the Fionn Loch. The track passes below the nothern cliffs of Ben Airidh Charr and the neighbouring mountain of Meall Mheinnidh and joins another track from Letterewe not far from the

Causeway between Fionn Loch and the Dubh Loch. The path at its western end is somewhat difficult to find and occasionally disappears in boggy ground. It is, however, the shortest way from Poolewe to the Dubh Loch and the cliffs of Ben Lair, and was once part of the original track from Glen Carron by Kinlochewe and Letterewe to Poolewe.

8. Ascent of Baeish Bheinn, 22 miles. Take the Loch Maree road through Kerrysdale and past Kerry Falls to Loch Bad an Sgalaig. About 600 yards beyond the loch a path goes off to the right, crossing the stream by stepping-stones. Take this track, which ascends along the eastern side of Meall a' Ghlas Leothaid (Hill of the Grey Slope), and in $1\frac{1}{2}$ miles reaches the stream which is the main feeder of Loch Bad an Sgalaig. Keeping this stream on the right for nearly 2 miles, Loch na h'Oidhche (Loch which fishes best by night) lies close at hand in the wide trough ahead; it is, however, not seen from the path at this point. Before reaching the latter loch turn across the stream and begin to climb the slopes of Baeish Bheinn, which rises straight ahead. This is best accomplished by following the course of a tributary burn which flows east from the mountain and joins the stream we have crossed. This burn has its source at the head of a corrie 2250 feet up, from whence it is easy to climb south-west to the summit ridge, and to reach the narrow col immediately north of the main peak. The top of the mountain consists of a ridge extending for $1\frac{1}{2}$ miles from north-west to south-east; the cairn on the northern end is 2417 feet above the sea, and commands a fine view to north and west.

The highest point is, however, at the southern end, where the summit is guarded by precipitous slopes, and should be approached with caution. The site of the cairn lies at a height of 2869 feet, and from it in clear weather magnificent views are to be obtained. Immediately below to the south lies Loch a' Bhealaich with its extension Loch a' Ghobhainn; beyond them rise the steep flanks of mighty Ben Alligin and of Ben Dearg, with Loch Torridon beyond.

South-east and apparently close at hand are the wild mountains which cluster round Ben Eighe, the sharp peaks of Liathach and Ruadh Stac Mor prominent above them. Loch na h'Oidhche is just below to the east; from its shores rise the precipitous slopes of Ben an Eoin (the Bird Mountain), which hides part of Loch Maree. Loch Maree lies in the trough beyond, with its guardian mountains along the eastern shore. Behind these again are the Teallach hills of Dundonnell and the high peaks of Fannich.

The chief glory of Baeish Bheinn is the widespread seascapes which open out to the west; the mountain is certainly the best point of vantage from which to overlook the coast of Gairloch. The sea-loch itself, with Longa at its mouth, is spread out below; the villages of Strath, Sand and Badachro on their respective peninsulas stand out clearly. Beyond is the blue expanse of the Minch, with the long extending coast of Skye and of the Lews; the small islands to the north of Skye and the Shiant Isles are clearly seen.

The distant view to the east shows a mass of peaks, not always easy to identify. The summit of Slioch peers above Ben an Eoin; west of it is Ben Airidh Charr and the mountains about the Fionn Loch.

The return journey may be made by the same route, or direct to Loch Maree Hotel. In the latter case the route is past the north end of Loch na h'Oidhche and round the northern flanks of Ben an Eoin into the wooded glen of the Talladale River. The latter is then followed to the main road opposite the hotel.

Note.—If time permits it is pleasant to traverse the whole summit ridge from south-east to north-west, where the great precipices of the Raven's Crag fall towards the Dubh Loch.

It is possible to descend the grass slopes of the adjacent north-east corrie and thence to strike across country to the isthmus between the Dubh Loch and Loch Bad an Sgalaig, from whence a track leads to the road. This is a rough and tiring scramble, but avoids the necessity for retracing one's steps to the Loch na h'Oidhche path.

CHAPTER XII

DUNDONNELL, STRATH NA SHEALLAG AND FANNICH

MAPS.—*O.S. Popular Edition, 1 inch, sheets* 19 *and* 26. *Bartholomew's Half Inch, sheets* 54, 55 *and* 58.

THE wide, sunny bay of Gruinard terminates to the east in Stattic Point, and is succeeded by the long, narrow inlet of Little Loch Broom. From the half-mile-wide strait where it joins the Minch this sea-loch winds inland for 8 miles; at its head is the well-wooded Strath Beag, shut in on three sides by high mountains. A narrow-necked peninsula, dominated by frowning Ben Gobhlach, separates the loch from the greater Loch Broom. Near its extremity along the flat shore by the mouth of the loch, stands the village of Scoraig, with its church and school, connected by a ferry with Badluchrach on the southern shore. The southern side of Little Loch Broom slopes gradually up from the sea and carries many crofts; besides Badluchrach it possesses the villages of Durnamuck and Badcaul and the hamlet of Badbea. South of Badbea rises Sail Mhor, an outlying buttress of the rugged Teallach group. The latter lies well back from the coast and is not visible from the loch-side.

Dundonnell owes much of its beauty to the Strath Beag River, which rises in Creag Rainich, at the head of Strath na Sheallag, and has carved out the splendid defile down which it hurries to Strath Beag. The wooded slopes and high precipitous hill-sides of the upper strath are very striking, as is the deep and narrow chasm close to the road through which, many feet down, the river flows. Lower down, by the river-side, is Dundonnell House, an old residence of the Mackenzies; behind it the estate road goes north to Eilean Daraich, once known as Dundonnell Lodge, which stands above the meadows a mile from the sea. The hotel stands at the head of the sea-loch, not far from the post-office at Auchtascailt; the road from Poolewe to Braemore passes its door.

Dundonnell stands on the northern edge of a wide track of roadless country, which extends southwards to Loch Maree and eastwards as far as Garve. In this extensive area, which is bounded on the west by Gruinard Bay, are three fine groups of mountains, the far-stretching Strath na Sheallag and several large lochs. The splendid Teallach mountains behind Dundonnell rank with the Coolins of Skye as the most abrupt range in Britain: their splintered peaks rise to 3483 feet, and between their spurs sleeps Loch Toll an Lochain. "An Teallach" in Gaelic means "The Forge," and is applied to the whole range, the reference being either to the mists rising like smoke from the peaks, or to the lightning flashes in summer storms. It is interesting to find that a mountain range in South China is known as Taitan Yang (The Blacksmith's Anvil) on account of the frequent thunderstorms which occur in its vicinity.

The Teallach peaks look south across Loch na Sheallag to the steep black sides of Ben Dearg Mhor, whose eastern flanks rise from Glen na Muice. This is a deep glen leading south from Strath na Sheallag between high mountains. On the east are Ben a' Chlaidheimh, Sgurr Ban and Mullach Coire Mhic Fhearchair, on the west Ben Dearg and A'Mhaighdean extend towards Ben Lair and the Loch Maree hills. The "Cross-lying Hill" (Ben Tarsuinn) shuts in the glen on the south and separates it from Lochan Fada.

Strath na Sheallag begins at the north-east foot of Ben a' Chlaidheimh, and extends north-westward for 12 miles to Gruinard Bay. It contains Loch na Sheallag, 4 miles in length, and was at one time the home of a numerous population, which was displaced to make room for sheep. Like surrounding districts, it is now given up to deer, and the solitary houses at Larachantivore, Shenavall, and

Achneigie are occupied by stalkers. A private road following the course of the Gruinard River connects the foot of Loch na Sheallag with the main road at Gruinard.

The Strath na Sheallag River rises in the little Loch an Nid, at the western base of Creag Rainich, an isolated mountain which also gives birth to the Strathbeag, or Dundonnell River. In a glen to the east of this mountain is Loch a' Bhraoin, a sheet of water 3 miles long, connected by the Cuileig River with Strath More and Loch Broom. Past its eastern end runs the road from Dundonnell to Braemore, and to the south-east stand the Fannich mountains. These mountains stand in a compact group on the watershed of Ross-shire; their ground plan is a large cross with arms pointing north-east and south-west. The central peak, Sgurr Mor of Fannich, rises to 3637 feet, a height only exceeded in Ross-shire by An Riabhachan above Glen Cannich. Eight more of the Fannich peaks exceed 3000 feet, Sgurr nan Clach Geala (Peak of the White Stones), reaching 3581. With their fine peaks, dark corries and high-lying mountain lochs, the Fannich mountains are indeed a noble group.

Loch Fannich is a crescent-shaped loch, some 7 miles long, lying at the southern foot of the range. It is being used in a hydro-electric scheme to supply water through a tunnel 3¾ miles to a power station at Grudie Bridge. As no dam is being built there will be no expansion of the surface area of the loch; it will, rather, be reduced during dry periods, although various aqueducts increasing the catchment area should help to stabilize the level. On the northern shore of the loch is the shooting lodge of Fannich, from which a private road goes east along the loch shore, and down the Fannich River to Lochluichart. At the west end of Loch Fannich stands Cabuie Lodge, named after the Cadha Buidhe or Yellow Pass, which is reached by an estate road from the south. This road leaves the main county road some 2 miles east of Achnasheen, crosses the hills to Loch Fannich and follows the southern shore of that loch for nearly 4 miles to Cabuie. From the house at Nest, half a mile east of Cabuie Lodge, a hill-track goes north through the mountains, crosses a pass of 1850 feet, and descends to the foot of Loch Bhraoin.

Although no roads traverse this Dundonnell-Fannich district, it is bounded on the north by the narrow Dundonnell-Braemore road, and by the main Ullapool road from Braemore to Garve. The latter crosses the Dirrie More, a bleak stretch of moorland along the watershed by Loch Droma. In the absence of other roads the hill-paths are of particular value, especially those from Loch Maree to Dundonnell, which are described below.

The Dundonnell district belonged at one time to the Earls of Ross, by one of whom it was made over to Celestine of Lochalsh. Later it was acquired by Alexander of Glengarry, who married a daughter of the Lochalsh Macdonalds, and was for many years at feud with the Mackenzies of Kintail. Dondonnell became a Macdonnell island in a sea of Mackenzie territory, separated by long miles of ocean from Loch Hourn and Glengarry, and within easy reach of the unfriendly clans of Fraser, Mackenzie and Munro. At last the Glengarry chief, finding the position untenable, surrendered all his rights in 1603 to Mackenzie of Kintail, and Dundonnell was added to the wide belt of Mackenzie lands which stretched from Kintail to Loch Broom. For many years Clan Kenneth continued to flourish; even when Seaforth, after the Risings of 1715 and 1719, lost his estates, the younger branches of the clan were not affected, and even added to their possessions. In the first years of the nineteenth century practically the whole of Wester Ross was in the hands of Mackenzie proprietors. A hundred years have made great alterations in this respect, Gairloch being one of the few districts where the old family still holds sway.

COMMUNICATIONS

Rail.—The nearest railway station is Garve, on the L.M.S. line from Inverness to Kyle. Achanalt and Achnasheen can also be reached by hill-paths from Dundonnell.

Road Services.—A mail motor, which can take a few passengers, leaves Dundonnell each morning to connect at Braemore with the Ullapool-Garve motor service. Passengers wishing to use this service from Braemore to Dundonnell should make arrangements in advance through the Dundonnell Hotel.

ACCOMMODATION

Hotels at Dundonnell, Achnasheen, Altguish and Garve. Other accommodation at Achanalt, Durnamuck, Badcaul, and possibly at Badluchrach.

WALKS

(a) *By Road*

1. Gruinard to Dundonnell and Braemore, 25 miles. Gruinard House stands by the shore of a pleasant bay, sheltered to the east by woods of pine, through which the Gruinard River makes its way to the sea. North of the estate buildings the road continues along the shore, passing the pier, and bending inland above the sandy bay of Mungasdale. Now the route is eastward, up a long ascent and then along the ridge which separates Gruinard from Little Loch Broom. From the highest point reached by the road, at 585 feet, there is a fine view northward across the narrow sea-loch and over Scoraig to the hills of Coigach. Ben Gobhlach stands up in isolated majesty in the peninsula between the two Lochs Broom, and to the east, hiding the greater peaks of the Teallach group, is the semicircular summit of Sail Mhor. The road now swings down a long hill which brings it to the shore of Little Loch Broom, passing on the left the end of a road leading by Durnamuck to the shore-side township of Badluchrach, and the few houses at Badcaul and Badbea. Crossing a stream, on which are some fine waterfalls not visible from the road, the route lies south-east to the head of the loch, where the hotel of Dundonnell stands by the roadside at the mouth of Strath Beag.

Continuing up the glen past the post-office, the road enters the woods and bends southwards, up the swiftly narrowing valley of the Strath Beag River. By leaving the road at a point a little beyond the third milestone from the hotel, and going a short way along a path to the left, the walker can reach the spot where a plank bridge crosses the narrow and vertical-sided gorge in which the river runs. So narrow is the cleft and so far down the stream, that one might easily pass over it without realising that it was there; it would be an ill place to come across on a dark night.

Presently the road bends to the east and begins to climb in earnest; the rocky walls in front seem to leave no opening, and it is only by describing a great semicircle that river and road together emerge from the deep defile and reach the moorland beyond. At a point nearly 5 miles from Dundonnell the road crosses to the opposite bank of the river, and goes steadily south-east, passes the deserted building which was once the Fain Inn, and reaches the summit level at 1109 feet. Along this somewhat desolate stretch of moorland road the Fannich mountains in front form the only attraction; looking back, however, there is a magnificent view of the great Teallach peaks a few miles to the north-west. Then Loch a' Bhraoin comes in sight on the right front, the road describes a right-angle and leads north-east down the left bank of the Cuileig River, crosses it, and again makes a right-angled turn, this time to go south-east up the southern side of a glen, across which can be seen the main road to Ullapool. This is the glen of the Droma River, which flows at the bottom of a tremendous gorge, into which it falls over the lofty Fall of Measach. The road from Dundonnell keeps along the upper side of the slope above the gorge, swings sharply north to cross the river by a stone bridge, and joins the main road to Ullapool or Garve at the gates of Braemore House.

2. Dundonnell Hotel to Ullapool, by Altnaharrie Ferry, 6½ miles. This is the most direct route to Ullapool, saving as much as 17 miles as compared with the ordinary route via Braemore. It is, however, a narrow, little-used and stony road, which descends to the ferry down a slope of excessive steepness. It is very definitely unsuitable for motor traffic and is just passable for cyclists; motor-cyclists should go round by Braemore. The remains of an ancient Ford car

abandoned by the road-side not far from the Dundonnell end may serve as a warning to over-sanguine motorists!

Leave the main road opposite the post-office of Dundonnell, and go through a gate along a road which leads through the policies of Eilean Daraich (still shown on the map by its former name of Dundonnell Lodge), past the mansion and eventually back to the main road. Instead of continuing along this road, turn left at the first road fork beyond the mansion, and again north, through another gate, out on to the hill-side. The road then goes north along the slopes of Beinn nan Ban, climbs gradually to 750 feet, passes the junction of another road leading down to Badralloch on the north shore of Little Loch Broom, and crosses the summit level past little Loch na h'Airbhe. By tramping west from this point it would be possible to climb Ben Gobhlach, whose isolated position on a sea-girt promontory should command exceptionally fine sea and mountain views. From the head of the descent to Altnaharrie an excellent bird's-eye view of Ullapool and of Loch Broom is obtained; it is about a mile to the seashore, and cyclists will find it necessary to walk. To call the ferryman, who lives in the last house on Ullapool Point, it is usual to light a fire on the beach, but it is better to have advised him in advance by letter or telegram. It is not always possible to cross the ferry here, especially in strong south-easterly winds, for the boat used is an open rowing boat. The house near the shore, which was once the inn of Altnaharrie, is now a private residence, which is often closed during the winter months. It does not offer accommodation to travellers.

(b) *By Hill-tracks*

1. Letterewe to Dundonnell, 21 miles. This is one of the finest mountain walks in Scotland, ranking with the Larig Ghru, the Corrieyarrick and those from Glen Affric to Kintail. In its course from Loch Maree to the sea it traverses every kind of Highland scenery, crosses three passes and fords two rivers. It is best traversed from south

to north, so as to arrive at Dundonnell when the sunset is lighting up Little Loch Broom and the stags are out on the slopes above Glen a' Chaorachain.

Leave Letterewe by the path which climbs to the Beallach Mheinnidh, and descends past the end of Ben Lair to the Dubh Loch Causeway. Cross the latter and leave on the left the keeper's house at Carn Mor, climbing along the hill-side above the Dubh Loch to reach the summit of the pass at 1670 feet. Passing on the right the double Lochan Feith Mhic 'Illean the path goes east across the flat watershed, and descends steeply with many windings into Glen na Muice Beag (The Little Glen of the Pig). From the brow of the descent the northward view is very fine. Ben Dearg Mor rises close in front, with Ben a' Claidheimh (Mountain of the Sword) on the right; between them Glen na Muice runs north to Strath na Sheallag, above which tower the steep slopes of Sail Liath, the end peak of the Teallach group. The path goes down Glen na Muice Beag, turns north along the larger Glen na Muice, passes a suspension bridge and reaches the stalker's house at Larachantivore, in Strath na Sheallag. Here the river must be crossed, either by stepping-stones, or by the bridge which we have passed, and a course set across the bog for Shenavall, another stalker's house, which can be seen across the strath on the farther bank of the Strath na Sheallag River. The way lies across a peat-bog, after which the river must be forded (not always an easy matter), and another path reached just below Shenavall. This path leads east up the north bank of the river, passes another keeper's house at Achneigie, and then bends south as if to ascend the glen to Loch an Nid. Here, by the side of a small wood, another path diverges, and soon doubles back to climb north along the hill-side. This is the Dundonnell track; it climbs out of the valley and goes north across a high plateau, overlooked on the west by the Teallach mountains. Near the summit a small loch is passed on the left, then the track attains its highest level of 1300 feet and begins its descent to Glen Chaorachain. Dropping sharply into the head of the glen, which is cut off by a high ridge from the base of the Teallachs to the west, the track crosses the stream and leads on through the woods to join the road 2½ miles south of Dundonnell Hotel. Glen a' Chaorachain is very delightful even in winter; its slopes are well wooded, the hills rise high on each side and a brawling river runs far below. This is a wonderful place for deer, which are best seen in the gloaming feeding among the trees beside the path, or on the hill-slopes above.

Note.—From Shenavall to its junction with the Dundonnell track the path makes a considerable detour, which can be avoided by striking north-east from Shenavall across the base of Sail Liath. The way lies up the ravine behind the house, following the stream towards its source, and then bearing east-north-east to join the Dundonnell track not far from its highest point. The way is marked by small cairns, and by the hoof-marks of horses, for it is used by stalkers and shepherds going with pack-ponies to Dundonnell, and by one shepherd who herds his sheep on horseback; it is, however, not always easy to keep to the track.

It is sometimes possible to secure accommodation at the stalker's houses at Larachantivore and elsewhere, which enables long days to be spent among the mountains. This is, however, dependent on the time of the year, and is not possible during the stalking season, when the forests are closed to strangers, except in so far as they may be traversed by right-of-way paths. The house at Achneigie, however, is never available for this purpose, being fitted up as shooting quarters for the owner of the Dundonnell Forest.

2. Dundonnell to Kinlochewe, 21 miles. This is an alternative route to Loch Maree, which does not necessitate the crossing of that loch to reach a hotel. It traverses two passes instead of the three crossed by the Letterewe route, but has the disadvantage that for 3 miles in the middle of the walk there is no track to follow.

Leave Dundonnell by the road up Strath Beag, turning off after 2½ miles by the path up Glen Chaorachain, and climbing out of that glen, crossing the high plateau and descending into Strath na Sheallag. From the plateau the walker can look south across Strath na Sheallag and see his track going up the glen to Loch an Nid in the distance. Descending by a steep path into Strath na Sheallag, the path goes south along the east side of the River

Nid, following it up to its source in Loch an Nid, and along the glen beyond. At the head of this glen is Beinn Beag, one of the line of mountains which runs east to the head of Loch Fannich, and divides the Strath na Sheallag basin from that of Lochan Fada and Loch Fannich. Through these mountains penetrate three passes, the western one being the Beallach na Croise, from the northern side of which a stream flows down to Loch an Nid. Leave the path where it bends to the east and follow the stream up to the pass. On the southern side is the head of another stream, which should be kept to the left, and a course laid for the extreme east corner of Lochan Fada, where a path begins. This path goes south past two lochs and down Glen na Muice to the cottages known as the Heights of Kinlochewe, crossing the river a mile before it reaches them. From the Heights a road leads south-west down the Bruachaig River to Kinlochewe.

3. Loch a' Bhraoin to Gruinard, via Strath na Sheallag, 22 miles. The first 8 miles of this route are along high ground among the mountains, the remainder is down Strath na Sheallag, with high mountains on each side.

Leave the Dundonnell-Braemore road at the ednb near Loch a' Bhraoin and go down by a fishing road to the loch shore. A path leads along the northern shore to the head of the loch, passes the house of Lochivraon and continues west along the river. Crossing a tributary, it slants up along the hill-side, bends north to reach Loch an Nid, and goes on down the glen to Strath na Sheallag. Then it bends west and follows the north bank of the river past Achneigie to Shenavall. Here it is necessary to ford first the Strath na Sheallag River and afterwards that flowing from Glen na Muice in order to reach the path which leads along the south-west shore of Loch na Sheallag. There are no bridges on the former river, and that on the latter is nearly a mile up-stream. Then the way is along Loch na Sheallag for 4 miles, with the Teallach hills on one side and the two Ben Deargs on the other. At the foot of the loch an estate road begins, which follows the Gruinard

River down its course between the hills and joins the main road close to the bridge a mile to the south of Gruinard House. The view up the strath from the road, with the big mountains looming up in the distance and the river swirling along in wide curves through its level valley, is one not easily forgotten.

4. Loch a' Bhraoin to Achanalt, via Loch Fannich, 15 miles. This is a fine walk through the Fannich mountains, and round the head of Loch Fannich. It is the shortest route for walkers from Dundonnell to the railway.

Leave the road at the bend near Loch a' Bhraoin, (which may be reached by means of the morning mail motor from Dundonnell to Braemore), walk down to the loch and cross the two streams which flow out of it. The path then ascends to a third stream, which it presently crosses and continues to climb up the east side of the glen leading into the hills. Steadily climbing, the track passes between the slopes of Sgurr Breac on the west and Sgurr nan Clach Geala on the east, and reaches the summit of the pass at a height of over 1850 feet. Crossing the summit level and again climbing the hill-side on the west it reaches 2000 feet, only to descend at once along the course of the Allt Leac a' Bhealaich into a wider glen below. Crossing by a bridge over the Allt Leac a' Bhealaich, it goes south down the main glen to the cottage of Nest, near the shore of Loch Fannich, where a road begins.

Two rivers fall into the west end of Loch Fannich, one from the north and the other from the west; between them in the delta stands Cabuie Lodge. Starting at the cottage of Nest, the road crosses the River Nid by a bridge, passes close to Cabuie Lodge, crosses the second river and goes south-east along the loch shore for 3½ miles. Then it turns south and begins to climb between the hills on its way to join the main road at the twenty-seventh milestone from Dingwall. Half a mile south of the loch shore a path diverges on the left, ascends over the shoulder of Meallan Odhar, on a course roughly parallel to the road below and descends to 1000 feet. At this point, which is less than a mile from the main road, the path forks, one branch going down the hill-side to join the main road, the other bending east and slanting down through the Strathbran plantations to reach the road close to the twenty-fifth milestone from Dingwall. The railway station at Achanalt is 2 miles along the road to the east.

5. Dundonnell to Loch Toll an Lochain and back, 11 miles. Loch Toll an Lochain is a small rock-basin lying at the base of the Teallach peaks at a height of 1700 feet. It can be reached from the track leading up Glen Chaorachain, but the most direct route is to follow the course of the Allt Garbh from the road to its source in the loch.

Leave the road where it crosses the stream at a point 2¼ miles south of Dundonnell Hotel and follow its course, along the eastern bank, up the deep hollow through which it flows. For the last mile the route is to the west, for the loch lies in a corrie which opens to the east, with high black cliffs on three sides. Above the western shore towers Sgurr Fiona, the monarch of the Teallach peaks, with pinnacles and buttresses on either side. To the south is Sail Liath, the end peak of the range, between which and the next peak is the lofty pass named Cadha Gobhlach. The northern wall of the corrie is formed by the high ridge extending from Bidean a Ghlas Thuill (the Little Sharp-pointed Peak of the Grey Hollow), to Glas Meall Liath (the Pale-grey Hill). The Teallach peaks are considered to be the wildest range on the Scottish mainland; they provide excellent climbs for skilled mountaineers, and are a favourite climbing ground in the spring and early summer. As the height of Sgurr Fiona, the second highest summit, is 3474 feet, it enjoys an exceptionally extensive view over the western sea-board, and inland to the ranges of Central and Easter Ross. Photographers should note that by reason of its position Loch Toll an Lochain is best photographed in the morning, before the sun has worked round to the west; it is, in any case, not an easy subject to do justice to, the cliffs rising so high above the shore on which one is standing.

CHAPTER XIII

Loch Broom, Ullapool and Coigach

Maps.—*O.S. Popular Edition, 1 inch, sheets* 15, 19 *and* 20.
Bartholomew's Half Inch, sheet 58.

Loch Broom is the most northerly of the large sea-lochs of Ross-shire; like Loch Torridon it opens north-west into the Minch, widening into a broad, island-studded gulf from the long, narrow fiord of its upper reach. It is 14 miles from Loch Broom Manse, at the head of the loch, to Rudha Dubh Ard, opposite Horse Island, where the loch proper ceases. The coast continues north-west for another 10 miles to the point of Rhu Coigach, which forms, with the Greenstone Point to the south, the horns of the broad gulf into which Gruinard Bay and the two Loch Brooms open. This gulf, which appears to have no distinctive name of its own, contains a number of large and small islands, known as the Summer Isles. The main group of these islands lies to the south of the Coigach promontory, seaward from Baden Bay; of these Tanera More and Tanera Beg are the chief. Isle Ristol is situated to the north and close to the coast, Priest Island and Eilean Dubh well out to sea and Horse Island off the point of Rudha Dubh Ard, the north-east limit of Loch Broom. The large island called Isle Martin lies at the mouth of Strath Kanaird and encloses a sheltered bay named Loch Kanaird.

At the head of Loch Broom is the sheltered valley of Strathmore, through which the Broom River runs. From Braemore Lodge, where it quits the bleak uplands of the Dirrie More, to its junction with Loch Broom, is a distance of 5 miles, and in that space the river has plunged over the lofty Fall of Measach, foamed along the bottom of a deep gorge, between sheer cliffs of rock and descended into the level green valley to flow past woods and gardens to the sea. Strath More is one of the most sheltered spots on the West Coast; the mild climate is favourable to the production of flowers and shrubs, and the fine woodlands, some of which have now been felled for timber, make a wonderful contrast to the bare hill-sides a few miles to the east. The mansion of Braemore, whose lodge gates are close to the bridge at the cross-roads for Dundonnell, was built by the great engineer Sir John Fowler in the second half of the nineteenth century. It stands in a magnificent position high above the road on the eastern side of the glen, looking west to the Teallach mountains. The light suspension bridge which crosses the gorge of the Droma below the falls was also erected by this proprietor.

The road from Garve comes down Strath More and goes north along the eastern side of Loch Broom, keeping high above the shore. The loch is long and narrow, with steeply shelving shores; along the western side are several crofting townships, but no main road. On the eastern side is Inverlael, with its lodge and school, situated near the head of the loch at the mouth of a transverse glen, which runs south and east into the mountains. These are the extensive group culminating in Ben Dearg (3547 feet); although their foothills approach Loch Broom the main peaks lie far back and are not visible from the road. Further north, where the loch bends slightly to the west, the road passes Leckmelm, and soon comes in sight of Ullapool. The town stands on a flat peninsula projecting into Loch Broom, which is here three-quarters of a mile wide; a long row of houses extends above the beach, from which a stone pier juts out. Even from a distance Ullapool has an individuality of its own; the streets run at right angles to each other, and there is an air of regularity not often found in Scottish towns. The reason is that Ullapool was laid out in 1788 as a model town by the British Fisheries Society, who intended it to become the fishing and curing centre of the West Coast. It is to-day a pleasant sea-side village, well provided with places of accommodation, and forms an excellent centre for exploring Loch Broom, Coigach and the Summer Isles.

Beyond Ullapool the road climbs a long hill parallel to the coast, descends into the glen of the Allt an t'Srathain and climbs over a second ridge to drop down a winding hill to the seashore opposite Isle Martin. A long level spit runs out toward the island, with a solitary house at its extremity; across its base goes the road, turns east to ascend the glen of the River Glutton and descends a long steep hill into Strath Kanaird. The land-locked bay between Isle Martin and the road is known as Loch Kanaird; across it to the north the mountains sink to the sea in sheer cliffs of grey rock, backed by the tremendous ridge of Ben More Coigach. This is the southernmost of the mountains of Coigach, those curious isolated hills which make this north-west region of Ross-shire so unique. It is a high ridge extending from east to west, and ending in the sea; seen from the road south of Ullapool it hangs like a gigantic curtain across the northern sky. From this main ridge other spurs run northward, surrounding the little Lochan Tuath and ending above the southern shore of Loch Lurgainn. Loch Lurgainn and Loch Baddagyle extend for 6 miles along the depression to the north of the Ben More Coigach group; from the northern shore of the former rises Stack Polly, more correctly known as An Stac, whose extraordinary crest of ragged rock-pinnacles gives it the air of an angry porcupine. At the east end of the loch stands the shapely mountain of Cul Beag, along whose foot goes the road from Drumrunie Old Lodge to Achilti-buie and to Lochinver. North of Cul Beag, overlooking the far-winding shores of Loch Sionascaig, is the sister-mountain of Cul Mor, a double-peaked height of 2786 feet. Cul Mor looks east towards Elphin, just across the Sutherland border which, with its companion village of Knockan, stands near the foot of Loch Veyatie and close to three other famous fishing lochs of Assynt.

The word " Coigach " signifies " a fifth," the Coigach district being the north-west fifth of Ross-shire. Consisting of the blunt-nosed promontory of Rhu More, ending in the headland of Rhu Coigach, and of an inland region of mountain, loch and moorland extending to the Assynt border, it is one of the least populated districts of the West Coast, with the seaside township of Achiltibuie as its only centre of population. This is a large village on the shore of Baden Bay, opposite the island of Tanera More; it possesses an excellent hotel and is a fine centre for loch and sea fishing. A narrow and circuitous road connects Achiltibuie with Ullapool; it goes north to the head of Loch Owskeich (Osgaig), then south-east by Loch Baddagyle and Loch Lurgainn to join the Ullapool-Inchnadamph road at Drumrunie Old Lodge, where it turns south to reach Ullapool by way of Strathkanaird and Ardmair. At the western end of Loch Baddagyle it sends off a branch to the north, which climbs over a ridge and descends to Inverpolly Bridge, near the head of the inlet known as Loch Polly. From this point the road switchbacks across a tumbled region of lochs and grey, rocky hills, passes to the west of Loch Sionasgaig, descends a wooded glen to the seashore, once more turns inland, and drops down a long steep hill to the glen of the Kirkaig River and to Inverkirkaig and Lochinver beyond.

Strath Kanaird extends eastward into the hills past Langwell to Loch a' Chroisg, which lies between the low Cromalt Hills on the Sutherland march and the Rhidorroch Forest to the south. Eastward from Ullapool stretches Glen Achall, with its lovely woods; down it flows the Rhidorroch River, coming from Glen Douchary in the south, and passing through beautiful Loch Achall and by Rhidorroch Lodge to reach the sea at Ullapool. Up Glen Achall runs an estate road leading east across the watershed to Loch nan Daimh, and thence by way of Glen Einig to Oykell Bridge on the road to Lairg. The centre portion of this route is more of a hill-track than a road and hardly fit even for cycles, but for pedestrians it offers a magnificent cross-country route between east and west.

The Loch Broom district in mediæval times formed part of the district of North Argyll and belonged to the Earls of Ross. It was probably never densely populated, even prior to the period of the " improvements," but the western shore of the sea-loch has been inhabited from very early times. Above the beach, opposite Corry Point on the other shore of the loch, are the remains of Dun Lagaidh and a mile to the south those of Dun an Righ Ruaidh, both built by the early inhabitants as fortified towers or brochs. Whether Pictish or pre-Pictish is not yet known, but it is probable that similar towers in other districts were in occupation when the Romans held Southern Britain. There is little left of Dun Lagaidh, but the masonry of Dun an Righ Ruaidh (Fort of the Red King) is still in good preservation.

The Summer Isles were inhabited in early times, as is evidenced by the name of Priest Island by which the most westerly one is still known. Here, in all probability lived a cleric of the old Pictish Church, one of those Celle Dhé, or Servants of God, who are usually termed Culdees. Long after the original Pictish Church had lost its identity, these devoted followers of Christ laboured among the far islands and promontories of the west. The remains of bee-hive huts and of stone cells which are still to be found in some of the islets of the North owe their origin in many cases to these ministers of an earlier Church, and not to the followers of Columba.

After the fall of the Lords of the Isles, and the decline of Macdonald power in the North, the Loch Broom district came into the possession of the Mackenzies. Coigach, however, belonged to the Macleods of Lewis and Assynt and was still in their possession at the close of the sixteenth century. There are still Macleods in Coigach, but the Siol Torquil, or Macleods of Lewis, Assynt and Coigach, became extinct during the troubles of the seventeenth century.

Communications

Rail.—Garve, on the L.M.S. line from Inverness to Kyle of Lochalsh, is the nearest station.

Steamer.—A steamer from Glasgow calls at Ullapool every ten days.

Road Services.—A mail motor, carrying passengers, runs daily in each direction between Garve and Achiltibuie, via Ullapool.

There is also a second passenger service starting from Achiltibuie and running through Ullapool to Garve and back.

Accommodation

Hotels (2) at Ullapool and Achiltibuie. Also at Garve and Altguish on the road to Ullapool. Other accommodation at Ullapool and Knockan, and possibly at Achiltibuie.

Youth Hostels at Ullapool and Achininver, 2 miles south of Achiltibuie.

Walks

(a) *By Road*

1. Garve to Ullapool, 32 miles. This is the mail route to Ullapool, but it is not recommended to walkers. The latter should use the motor service as far as Braemore, visit the Fall of Measach (Corryhalloch), which is now National Trust Property, and walk down Strath More and thence to Ullapool.

The road leaves the railway station at Garve, goes north past the hotel and through the village, leaving the main road to Achnasheen about a mile from the station. Making a wide curve to north and east it strikes up Strath Garve, crosses to the east bank of the Blackwater River and goes on up the glen, with the heights of Little Wyvis above on the east. Climbing an easy gradient the road curves north-west past the woods of Inchbae Lodge and the entrance to Strath Rannoch, crosses a bridge and in 2 miles passes the entrance to Strath Vaich. A private road leads up this glen, connecting with hill-tracks to Oykell Bridge and Bonar

Bridge. It is not open to motorists, but can be used by pedestrians. Bending south and again west the road passes the Altguish Hotel and begins the long climb to Loch Droma, with the river, now known as the Glascarnoch, in the glen below on the right. Presently a broad corrie opens up on the north, with the lofty summits of Ben Dearg and Cona Mheall overshadowing its upper end. In a high recess between the two mountains, invisible from the road, lies Loch a' Choire Ghranda, one of the high-lying rock basins of the type of Loch Toll an Lochain near Dundonnell.

Loch Droma lies at a height of 900 feet on the summit level of the Dirrie More; above it to the left are the outlying spurs of the Fannich mountains and on the north the lower slopes of Ben Dearg. The road goes along its northern shore, affording splendid views of the distant Teallach peaks in front and descends gradually to the head of Strath More. Here, at the gates of Braemore Lodge, the Dundonnell road diverges to the left, crossing the Droma River some distance above the Falls. These can be visited by going through a gate on the left some way down the road to Ullapool, and descending a path to the edge of the gorge from which the Fall is visible. A second path, diverging to the left, leads to a suspension bridge spanning the gorge some distance below the Fall. The volume of water is not great, but the narrow wooded gorge, with its vertical rock walls, is most impressive. There is another and lower Fall higher up the river.

Now for 5 miles the way lies down Strath More, the road passing along or through woodlands, by the gates of Inverbroom Lodge and on to Inverlael at the head of Loch Broom. Some way south of Inverlael Lodge a bridge crosses the river and leads to the church and manse of Lochbroom. Keeping well above the loch the road goes north to Leckmelm, bends west above the shore and swings down a hill to enter Ullapool from the east.

2. Ullapool to Knockan and Inchnadamph, 22 miles. This road connects Ullapool with the road up Strath

Oykell to Inchnadamph and Lochinver, and was for many years the only route to the latter place. It leaves Ullapool at its eastern end and goes north to the bridge across the Ullapool River, bends to the west and climbs a long hill parallel to the coast. Descending into Glen Strathain, the road again ascends to cross a ridge and drop down a winding hill to the seashore opposite Isle Martin. Passing Ardmair and along the shore of Loch Kanaird, the way lies inland up the glen of the Glutton River, climbs round a corner at its head and goes down a long and steep hill into Strath Kanaird. Crossing the River Kanaird and slanting up the opposite side of the valley through the village, the road reaches a more level stretch, across which Cul Beag comes into view. From the roadside near Drumrunie Lodge, which is built on a hill to the right, there is a fine view up the glen to Stack Polly, with the Coigach peaks on the left and Cul Beag heaving its great bulk into the sky on the right.

At the Old Lodge of Drumrunie the Achiltibuie road goes off to the left; the main road ascends to the north, bending north-east along the base of Cul Mor and crossing the Sutherland boundary near the summit level. A gradual descent leads to the villages of Knockan and Elphin, which stretch for about 2 miles along the road-sides; from this point Suilven and Canisp are both visible in the north-west and the large lochs of Veyatie and Cam Loch are not far away. Swinging to the east, the road joins that from Strath Oykell at Ledmore, a little to the north of Loch Borrolan, and goes north across the Ledbeg River and past Loch Awe towards Inchnadamph. The River Loanan flows from Loch Awe down a glen to Loch Assynt; above it is a line of fine limestone cliffs and far in front, beyond the head of Loch Assynt, towers Glas Bheinn. Inchnadamph stands on a level space at the head of the loch; the road passes in front of the hotel and goes on to Lochinver.

3. Drumrunie Old Lodge to Achiltibuie, 14 miles. This road leaves the road to Inchnadamph below the Old Lodge of Drumrunie, which stands at the foot of Cul Beag. It

leads westwards across a spur of that mountain, swings down a hill to the shore of Loch Lurgainn and follows the eastern and northern shores of that crescent-shaped loch, past the lonely shepherd's cottage at the foot of Stack Polly, and so to Loch Baddagyle beyond. In crossing from the one loch to the other a fine view is to be obtained by looking back. Cul Beag on the one hand and Beinn Eun and Ben More on the other are separated by the dark loch; high above on the left are the scree slopes and ragged pinnacles of Stack Polly.

Skirting the northern shore of Loch Baddagyle and continuing along Loch Owskeich to its foot, the road turns west to the head of Achnahaird Bay, an inlet of the wide bay of Enard. Here it turns sharply to the south, passes along the eastern side of Loch Baa and Loch Bhattachan, and reaches the shore of Baden Bay at a point 2 miles to the north of Achiltibuie Hotel. From the hotel the road continues south-east for about 4 miles, ending at Coulnacraig on the seashore at the western foot of Ben More Coigach.

(b) *By Hill-paths*

1. Ullapool to Oykell Bridge Hotel, 19 miles. This route leaves the main road to Inchnadamph on the east side of the bridge across the Ullapool River, and leads east along the river to the foot of Loch Achall. Here it crosses to the northern bank and goes on along the north shore of the loch, past Rhidorroch Lodge and up the beautifully wooded Glen Achall beyond. Eight miles from Ullapool is Rhidorroch Old Lodge, which stands in a loop of the river on the southern bank. Beyond the lodge the road begins to climb, still keeping to the north bank, and soon bends north-east to cross the watershed to Loch na Daimh. Attaining its highest level of 820 feet near the head of that loch, it goes down the glen beyond it to the transverse glen of the Rappach Water, fords the River Poiblich and goes down the south bank of the Rappach to Duag Bridge, at the head of Glen Einig.

From this bridge there are two routes to Oykell Bridge,

by the north or the south side of Glen Einig. For the former it is necessary to ford the Rappach Water, which here changes its name to the River Einig, and to proceed for 2 miles by a path along the north bank as far as the Oykell River. Here the track turns north, crosses a small tributary of the Oykell, and reaches the main road at Oykell Bridge. The other track crosses Duag Bridge, ascends through the woods along the side of the glen, crosses a stream in the woods, and reaches the cottages of Amat, south of Oykell Bridge. From here a path leads to a bridge over the Einig River and joins the path on the north bank. The main track fords the Einig some distance below the bridge and leads up the Oykell to Oykell Bridge. It should be noted that while the southern track is actually a cart road, which begins at Coire Mor 6 miles to the south, that on the north side of the glen is merely a path.

2. Ullapool to Achiltibuie along the coast, 14 miles. This is the most direct land route to Achiltibuie; for the middle portion of the journey the way lies along the foot of the cliffs close above the sea and is in places somewhat hazardous. It was the route taken by the Achiltibuie postman in former years, but is now rarely traversed. Leave the town by the Inchnadamph road, turning off at the first milestone along a track which goes north-east over the hills, passes between two pairs of lochs, and drops down the hill-side into Strathkanaird. Rejoining the road immediately to the south of the bridge, the way lies across the latter, and then along a path to the left, keeping south of a schoolhouse, and making for a bridge across the Runie River, above its junction with the Kanaird. From this point there is no defined track, the way lying west along the foot of the hill to the sea. Passing north of the old fort at the north-east corner of the bay, the walker must make his way as best he can between the cliff and the sea for 4 miles, crossing the stream which runs into the bay known as Geodha Mor and rounding the western end of Ben More Coigach. In another mile three streams are crossed in succession and the beginning of a road is reached.

This road turns inland past the cottage at Culnacraig, ascends along the hill-side above Horse Sound, passes to the east of Badenscallie, and on by Polglas to Achiltibuie. The great feature of this walk, apart from its difficult nature along the cliffs, is the extensive sea-views which it commands. Ben Gobhlach in particular is a prominent object in the south, as are the Summer Isles out at sea.

3. Inverlael (head of Loch Broom) to Dundonnell Hotel, 8½ miles. This is a short-cut from Loch Broom to Dundonnell, which can be used when the ferry is impassable. By taking the morning mail motor as far as Inverlael, the walker bound for Dundonnell can avoid the long road circuit by Braemore, and obtain views of the Teallach peaks from the divide between the two glens. Go south from Inverlael Lodge to the bridge over the Broom River, cross it, and keep straight on, past the turn north to the church and manse, to the cottages of Croftown below the hill-side. At the back of the cottages a track begins, slanting southwards up the hill-side, and in a short time doubling back to climb in a north-westerly direction past two small lochans on the heights to the shore of the little Loch an Tiompain. From this sheet of water, which lies at a height of 1249 feet above the sea, the path ascends for another 100 feet and begins its descent to Strath Beag, keeping along the slopes on the north side of the glen of the Allt a' Chairn. Passing to the north of a little hill, the track enters the woods and emerges at the bridge to the south of Dundonnell House, where it joins the main road. Dundonnell Hotel is 2½ miles along the road to the north.

CHAPTER XIV

LOCHINVER AND ASSYNT

MAPS.—*O.S. Popular Edition*, 1 *inch, sheet* 15.
Bartholomew's Half Inch, sheet 58.

THE district of Assynt forms the south-west portion of the
modern County of Sutherland: it is divided from the
Ross-shire district of Coigach by the River Kirkaig, Fionn
Loch and Loch Veyatie, and extends northward to
Eddrachillis Bay and Loch Cairnbawn. The beautiful
Loch Assynt is the largest of its many lochs; from its
western end flows the rushing Inver, which falls into the
sea below Lochinver Bridge.

Assynt is a region of low grey hills of archæan gneiss,
set with brown heath, bracken and heather, and studded
with countless lochs and tarns. This is the oldest of British
rocks, smoothed and rounded by the centuries and scored
by glaciers; its rounded bosses form the plateau of Assynt.
From this plateau rises abruptly a group of great mountains,
each standing clear of its fellows in lonely grandeur. Ben
More Assynt is the highest summit; it rises to the east of
Loch Assynt, and is the main peak of a considerable range
which extends north-west to Glas Bheinn. Ben More is
3273 feet high; its summit is capped with white quartzite
and is the highest point in Sutherland. North of Loch
Assynt the mighty mass of Quinag towers above Kyle Sku
and looks east to Glas Bheinn and Ben Leoid. Its name
Cuineag signifies a water-stoup or a milking pail, which
its outline is said to resemble; with its three great peaks
and deep northern corries it is one of the most majestic of
Highland mountains.

Suilven, which has been nicknamed the Sugar Loaf, is undoubtedly the most outstanding of the mountains of Assynt: it stands in Glen Canisp, south-east of Lochinver, and 2 miles from the shapely peak of Canisp. Suilven is a ridge of rock about $1\frac{1}{2}$ miles long, rising abruptly from a lower plateau; at each end are rocky peaks, with a lower one between. Seen from east to west it presents the appearance of a gigantic tower of rock, apparently inaccessible, but from north or south it takes on the form of a brobdingnagian elephant. Viewed from the moors on the Lairg road its two peaks look like the fangs of a gigantic tooth. The name Suilven is a Gaelic-Norse hybrid, meaning " Pillar-fell "; the mountain is indeed a watch-tower of rock overlooking the coast lands of Assynt and Coigach from its elevation of 2398 feet.

Assynt's mountains stand well back from the coast, except where Loch Cairnbawn penetrates inland at the base of Quinag. The coast is low and rocky, indented with small sea-lochs and bays, and guarded by numerous islands. The bay of Lochinver is itself an inlet of the wide Enard Bay, which extends from Coigach Point to Stoer Head, and contains Loch Kirkaig, Loch Roe and the fine sandy bays of Achmelvich and Stoer. Beyond the peninsula of Stoer, with its powerful lighthouse and numerous villages, is the wide, island-studded bay of Eddrachillis, whose fretted southern shores sweep east past Oldany Island to Loch Cairnbawn and Kyle Sku. Here is the narrow strait, crossed by the ferry to Kyle Strome, where Loch Cairnbawn divides into two arms which penetrate far up into the mountains and are known as Loch Glendhu (Black Glen) and Loch Glencoul (Back-lying Glen).

Lochinver is now the most important centre in Assynt, and has taken the place of the former capital of Inchnadamph. It is a fishing village at the mouth of the River Inver and has shops, churches, a hotel and a steamer pier. The former fine Culag Hotel, once the residence of the Duke of Sutherland, was burnt down some years ago and is still a ruin. The main industry of Lochinver consists

in catering for summer visitors and for the tenants of
shooting lodges, for the deep-sea fishing has ceased to be
remunerative. A road along the northern shore of Loch
Assynt connects the village with Inchnadamph, Strathoy-
kell and Lairg: another, by Inverkirkaig and Inverpolly,
leads south to Achiltibuie and Ullapool. A third road,
narrow, hilly and winding, switchbacks northwards along
the coast to Stoer, Drumbeg, Unapool and Kyle Sku.

Inchnadamph (Stag's Meadow) stands at the head of
Loch Assynt on the Lairg-Lochinver road. Its situation
in a green strath at the junction of two rivers and a loch
marks it out as a natural centre, and it was for long the
chief village in Assynt. With its church, school, post-office
and good hotel, it provides an attractive halting-place
amid magnificent surroundings; behind it rises the range
of mountains of which Ben More and Conamheall are the
crowning heights, and to the west are the long vistas of
Loch Assynt. Two miles to the north, on a promontory
of Loch Assynt, is the ruin of Ardvreck Castle, from which
the Macleods ruled Assynt; a mile further on, at Skiag
Bridge, a mountain road strikes off for Unapool and Kyle
Sku ferry. This road climbs round the eastern base of
Quinag, and affords fine views of his corries, and of the
other mountains of Assynt. The ferry at Kyle Sku, which
during the season can transport motor-cars, leads to Kyle
Strome and Scourie, and thence to Laxford Bridge,
Rhiconich and Durness, and is a vital link in the road
system of the north-west.

From Ledmore, some 6 miles south of Inchnadamph, a
secondary road leads south by the villages of Elphin and
Knockan to Strathkanaird and Ullapool, passing on the
eastern side of Canisp, Suilven and the isolated Coigach
mountains.

Assynt was once ruled by the Norse sea-rovers, who have
left their traces in such place-names as Kirkaig, Stoer,
Oldany and Suilven, the latter being a Norse-Gaelic
hybrid. That they held the coastal districts is certain, but
it is probable that in the inland mountain fastnesses the

PLATE VII   LOCH ASSYNT WITH THE RUIN OF ARDVRECK C

The castle, which stands on the peninsula i
captor of Montrose and last chief of Assynt.

Photograph by R. M. ADAM

istance was the home of Neil Macleod, the
in is that of Calda House.

Gaels were able to hold their own. Later came the Macleods, themselves of Norse origin, who ruled the district until well into the seventeenth century. These were the Siol Torquil, or Macleods of Lewis, and quite distinct from the Siol Tormod of Skye and Harris. They were a warlike race, constantly at feud with their northern or eastern neighbours; their conflicts with Sutherlands, Murrays and Mackays seem to have continued for nearly three hundred years. In the year 1406 the Macleods invaded Strathnaver to avenge an insult to the sister of their chief, who had married a Mackay. On their return, laden with booty, they were overtaken in Strath Oykell by the incensed Mackays, and a fierce battle ensued, in which the northern clan was victorious. Only one Macleod is said to have returned to Lewis to tell the tale of Tuiteam Tarbhach, " the Place of Slaughter."

A burn in the mountains behind Inchnadamph, still called the Mackay's Burn, once played a decisive part in the clan warfare of long ago. The story goes that a warband of Mackays, crossing the hills into Assynt, came on a lonely bothy tenanted by a solitary Macleod. Outcast from his clan for some crime, and bitterly resentful, the renegade agreed to guide the raiders by a secret track through the darkness, so that they might reach the unsuspecting Macleod village before dawn. The way led across a gorge, where it was necessary to leap to a midway rock, and thence, by a change of direction, to the farther bank. The Macleod crossed first, and called to the Mackays to follow, but took care not to indicate the change of direction. Each Mackay in turn leapt to his death, and thus the outcast saved his sleeping clansmen.

The castle at Ardvreck on Loch Assynt was the home of Neil Macleod, the captor of Montrose and last chief of Assynt. His fortunes rapidly declined after the execution of the Great Marquis, and eventually Assynt was lost to the Macleods for ever. There is some doubt as to his conduct in allowing Montrose to be surrendered to his enemies, for Neil Macleod was on the side of the Covenant;

but he sinned against the Highland law of hospitality in giving up a fugitive on his lands, so that the bitter curse of Ian Lom, the Keppoch bard, seems to be fully justified. Neil Macleod goes down to history as the betrayer of Montrose, and shares with Mentieth, who betrayed Wallace, the scorn of posterity.

Communications

Railways.—There are no railways in Assynt, Lairg and Invershin being the nearest stations.

Steamers.—A cargo steamer from Glasgow calls regularly at Lochinver, and cruising steamers call during the season.

Road Services.—A mail motor van runs daily in each direction between Lairg, Inchnadamph and Lochinver. There is also a passenger service from Invershin, which joins the Lairg route at Rosehall. This is a daily service from June to September, and on Tuesdays, Thursdays and Saturdays during the rest of the year. The mail service is continued from Lochinver to Stoer, Clashnessie and Drumbeg.

Accommodation

There are hotels at Altnacealgach, Inchnadamph, Kyle Sku, Lochinver, and a temperance hotel at Drumbeg. Other accommodation in private houses or boarding-houses at Lochinver, Stoer, and Knockan, near Elphin.

Walks

(a) *By Road*

1. Drumrunie Old Lodge to Lochinver, by Loch Lurgain, 20 miles. This road quits the Ullapool-Inchnadamph road at Drumrunie Old Lodge, 12 miles from Ullapool, and runs west along the base of the mountain Coul Beg, descends to the basin in which lies crescent-shaped Loch Lurgain, and curves around the loch below Stack Polly, with its extraordinary crest of splintered pinnacles, and on to Loch Baddagyle. The northern side of Ben More Coigach and his satellite mountains is well

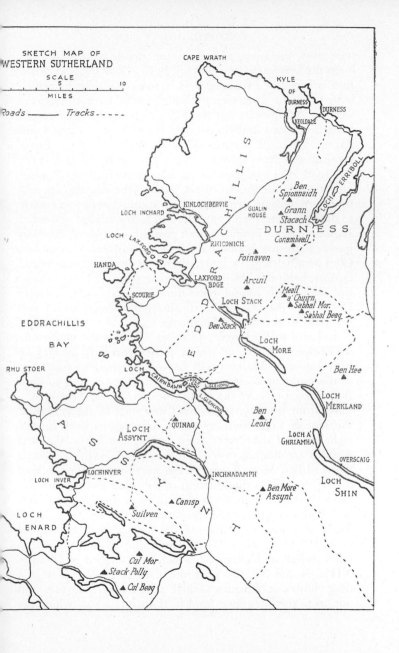

SKETCH MAP OF
WESTERN SUTHERLAND

SCALE
5   10
MILES

Roads _____   Tracks _ _ _ _

CAPE WRATH

KYLE
OF
DURNESS
DURNESS
KEOLDALE

A CHILLIS

LOCH ERRIBOLL

Ben
Spionnaidh
Grann
Stacach
Conamheall
DURNESS
Foinaven
Arcuil

KINLOCHBERVIE

LOCH INCHARD
GUALIN
HOUSE

LOCH LAXFORD
RHICONICH

HANDA
LAXFORD
BDGE

SCOURIE

Meall
a' Chuirn
Sabhal Mor:
Sabhal Beag

Loch Stack
Ben Stack

LOCH
MORE

EDDRACHILLIS
BAY

Ben Hee

RHU STOER
LOCH
CAIRNBAWN
KYLE
L. GLENDHU
L. GLENCOUL

LOCH
MERKLAND

Ben
Leoid

LOCH A'
GHRIAMHA

QUINAG
LOCH
ASSYNT

OVERSCAIG

LOCHINVER

A S S
Y N T

INCHNADAMPH

LOCH INVER

Canisp

Ben More
Assynt

LOCH
SHIN

LOCH
ENARD

Suilven

Cul Mor
Stack Polly
Cul Beag

seen from the road, and from the divide above the two lochs the rearward view of Stack Polly, Coul Beg and Beinn Eun is very fine. Baddagyle is less striking than its neighbour Lurgain: at its western end the road continues north-west for Achiltibuie, but the Lochinver road turns sharply back to the east and climbs over into the glen of the Polly River. From the summit ridge Stack Polly appears like a gigantic couchant sphinx. From Inverpolly to Lochinver the road rises and falls amid numerous lochs and rocky hills, descending the Strathain Glen to the sea, and skirting the shore, only to turn inland up a long ascent and finally to descend a steep and winding hill to the bridge across the Kirkaig River. From the high ground over which the road passes there are occasional views of Suilven, Canisp and Coul Mor, with Stack Polly, already losing its characteristic outline, behind in the south. Passing through Inverkirkaig, the road twists inland once more, passes Loch na Doire Daraich with its strangely-situated schoolhouse, and descends to the bay of Lochinver.

2. Lairg to Lochinver, 47 miles. This is the mail route to Lochinver, part of which passes through country of little interest. Walkers will be well advised to make use of the motor services as far as Inchnadamph, and to walk thence by Loch Assynt to Lochinver. Lairg Station is 2 miles from the town; the road descends to the bridge at the foot of Loch Shin, crosses it, and turns back up the right bank of the river. After leaving the latter, the next 8 miles are mainly over open moorland, with occasional views of Ben More Assynt to the north-west; then follows a long descent to the junction of the road from Invershin. Here the road bends south-west to cross the Cassley River, and continues westward, past the battlefield of Tuiteam Tarbhach, up the course of the Oykell to the hotel at Oykell Bridge. Here is the beginning of a hill-track to Glen Achall and Ullapool, which is described in Chapter XIII., Route No. (b) 1. From Oykell Bridge there is a long climb out of Strath Oykell, past Lubcroy Lodge, and out on to the open moorland to the west, across which the

isolated mountains of Canisp, Suilven and Coul Mor have now come into view. Loch Craggie is passed on the left, and the watershed is crossed to Loch Borrolan, by the side of which stands the fishing hotel of Altnacealgach. The name means " the Cheats' Burn," and is a reminder of a boundary settlement of long ago, when the Ross-shire representatives, with earth from Balnagown in their shoes, swore that while pacing out the county boundary they had never left Ross-shire soil! The long narrow " peninsula " which Ross-shire now thrusts northward into Sutherland, is a legacy of this sharp practice.

Two miles beyond the hotel a secondary road goes off to Elphin, Knockan and Drumrunie Old Lodge, where the western road from Lochinver to Ullapool is joined. The Inchnadamph road bends northwards, crosses the Ledbeg River, where marble was once worked, and continues past Loch Awe down the glen to Inchnadamph, below a fine range of limestone cliffs, with Conamheall and Ben More Assynt prominent in the east. Passing the hotel, bridge and post-office, the road bends west to skirt the shore of Loch Assynt, past the ruins of Calda House and Ardvreck Castle, to Skiag Bridge, where the Kyle Sku road diverges to the north. The Lochinver road continues to rise and fall along the northern shore of the loch, passes Loch Assynt Lodge, and bends to the south-west where the loch turns at right angles in its western reach. The eastward view from this point is very fine, extending up the length of the loch to Inchnadamph and its guardian mountains. At the west end of Loch Assynt the road begins to descend, and follows the right bank of the River Inver down to the sea at Lochinver, which is 5 miles from Little Assynt at the end of the loch.

3. Lochinver to Stoer, Drumbeg and Unapool, 22 miles. This route, like that to Inverpolly, traverses the coastal region of low, grey, gneiss hills; though it runs at no great distance from the shore, the sea is only occasionally visible, but from Cnoc Poll, near Stoer, is to be seen in clear weather one of the most magnificent views of sea and mountain in

all Scotland. Leaving the Inchnadamph road half a mile beyond the Inver Bridge, the Stoer road bears north-west for 1½ miles, descends to a glen and a bridge, where the local road to Achmelvich goes off to the left, and again climbs north and then west. Crossing an awkward transverse ridge in a series of zigzags, it continues past Loch an Ordain down to the sandy bay of Clachtoll. Just west of the loch a burn flows below the road and disappears through a cleft in the rocks on its way to the sea. On this burn, though invisible from the road, stands an old mill where corn used to be ground. Beyond Clachtoll is a reedy lagoon where moorhens hide: on the left are the sand-hills of Stoer Bay.

Stoer village stands on a hill-side, with extensive views to the south and west. For the finest views of all the wayfarer should leave the road and walk north-west for three-quarters of a mile to the summit of the low hill of Cnoc Poll. From this eminence of 352 feet he may see, in clear weather, the coast of Assynt and of Wester Ross, of Lewis and of Northern Skye, with the mountains of the West Coast from Canisp and Suilven to the giants of Torridon. Behind him, to the north, is the Stoer peninsula, with its lighthouse on Stoer Head and its numerous crofting townships. The road crosses the base of this peninsula to Clashnessie Bay, traverses a rock-cutting high above the sea and winds inland, past several lochs, to Drumbeg, where there is a small hotel. On the rocky coast, close to the mouth of Loch Nedd, the empty hull of the luxury Liner *Bermuda* drove ashore in the spring of 1933. She was on her way to the Forth to be broken up, broke adrift from her two tugs between Handa Island and Cape Wrath, and drifted in unhurt to her last berth near Drumbeg.

From Drumbeg onwards the road surface deteriorates: the route is along the inlet of Loch Nedd, across the foot of Glen Leirg and of Glen Ardvar, turning east along the side of Loch Cairnbawn to Torgawn. The heads of these two glens penetrate below the steeps of Quinag, whose north-west peak dominates this region, and is the focus of the landward views. From about Glen Ardvar the sea views also are of great beauty, the islands and shores of the bay of Eddrachillis forming one of the most magnificent sea-scapes in the whole country. A Sutherland man, who is well qualified to express an opinion, has told the writer that he knows of no more beautiful sight in Sutherland than the westward view from this point in the light of a summer evening. From Torgawn the road turns inland, crosses higher ground past Loch Unapool, and joins the road from Inchnadamph some 3 miles south of Kyle Sku.

4. Skiag Bridge to Kyle Sku, 7 miles. This road leaves Loch Assynt at a point 2 miles north-west of Inchnadamph Hotel, and climbs steadily to the pass (813 feet) between Quinag and Glasven. (From a point 1 mile short of the summit a track leads west to the top of Spidean Coinich, the southern peak of Quinag.) The descent on the north side is steep and has sharp bends; the road crosses and recrosses the Unapool Burn, skirts the shore of Loch Glencoul, with fine views up that loch to Ben Leoid's prominent peak, leaves the village of Unapool to the right, and descends to the ferry and the little inn of Kyle Sku. Across the narrow kyle is the landing pier of Kyle Strome, from which a road goes north-west to Badcall and Scourie. Kyle Sku ferry, like that of Dornie, on Loch Alsh, is at the junction of three sea-lochs, amid magnificent scenery. Loch Glendhu and Loch Glencoul, which penetrate east and south-east among the mountains, are narrow lanes of deep water, above which the rocks rise steeply. No road leads to the solitary house at the head of Loch Glencoul; a rough track from Kyle Strome traverses the north shore of Loch Glendhu to the keeper's house at the foot of Ben a' Bhua.

(b) *By Hill-tracks*

1. Lochinver to Elphin, by Glen Canisp and Glen Dorcha, 16 miles. This route takes the walker through the heart of Assynt, between Suilven and Canisp, to the base of the Ross-shire mountain of Coul Mor.

Leave Lochinver by the estate road to Glen Canisp Lodge, where the track begins. It leads eastward, up the north side of the river, to its source in the mile-long Loch na Gainimh, skirts the north-east shore of the latter and traverses Glen Dorcha, crosses to the south side of the smaller Lochan Fada, and then goes due south to the shore of Cam Loch. It then skirts this large sheet of water, rounds its eastern end and joins the Ledmore-Elphin road $1\frac{1}{2}$ miles from Elphin post-office. The summit of Suilven is $1\frac{1}{2}$ miles to the south of this track, and Canisp rises straight from Glen Dorcha; Elphin is about 3 miles from the summit of Coul Mor.

2. Elphin to Inverkirkaig, by Fionn Loch, 14 miles. This route runs nearly parallel to the last one, along the depression to the south of Suilven.

Leave Elphin by the Ledmore Road, turning off in $1\frac{1}{2}$ miles to skirt the end of Cam Loch, and go west along its north-east shore for nearly 2 miles. So far the route has been the same as in No. 1, but now it lies west along Cam Loch, past a cottage called Bracklach, and along the base of Suilven to the Fionn Loch. This long, narrow loch has then to be passed, the path going along the north-east side, doubling round between it and a continuation to the north-west, and bending back to the south-east to reach the River Kirkaig at a point just below its exit from the loch. Thence the path goes west along the north bank of the river, past the fine Falls of Kirkaig, and follows the beautifully wooded glen down to the sea at Inverkirkaig. From thence to Lochinver is 3 miles by road.

3. Achiltibuie to Inverpolly, Inverkirkaig and Lochinver, 14 miles. This is a variation of the road route described in Chapter XIII. It follows the coast as far as possible, and is somewhat shorter than the road. For walkers it forms a link in the coast route along Wester Ross and Sutherland.

Leave Achiltibuie by the road to the north, passing Loch Bhattachan and Loch Baa, and turning east to Loch Owskeich. Where the road crosses the stream which connects that loch with Loch Garvie, a path strikes off round Garvie Bay, and crosses the River Polly near Inverpolly Lodge. Passing east of the lodge, this track goes north along the coast of Enard Bay, rejoining the Lochinver road at the seaward end of Glen Strathain, where the river is crossed. From here the road is followed to Inverkirkaig and Lochinver, as described in Route No. (a) 1.

4. Lochinver to Inchnadamph, by Glen Canisp and the south shore of Loch Assynt, 15 miles. This route commands fine views of Suilven from the west and north and of Loch Assynt, Canisp and Quinag. It has also the advantage of avoiding all main roads.

Leave Lochinver by the estate road to Glen Canisp Lodge and continue by the path up Glen Canisp for nearly 2 miles. At a point where the track skirts a projecting mass of high ground on the left and some distance before reaching the foot-bridge which is crossed on the way to Suilven, a branch track goes off to the north, climbs over the high ground, crosses the neck of water between two lochs, and makes for the rocky knoll of Cnoc an Leothaid. Crossing to the east of its highest point, with a magnificent rearward view of Suilven, the track descends to the Inver River, crosses its tributary the Allt an Tiagaich and strikes east along Loch Assynt. At first close to the shore, it soon cuts across the base of a broad peninsula, skirts the next bay and begins to slant up the hill-side, crossing the northern slopes of Beinn Garbh at a height of some 700 feet and finally descending to the shore at the head of Loch Assynt. Here the River Loanan has to be crossed, and Inchnadamph Hotel is reached in less than half a mile.

5. Altnacealgach Hotel to Ben More Assynt and Inchnadamph, by Loch Ailsh, Glen Oykell and the top of Ben More, 17 miles. This route leads through the fastnesses of Ben More, and necessitates a steep climb from Dubh Loch Mor to the summit ridge of Ben More. A long summer day with fine weather should be chosen, and maps, a compass, and adequate provisions should be taken.

Take the Lairg Road from Altnacealgach for nearly

3 miles, turning off to the north by a cart track which serves Ben More Lodge. This track crosses a tributary, and shortly afterwards the River Oykell and strikes up the east shore of Loch Ailsh to the lodge at its head. From the lodge a path leads for 7 miles up the east side of the River Oykell, finishing high up under Ben More Assynt on the shore of a small tarn called the Dubh Loch Mor. Due north of the loch is the high ridge connecting Conamheall with the summit of Ben More Assynt: along it runs the path from Inchnadamph. By climbing to this ridge the walker may reach the summit of Ben More, or by turning west he may descend over the top of Conamheall into the glen of the Traligil River, and thence reach Inchnadamph.

6. Inchnadamph to Quinag and Kyle Sku, by the Beallach a' Chornaich, 14 miles. This route takes the walker round the southern flanks of Quinag, and through the pass which separates the southern peak, Spidean Coinich, from the main mass of the mountain.

Take the Lochinver road from Inchnadamph for 5 miles, until past the promontory which juts into the loch due south of Spidean Coinich. Leave the road and climb towards that hill, when a track will be met going west, which soon afterwards turns north and ascends for a mile below the western flank of Spidean Coinich. Then it turns east and climbs to the high pass, called Beallach a' Chornaich, which crosses through the heart of Quinag. From the summit of the pass the track descends to the headwaters of a burn, and follows its south bank in a north-easterly direction, passes on the right two small lochs and reaches the road just south of the White Bridge on the Unapool Burn. It should be noted that from the west end of Loch nan Eun, the second of the two lochs, there is little or no track visible, and that the walker will have to take a line down the hill-slope direct to the White Bridge. From the latter part of this route fine views of Loch Glencoul and its background of mountains will be obtained.

7. Inchnadamph to Kyle Sku, by Glas Bheinn, 8 miles. This track, which leaves the road opposite Ardvreck Castle,

is a short-cut across the flank of Glas Bheinn, from which fine vistas to the west along Loch Assynt are to be seen.

Take the cart track which goes north from a point opposite the ruins of Ardvreck, taking care to quit it when it turns west to Achmore, and keep to the path which climbs north over the flank of Glas Bheinn. This path ascends to 1400 feet, descending to rejoin the Kyle Sku road 3½ miles north of Skiag Bridge. Kyle Sku is 4 miles to the north.

8. Round the base of Quinag, from Skiag Bridge, 17 miles. This route commands fine views of Quinag in its differing aspects, and of the islands and inlets of Eddrachillis Bay.

Take the Kyle Sku road at Skiag Bridge, turning off in a third of a mile by a track which diverges to the north west, crosses the Skiag Burn and goes west past two small lochs for 2 miles, below the slopes of Spidean Coinich. Bending sharply north to cross a burn, it shortly afterwards recrosses it higher up and divides into a north and a north-west track. The former leads to the Beallach a' Chornaich, already described in Route No. 6. The north-west path again crosses the burn and goes over to Upper Glen Leirg, follows the right bank of the Uidh an Leothaid nearly down to Loch an Leothaid and bends north, across an outlying spur of Sail Ghorm, descending to join the Drumbeg-Kyle Sku road near the head of Loch Ardvar. By going south-west along the road from this point, Drumbeg and Loch Nedd can be reached in 4 miles. The Kyle Sku road crosses the foot of Glen Ardvar, and goes east past the houses of Rientraid to the shore of Loch Cairnbawn, which is skirted as far as the next river at Torgawn. Here the road bends inland, crosses the river and climbs over past Loch Unapool to join the main road 3 miles south of Kyle Sku. From the latter part of this route there are fine views of Sail Ghorm and Sail Garbh, the two great northern peaks of Quinag, which tower up to the south, enclosing between them the deep corrie known as the Byre of Quinag.

ASCENT OF SUILVEN (2399 feet)

Leave Lochinver by the estate road to Glen Canisp

Lodge, and take the path up the glen for $2\frac{1}{2}$ miles beyond the lodge, where a foot-bridge crosses the river to the south. Cross this and climb out of the valley, heading south by east, until a chain of small lochans is reached, between which the path leads, making for the centre of the northern base of the mountain. A steep grass gully is seen to lead upwards from that point, and is the means of approach to the summit ridge. Climb up this gully, through long heather, passing to the left of the knob of rock which will be met not far from the start, and zigzagging where necessary to avoid difficult pitches or jutting rocks. The ridge of the mountain is reached at its lowest point, between the middle and the western peaks; it is in places very narrow, but affords a safe passage in a westerly direction to the summit of the mountain. This is a small convex plateau, surrounded on three sides by precipitous cliffs, and known as the Grey Castle. From it the mountain is seen as a narrow, steep-sided ridge with the middle and eastern peaks standing against a background of loch-studded moorlands.

Its isolated position and precipitous sides have made Suilven the watch-tower of Assynt. The Norsemen knew it as the " Pillar-fell," and the description is an apt one. From the Grey Castle one may see on a clear day the coast, and lochs, and mountains of Assynt, Eddrachillis and Coigach, from Handa Island and Quinag to Ben More Coigach. In the west and south is the Minch, with the distant peaks of Harris and the far blue headlands of Skye; nearer at hand, beyond the islands of Loch Broom, stretch the long promontories of Ross-shire.

The return should be by the same route as the ascent: under no circumstances should the descent of the Grey Castle be attempted, for that is difficult and dangerous even to trained rock-climbers. It is possible to descend by a grass gully into the glen of the Fionn Loch, on the south of the mountain, and to return to Lochinver by way of the Kirkaig glen. This route is much longer and does not appear to have any advantages over the shorter one through Glen Canisp.

CHAPTER XV

Scourie, Eddrachillis and the Reay Forest

Maps.—*O.S. Popular Edition, 1 inch, sheets 9 and 16.
Bartholomew's Half Inch, sheet 58.*

To the east and north of Assynt lies the district of Eddrachillis, a rugged region of grey rock extending nearly to Cape Wrath. Its coast is fringed with islands and broken into lochs and bays: inland are countless lochans and a series of fine fishing lochs. Along the eastern border stretches the long range of the mountains of the Reay Forest; from Ben Hee in the south to Foinne Bheinn in the north its length is 14 miles. To the west of this range, with the Ben More group as its southern neighbour, a second belt of mountains extends from Ben Leoid towards Ben Stack. Between these two parallel ranges is the long, narrow depression which runs from Loch Shin to Loch Laxford and contains the chain of large fresh-water lochs known as A' Ghriamha, Merkland, More and Stack. Along this depression, too, runs the road from Lairg to Laxford Bridge, by which the mails reach Scourie.

The coast of Eddrachillis extends from Loch Cairnbawn to the outlet of the River Geisgeach, 4 miles south of Cape Wrath. The southern portion of this sea-board is broken and indented, and fringed with islands and skerries; from Loch Cairnbawn to Loch Inchard a succession of bays and sea-lochs penetrates deep into the land. Loch Cairnbawn and the bays of Calva, Badcall and Scourie are inlets of the great bay of Eddrachillis, in the south: further north lies the Island of Handa, with its bird-haunted western cliffs, divided from the mainland by the narrow Sound of

Handa. Still further to the north the two great fiords of
Loch Laxford and Loch Inchard cut deep into the land,
enclosing between them a rugged district known as the
Ceathramh Garbh or Rough Quarter, which is still further
cut up by the inlets of Loch Dougal and Loch a' Chataidh.

Along this coast lives the greater part of the population
of Eddrachillis, for the interior is given up to deer and
grouse. Badcall, Scourie, Rhiconich and Kinloch Bervie
are the chief centres, and there are numerous cottages in
the Scourie district, and along the north shore of Loch
Inchard, as far as Sheigra. From this point to Cape Wrath
the coast is uninhabited and trackless: there are no longer
any sea-lochs or inlets, for only the wide expanse of Sand-
wood Bay breaks the long even line of cliffs. Inland, in this
furthest peninsula of Scotland, the low brown mountains
of the Parph roll northwards to Durness.

The main road which serves the district is that from Lairg,
on the L.M.S. line from Inverness to Wick, which leads
along the north-east shore of Loch Shin, then by Lochs
Merkland and More, and below Ben Stack to Laxford
Bridge. Here it divides, one branch going south-west to
Scourie and thence to Badcall and Kyle Strome. The
other goes north to Rhiconich, on Loch Inchard, and
thence across a high, bare watershed to Strath Dionard
and down to Durness on the north coast. A branch road
leads from Rhiconich along the north shore of Loch
Inchard to Kinloch Bervie and Sheigra.

Scourie, which stands at the head of a narrow bay, is
the chief place in the district. Possessing an excellent hotel
and other accommodation for visitors, it has become a
favourite centre for loch fishing, and for visiting Handa
Island, with its wonderful bird-life and towering western
precipices. Three miles to the south, beside the sheltered
bay of Badcall, stands the church of Eddrachillis, looking
out to the islands of Eddrachillis Bay. Rhiconich, at the
head of Loch Inchard, used to possess the only hotel between
Scourie and Durness; this has now been converted into a
police station.

The early history of Eddrachillis is obscure; we know that it was once inhabited by the Picts, who occupied the whole of what is now the County of Sutherland, and were eventually dispossessed by the Dalriad Scots from Ireland. In the ninth and tenth centuries came the Norsemen from Lochlann, raiding and finally occupying the coast lands, and slaying or driving out the Gaelic-speaking inhabitants. The place-names which they left behind them in Eddrachillis remind us to-day of these grim sea-rovers, who talked of the Laxa Fiord (Salmon Firth), and of the conical "Stack" which towers up above the source of the Laxford River.

In the course of the twelfth century, when the Norse power was on the wane, a wave of Gaelic settlers came north from Moray and gradually reached Eddrachillis. These were the Mackays, then known as Clan Morgan, who were expelled from Moray by the Scottish king, and settled in Strathnaver under the protection of the Norse jarls of Orkney and Caithness. Eventually the whole of northern Sutherland, from Scourie to the border of Caithness, became Mackay territory and was known as Strathnaver, a term which included Tongue, Durness and Eddrachillis, as well as the strath of the River Naver. It was not until the seventeenth century, when Sutherland was created a county, that Assynt and Strathnaver were included in its bounds. Prior to that date the term Sutherland was applied to the south-eastern part of the modern county, which was the territory of the Murrays, the Gordons and the original Sutherlands.

COMMUNICATIONS

Rail.—There are no railways, the nearest station being Lairg on the L.M.S. line from Inverness to Wick.

Steamers.—There is no regular steamer service.

Road Services.—A mail motor, carrying passengers, runs each week-day in both directions between Lairg, Laxford Bridge and Scourie. A branch service between Laxford Bridge and Durness serves Rhiconich.

Accommodation

Hotels at Scourie and at Overscaig, Loch Shin. (The latter is situated on the mail route, but is outside the district of Eddrachillis.) Other accommodation at Scourie. There is no longer a hotel at Rhiconich.

Walks

(a) *By Road*

1. Lairg to Scourie, by Laxford Bridge, 44 miles. This is the mail route, which passes through several miles of rather featureless country. Walkers are advised to make use of the motor service as far as Loch More (26 miles), and to walk thence to Scourie.

Leaving Lairg Station, the road leads down into the town and proceeds along the north-east shore of Loch Shin, diverging from the Tongue road a few miles beyond Lairg. This is a long, narrow and somewhat featureless loch of the river type, beside which the road runs for 16 miles as far as the hotel of Overscaig. This well-known fishing hotel stands between the road and the loch; visitors may fish certain of the chain of lochs which lie to the north, as well as Loch Shin.

Beyond Overscaig the road quits Loch Shin and follows the eastern shore of Loch a' Ghriamha and Loch Merkland, behind which rises Ben Hee, the monarch of the Reay Forest. From the head of Loch Merkland a rough track strikes off through the mountains to the lodge of Gobernuisgach in Strath More. From the end of the loch the Scourie road turns westward, climbs to a height of 419 feet and descends to Loch More, which stretches for 4 miles in a north-westerly direction between the mountains. On the level ground at its lower end is Achfarry, where in former years the mail-cart changed horses. Here the road bends to the right to avoid the spreading base of Ben Stack, which rises above the loch of the same name, and dominates all the country towards Laxford Bridge and Scourie. The road now turns once more westwards, skirts the shore of

Loch Stack as far as Stack Lodge, approaches the Laxford River, and follows that famous salmon stream down to Laxford Bridge. Here it keeps on instead of crossing the bridge, and winds round many lochs and through low hills of gneiss to Scourie.

The Durness road crosses Laxford Bridge, skirts Laxford Bay and goes north to Rhiconich, at the head of Loch Inchard. Thence it climbs north-east over high bare moorland to Gualin House and descends Strath Dionard to Durness, 56 miles from Lairg.

2. Scourie to Kyle Strome, 12 miles. From Scourie Bay the road goes south and winds past two small lochs to the pleasant bay of Badcall, with its fine sea-views, and thence inland to the head of Calva Bay. Here it turns away from the coast up Glen Strathain, rising and falling through broken hill country to Duartmore Bridge. Three more miles lead to Kyle Strome, the last two being mainly downhill. For much of the way the road commands splendid views of the lochs and the Kyle below, and of the frowning northern face of Quinag.

(b) *By Hill-tracks*

1. Loch Merkland to Strath More, by Gobernuisgach Lodge, 8 miles. This track leads through the Reay Forest and connects the Lairg-Scourie road with that from Altnaharra to Loch Hope. It is one of the old drove roads, and was until quite recently practicable for motors.

One mile from the northern end of Loch Merkland, where a small peninsula projects southward into the loch, the track leaves the shore, crosses the Lairg-Scourie road, and follows the course of the Allt nan Albannach (Highland-man's Burn) north towards the mountains. Bending east to round the flank of Sail Gharbh, an outlying spur of Ben Hee, the path climbs to the Beallach nam Meirleach (859 feet), and passes for nearly 2 miles between a chain of three lochs and the steep slopes of Meall a' Chleirich (the Minister's Hill), which rise to the north. Gradually descending to-wards the north and later north-west, it reaches the shooting lodge of Gobernuisgach, turns sharply north-east down to Strath More, crosses the river, and in another mile joins the main road at a point 9 miles west of Altnaharra.

2. Loch More Lodge to Kyle Strome, 5½ miles. This is one of the shooting paths connecting Loch More with the coast. It climbs west from the lodge for 1½ miles, then turns south-west towards Ben Strome, rounds the southern slopes of that mountain and descends to the Scourie road, which it joins close to the lodge of Kyle Strome. At a point about 2¾ miles along this track, a branch goes off to the south to reach Kyle Strome by way of the shore. This track passes close to the foot of the big Loch an Leathaid Bhuain, and down the Maldie Burn to the sea.

3. Loch Stack Lodge to Duartmore Bridge, 5 miles. This is another of the shooting paths. It leads south-west past Ben Stack, crosses the hills by a number of lochs, and descends to the Scourie road at Duartmore Bridge, 3 miles north-west of Kyle Strome.

4. Achfarry (Loch More) to Gobernuisgach Lodge, 9 miles. This is a shooting path connecting the lodge at Loch More with that at Gobernuisgach. It starts 500 yards north of Achfarry, crosses the stream connecting Loch More with Loch Stack and goes north to the south-east corner of Loch Stack. Here two more streams are crossed, and finally, after crossing the Amhuinn an Loin, the track turns east up the course of that river. Climbing steadily due east, it reaches the pass (1426 feet) between Sabhal Beag on the north and Meall Garbh on the south, descends into the glen on the eastern side, crosses two streams, and reaches the road close to the lodge at Gobernuisgach.

5. Achfarry (Loch More) to Gobernuisgach Lodge, by Meall a' Chuirn (Meall Horn), and Glen Golly, 12 miles. This is an alternative to the last route, passing close under the northern spur of Meall Horn at a height of 1650 feet. The start is the same as in Route No. 4, but after crossing the Amhuinn an Loin a further stream, the Allt a' Chuirn, is crossed and its right bank followed up to its source, which lies high up on the western flank of Meall

Horn. Climbing still higher the path presently comes to an end, but by proceeding in the same direction (north by east) an eastward-flowing stream will eventually be crossed close to its head. Follow this stream downwards until the beginning of a fresh path is reached. This new track passes close to a small loch, crosses a north-flowing stream (the source of the Dionard River), and climbs eastward over high ground before descending past a waterfall to the head of Glen Golly. This glen runs south-east for 3 miles: at its foot, beyond two streams, is the lodge of Gobernuisgach.

6. Scourie-Tarbet-Foindle Mor-Scourie, 11 miles. This is a walk round the broad peninsula which lies to the north of Scourie Bay. It affords fine views of Handa Island and of the mouth of Loch Laxford.

A cart track leaves the main road half-way between the head of Scourie Bay and the foot of Loch a' Bhaid Daraich, leading north and shortly degenerating into a path. It leads along the lower slopes of the hills, in a direction parallel to the coast, as far as the bay of Tarbet. Handa Island rises beyond the Sound to the west, presenting its less elevated side to the view. It can be visited by boat from Tarbet, or from Scourie itself. The last inhabitants left the island many years since, and only a few sheep share it with the sea-birds. The views from its highest point are very extensive, resembling those obtained from Cnoc Poll in Assynt. The path now bends north-east to Fanigmore, on an inlet of the island-studded Loch Laxford, where it turns south-east to the clachan of Foindlemore, standing at the head of another inlet 1½ miles further on. Here the track turns inland and goes south between two lochs, to bend south-east and join the Scourie road near Claisfearn, 4 miles from Scourie.

7. Rhiconich and Kinloch Bervie to Cape Wrath, along the coast, 20 miles. This is a strenuous walk along an uninhabited stretch of coast-line, with not even a track for two-thirds of the way. The walker must take his own food and carry a tent, or blanket, for there is not a house between Sheigra and Cape Wrath Lighthouse. In good weather, however, the grandeur of the coast scenery will

well repay the labour of the cross-country journey.

From Rhiconich, 12 miles north-east of Scourie, a road goes west along the north side of Loch Inchard to Kinloch Bervie, with its church and post-office, and continues for another 4 miles to the hamlet of Sheigra. At this point the coast-line bends to the north opposite Eilean an Roin Mor, and the road comes to an end, and from here the walker must make his way along the coast as best he can. The only obstacles are the nature of the ground, and the numerous streams which have to be crossed. By keeping mainly to the cliffs, with occasional descents to cross streams, the walker should have little difficulty in reaching his goal. The light-house at Cape Wrath stands in an exposed position some 350 feet above the sea; it can be visited at certain times by per-mission of the chief officer. A rough road of 12 miles con-nects the lighthouse with Keoldale Ferry and Durness; but if time is not of importance the north coast may be followed to the same point, and far finer scenery enjoyed. When the Fleet is in these waters in the early summer, gun practice is sometimes carried out across the Cape Wrath peninsula; at such times the road to the lighthouse is closed.

8. Loch More to Glen Cassley, through the mountains, 26 miles. This is a hill walk for strong pedestrains; it includes 6 miles of hill-side with not even a rough track, and there is no hotel at Invercassley, where the route finishes. From the lonely house at Lochmoreside (which can be reached by the mail motor from Scourie) a path strikes south into the hills, climbs west of Ben Lice and of Meall na Leitreach, and ascends Strath nan Asinnteach to the little Loch Dubh at the foot of Ben Leoid. Here the path comes to an end, but the way lies due south, over a col, to the head-waters of the Fionn Allt, and down the east side of that stream to the two lochs of Fionn Loch Mor and Fionn Loch Beag. By keeping along the eastern shores of both lochs until well past the second one, the walker will pick up the head of a path which leads south along the Cassley River and right down Glen Cassley to Invercassley at its foot. The hotel at Oykell Bridge is 8 miles west of Invercassley.

CHAPTER XVI

Durness, Tongue and Strathnaver

*Maps.—O.S. Popular Edition, 1 inch, sheets 9 and 10.
Bartholomew's Half Inch, sheets 58, 59 and 60.*

ALONG the north coast of Sutherland, from Cape Wrath to the border of Caithness, stretches the country of the Mackays, otherwise known as the Reay country. It is a land of giant headlands stretching far into the northern sea, of shallow kyles and sandy bays, with one great sea-loch. Inland are lonely lochs set amid brown moorlands, each with its guardian mountain by its side.

In the west, where the precipices of Cape Wrath front the Atlantic, are the low, rolling mountains of the Parph, cut off from the habitations of men by the shallow, sand-choked Kyle of Durness and the wide green trough of Strath Dionard. Round the head of this strath rise the grey slopes of Foinne Bheinn and Conamheall; a line of great green hills extends northwards to the sea and forms its eastern wall. Gran Stacach (Cranstackie) and Ben Spionnaidh are the chief of these heights; their eastern slopes rise from Loch Eriboll and look across to Ben Hope. East of the Kyle of Durness are the sandhills of Balnakill Bay, where an ancient church stands in the shelter of the long curving promontory of Farrid Head. Two miles away is the village of Durine, straggling along the shore of Sango Bay and containing hotels, a post-office and the church of Durness. Here also are the ruins of one of the burnt-out hotels of which the Highlands can show so many examples. Three miles to the south, by the side of the Kyle of Durness, and close to the Cape Wrath Ferry, stands the hotel of Keoldale.

East of the Durness peninsula is the deep inlet of Loch Eriboll, extending for 10 miles towards the mountains and affording secure anchorage for the largest ships. The long white cliffs of Whiten Head shelter it on the north-east, and are continued along the north coast towards the Kyle of Tongue. Between Loch Eriboll and the latter is the Moine, a far-spread tract of high, bare moorland, which extends southward to the foot of Ben Hope. Across it runs the road from Durness to Tongue, circling Loch Eriboll and crossing the end of Loch Hope. The latter is a long, narrow, fresh-water loch, occupying the lower half of Strathmore, up which goes the road to Altnaharra. From its south-eastern shore rises Ben Hope (3040 feet), the highest mountain of Northern Sutherland.

The Kyle of Tongue is the easternmost of the three great inlets of the north coast: its shallow waters are full of sand-banks, and are crossed by a ferry at the point where a long spit of sand projects from the eastern shore. From this " tongue " (Norse: Teanga) comes the name of the district and of the Kyle. Well back from the head of the Kyle rises Ben Laoghal, an imposing ridged mountain with five great peaks. Below it to the east is the long, narrow Loch Laoghal, beside which runs the road from Altnaharra to Tongue.

The village of Tongue, whose correct name is Kirkiboll, stands above the eastern shore of the Kyle; it has a post-office, schools and churches, and a large hotel. Tongue House, which stands in wooded policies above the long spit of Tongue Ferry, was at one time the seat of the Lords Reay, chiefs of Clan Mackay, and is now the property of the Duke of Sutherland. Here at Tongue, as hardly any-where else in the Reay country, are trees and woodlands which flourish along the sheltered shores of the Kyle.

In Tongue Bay is the little group known as the Rabbit Islands; further out, beyond Kyle Rannoch, lie Eilean nan Ron (Seal Island) and Eilean Iosal. From here to the Caithness border extends a succession of bays and points, along which are strung the villages and scattered houses of the district. Bettyhill, among the sandhills at the mouth of the River Naver, Strathy on Strathy Bay, backed by the long finger of Strathy Point, and Melvich by the Halladale River, are the chief of these. Inland, traversed by the green straths of Naver and Halladale, are the brown, bare moors of Sutherland, rising in the south to the heights of Beinn Cleith Bric (Klibreck) and Beinn Armuinn.

Strathnaver extends for 23 miles from Altnaharra, at the head of Loch Naver, to Bettyhill and Torrisdale Bay. It is a wide green trough among the moors, through which the brimming Naver sweeps along to the sea. Loch Naver lies at the foot of Beinn Cleith Bric (Klibreck); it is 6 miles in length and has some woodlands along its shores. A road from Altnaharra follows its northern shore to the loch foot, and thence down the left bank of the Naver to Bettyhill, joining the Tongue road 3 miles south of the latter place. From the village of Syre, 4 miles north of Loch Naver, a branch road connects Strathnaver with the station of Kinbrace, on the Helmsdale River, 15 miles to the south-east.

Strath Halladale extends from Forsinard to Melvich Bay, and is of the same character as Strath Naver. The Halladale River once formed the boundary between Caithness and Sutherland, which now runs along the crest of the hills to the east. It is, like the Naver, a famous salmon river. The Naver flows from Loch Naver, and is soon joined by an important tributary, the River Mallart, which rises in Loch Choire. This loch occupies a long trough at the southern foot of Beinn Cleith Bric (Klibreck) and is 570 feet above the sea. Except to the north-east it is ringed by mountains, Beinn Cleith Bric to north and west, Beinn Armuinn and his fellows to the east and south. The loch extends for 4 miles and is connect3d by a narrow channel with the smaller Loch a' Bhealaich which lies further to the south-west. From the head of Loch a' Bhealaich a pass leads westward to the Crask, where the road from Lairg crosses the high ridge which separates the basins of Loch Shin and Loch Naver. This was always debatable land between North and South, between

Strathnaver and Sutherland, between Mackays and
Murrays; it is still the march between the parishes of
Tongue and Lairg. The Crask Inn is 8 miles from Altnaharra, towards which the Tongue road descends the long
dreary Strath Bagaisteach.

Altnaharra consists of a hotel, post-office, manse, church
and shooting lodge, which stand close to the head of Loch
Naver near four cross-roads. From it the Tongue road
climbs northward to Loch Laoghal, and the Strathnaver
road goes east along Loch Naver. Westward is the strath
of the River of Mudale, up which goes the road to Loch
Eriboll and Durness, climbing up past the foot of Loch na
Meadie to descend into the head of Strathmore. Strathmore
runs northwards along the base of Ben Hope; its lower
end is filled by Loch Hope, which discharges into Loch
Eriboll by the short River Hope. At the foot of Loch
Hope is Hope Lodge, set on a hill-side, where the Strathmore road joins the coast road from Tongue to Durness.
From a ford on the river near the head of Loch Hope a
rough and steep road crosses the hills to Eriboll; this forms
a short-cut for walkers bound to the west, but is no longer
practicable for vehicular traffic.

Northern Sutherland is served by three main roads,
two of which radiate from Lairg. These are the road to
Laxford Bridge, Rhiconich and Durness, and that by the
Crask and Altnaharra to Tongue. The third road comes
from Thurso along the north coast and connects Melvich
and Bettyhill with Tongue, Eriboll and Durness. A branch
road leads from Altnaharra to Hope Lodge and another
through Strathnaver to Bettyhill. A secondary road goes
up Strath Halladale from Melvich to Forsinard, and thence
to Helmsdale on the east coast; it sends off a branch from
Kinbrace to Syre in Strathnaver.

The ancient inhabitants of the Reay country were the
Picts, or Caledonians, who occupied the whole of Northern
Scotland and have left their traces on the face of the land.
The structures known as Picts' Houses are numerous in the
straths and along the shores of the kyles, and Pictish towers

(brochs) stand in Strathmore and Strathnaver. That of Dun Dornadilla, in Strathmore, though very much reduced in height, is a fine example of these towers of refuge. The Picts were a warrior race; they faced the legions of Rome, the Scots from Ireland, and the sea-rovers from Scandinavia, and were for a time successful. But at last, under the attacks of Scot and Norseman, the Pictish kingdom fell, when Kenneth Macalpine became the first king of Scotland. Then the Norsemen occupied the north-east coast and settled along the bays and kyles of the north, and in the fertile straths, while the Picts sullenly withdrew to the mountains of the interior. The Norse Power became firmly established in the north; they pushed southward along the east coast, and their jarls met and defeated the Gaelic rulers of Moray in several hard-fought battles. At one period the territory of the jarls of Caithness extended from Orkney to Dingwall, and the Beauly River was their frontier with Moray.

From this same province of Moray in the twelfth century came the Gaelic settlers of the Clan Morgan, seeking new homes in the north. They had fought for their ruler, Malcolm MacEth, in his struggle with the Scottish king, and were driven out from Moray by the victorious monarch. Jarl Harald was then the ruler of Caithness; he welcomed the newcomers and gave them lands in Strathnaver. When the Scottish king William the Lion came north to chastise the Norse earl, these Gaels from Moray fought side by side with the Norsemen at a great battle in Strathnaver. It was fought at Dalharald, near the foot of Loch Naver, where a stone called Clach an Righ marks the spot from which the king directed the fight. The battle went against the allies, who retired down the strath to the sea, pursued by the royal troops.

As years went on Clan Morgan grew in numbers and spread over the north, attracting to their ranks such of the Picts as still dwelt along their borders. No longer vassals of the Norse jarls, they had become a powerful ruling clan, called Mackay after their leader Iye MacEth. Early in

N

the thirteenth century came another irruption from Moray,
when the followers of Hugh Freskyn settled in Sutherland
and were quickly at enmity with the Mackays. Their
territory was the " Suder land " of the Norse settlers in
Caithness, which forms the south-eastern portion of the
modern county of Sutherland. These followers of Freskyn,
who soon became known as Murrays, had served in the
royal armies against the Mackays, and now, for more than
three centuries, a bitter feud raged between the two clans.
Forays and fighting were of constant occurrence, raiding
parties went south into Sutherland or north to Strathnaver,
and the Crask became a jealously guarded frontier. In
1433 the Murrays invaded Strathnaver in force, and were
met at Druim na Cuip, 2 miles south of Tongue, by Iain
Aberach Mackay, son of the old chief, with the men of his
clan. The Murrays were defeated, with the loss of their
leader, an ambush set on the slopes of Ben Laoghal com-
pleting their discomfiture; but a Sutherland archer slew
the old Mackay chief, who had gone out to succour his
wounded clansmen after the fight.

The Macleods of Assynt, too, were frequently embroiled
with the Mackays, as in the bloody Battle of Tuiteam
Tarbhach, in 1466. This was fought in Strath Oykell,
after the western clan had swept Strathnaver with fire and
sword, and resulted in the destruction of the invading force,
one Macleod alone escaping to tell the tale. The Sinclairs
of Caithness were not always peaceful neighbours of the
Mackays; at Altgawn in 1586, while the Caithness men
were pursuing a force of Gunns, they came upon a raiding
party of Mackays, who had already beaten off another force
of Murrays and Sutherlands. Making common cause with
the Gunns, the Mackays attacked and routed the Sinclairs,
and thus won two battles against different adversaries.

The seventeenth century, which saw so much fighting
in the rest of Scotland, proved more peaceful in Strathnaver,
for most of the Mackay fighting men were serving overseas
in the armies of Gustavus Adolphus. Their leader, Sir
Donald Mackay, was created Baron Reay and served

Charles I. in the Civil War. The Mackays took the Hanoverian side in the Risings of 1715, 1719 and 1745, and Hugh Mackay of Scourie commanded Dutch William's troops at Killiecrankie in 1689.

Towards the end of the eighteenth century the marriage of the Countess Elizabeth of Sutherland to the Marquis of Stafford inaugurated the Leveson-Gower connection with Sutherland. Within fifty years that family had acquired almost the entire county of Sutherland, the Reay estates coming into their possession in 1829. The " Sutherland Clearances," which depopulated Strathnaver, Kildonan, and other districts, were carried out during this period, and have left a dark stain on the memory of those responsible for the methods employed. This removal of the inhabitants of entire villages to make room for large sheep farms is now recognised to have been economically, as well as morally wrong, although at the time it was met with approval. Robert Chambers, writing in 1824 in his *Picture of Scotland*, refers to the " Clearances " in the following words: " Of late years, however, the landlords have very properly done all they could to substitute a population of sheep for the innumerable hordes of useless human beings who formerly vegetated upon a soil that seemed barren of everything else." It is good to think that modern administrators have at last reversed this policy, and that to-day new houses are being built in Strathnaver.

COMMUNICATIONS

Rail.—There is no railway in the district. The nearest stations are Lairg, Forsinard and Kinbrace, on the L.M.S. line to Wick.

Steamer.—There is no regular passenger service.

Road Services.—1. Lairg-Laxford Bridge-Durness, daily in each direction.

2. Lairg-Altnaharra-Tongue, daily in each direction.

3. Thurso-Melvich-Bettyhill-Skerray, daily in each direction.

4. Kinbrace-Syre-Skail (Strathnaver), daily in each

direction during summer, and three times a week at other times.

Accommodation

Hotels at Durness, Keoldale, Tongue, Bettyhill, Strathy, Melvich, Altnaharra and the Crask.

Other accommodation at Durness, Portnancon and Heilem (Loch Eriboll), Tongue and Skail.

Youth Hostel near Tongue, on the point of land from which the ferry runs.

Walks

(a) *By Road*

1. Lairg-Laxford Bridge-Durness, 56 miles. This route is described in Chapter XV., Route No. 1. It is not recommended to walkers (except as stated below), who would do better to use the motor service. The middle section of the route, from Loch More to Laxford Bridge, passes through fine scenery, but accommodation is a difficulty, for there is no hotel nearer than Scourie, once Overscaig is passed. If, however, a walk is decided upon, it should be from Rhiconich to Durness, climbing the long ascent to Gualin House, with fine views of Arcuil and Foinne Bheinn on the right hand. The prominent mountain behind Gualin is Farrmheall (1709 feet), from whose summit one looks north towards Cape Wrath. Just beyond Gualin House begins the descent to Strath Dionard, whose head lies back among the hills to the right. Crossing the Dionard River at the Drochaid Mhor, the road soon reaches the Kyle of Durness, and follows its east shore for 3 miles. Leaving the hotel and ferry of Keoldale away to the left the road ascends a brae, bends a little to the east, and arrives at Durness.

2. Lairg to Altnaharra and Tongue, 39½ miles. This is the mail route to Tongue. Walkers are recommended to use the motor service as far as Altnaharra, and to walk from that point. The road starts from Lairg Station, descends to the town, and goes north along Loch Shin. Two miles from Lairg the Laxford Bridge and Scourie

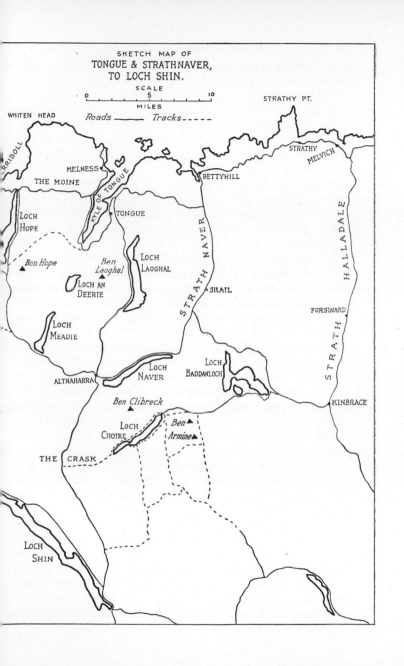

SKETCH MAP OF
TONGUE & STRATHNAVER,
TO LOCH SHIN.

SCALE
0   5   10
MILES

Roads ——   Tracks ─────

STRATHY PT.

WHITEN HEAD

RRIBOLL

MELNESS

THE MOINE

KYLE OF TONGUE

BETTYHILL

STRATHY
MELVICH

LOCH
HOPE

TONGUE

Ben Hope

Ben
Laoghal

LOCH
LAOGHAL

STRATH NAVER

STRATH HALLADALE

LOCH AN
DEERIE

SKAIL

FORSINARD

LOCH
MEADIE

LOCH
NAVER

LOCH
BADDANLOCH

STRATH

ALTNAHARRA

Ben Clibreck

KINBRACE

LOCH
CHOIRE

Ben
Armine

THE CRASK

LOCH
SHIN

road diverges to the left, the Tongue road continuing north up the wide Strath Tirry. Three miles further on, just before a bridge is crossed, a rough track goes off to the right along the Feith Osdaill. This is the start of a hill-track to Loch Choire through the Ben Armuinn Forest. The main road continues past Rhian Bridge, mounting in long gradual sweeps to the Crask Inn. Though this part of the road is somewhat monotonous, it commands fine views of the distant mountains. Across the moor to the west rises Ben More Assynt: from it to the north and east sweeps a great semicircle of peaks, among which Ben Leoid, Ben Hee, Ben Klibreck and Ben Armuinn are prominent.

Beyond the Crask the road swings down Strath Bagais-teach to Altnaharra, passes the hotel and the junction of the Strathnaver and Strathmore roads, and climbs over a high bare moorland with wide views to north and south. Descending to the foot of Loch Laoghal, it follows the west shore of that loch, passing along the foot of a spur of the craggy Ben Laoghal, and mounting past Loch Creagach on to the open moor which overlooks the Kyle of Tongue. From this height there is a fine view of the Kyle and its islands, with Ben Laoghal at its head and Ben Hope tower-ing up in the west. The road now begins to descend, swings down a long hill, turns sharply to the left, and curls round past the hotel to the post-office of Kirkiboll, or Tongue village.

3. Durness to Tongue, Bettyhill and Melvich, 59½ miles. Although this is the north coast road, it runs for much of its course at some considerable distance from the shore, the north coast being only skirted for a few miles east of Durness and again between Bettyhill and Melvich. The fine inlet of Loch Eriboll and the Kyle of Tongue are seen to great advantage, and there is a good view of Loch Hope from its lower end. By making use of the ferries to cross Loch Eriboll and the Kyle of Tongue the length of the walk can be materially reduced.

Leaving Durness the road runs along low cliffs of limestone, and over the top of the celebrated Cave of Smoo. This is a large subterranean hall into which, through an opening in the roof, a stream pours its waters. Communicating through an arched opening with an outer cave on the shore, it can only be reached by means of a boat, a deep pool barring the way. A notice on a gate near Smoo House indicates the path to the shore.

After passing Smoo the road keeps high above the shore, with its sandy bays and rocky points, rounds the last spur of the mountains, which is known as Ben Ceannabeinne (head of the mountain range), and turns south towards Loch Eriboll. A secondary road diverging to the east leads to the little harbour of Rispond, at the mouth of the loch, which was once the centre of a curing industry. The main road continues southwards and presently opens up a view across Loch Eriboll, with Ben Hope rising beyond its western shore. Seven miles from Durness is the short byroad leading to Portnancon, from which a ferry crosses the loch to Heilem on the eastern side. The main road continues south along the base of Ben Spionnaidh and Gran Stacach to the head of the loch, crosses the foot of Strath Beag and passes between the shore and the towering rock known as Creag na Faoilinn. Turning north-east inland, it climbs to the village of Eriboll, and swings round sharp corners down a steep descent to the shore, leaving the road to Heilem ferry on the left and curving round, up another long hill, to turn eastwards towards Loch Hope. From the high ground between the two lochs there is a fine view to the south along Loch Hope, with Ben Hope's western precipices rising above its margin; the road crosses the Hope River, turns south, and ascends a long hill, past Hope Lodge, up to the brown wilderness of the Moine. Midway on this wind-swept expanse, at a height of 741 feet, stands the Moine House, once an inn for travellers but now a private residence. It is a bleak spot, but enjoys a glorious mountain view. South-west are the mountains of Durness and the Reay Forest, southward is Ben Hope, and to the south-east the five peaks of Ben Laoghal stand dark against the sky. Far to the east are the two Ben Griams, and the blue triangle of Morvern in Caithness: to seaward lie the nearer islands of the Orkneys.

From the Moine there is a long descent to the Kyle of Tongue, where the road turns south along the shore. Just beyond the turn is the ferry pier from which one may cross to Tongue. If the tide is low the passenger may have to land on an island, and cross to the Tongue mainland by means of stepping-stones. The main road circles round the head of the Kyle, crosses the Kinloch River, and climbs inland between two lochs before crossing the Rian Burn and reaching Kirkiboll (Tongue village). The ruined stronghold crowning the end of a ridge to the west is Castle Varrich, once occupied by the Mackays.

Keeping uphill to the right past the hotel, the road curves east, and then turns sharply to the north, leaves Tongue House and the ferry below on the left, and swings east above the shore round the northern base of the rugged Watch Hill of Tongue. Along this part of the route are fine seaward views over the islands of Tongue Bay, but presently the road turns inland to cross Strath Teanga, and rises and falls over desolate moorlands towards the east. After descending to cross the Alltan Dearg and then the Borgie River, the road climbs a third long hill, and drops down the far side into Strathnaver. From the foot of the hill a branch road goes off up the strath and on to Altnaharra; but the main road passes down the left bank of the river, crosses the Naver and continues north for about a mile to Bettyhill, which stands in a pleasant situation above the sandhills at the river mouth. From this point to Melvich the road is continually rising and falling, crossing the numerous streams of the district and the intervening moors. Farr Church, Armadale, and Strathy are passed on the way, and there are fine views of Ben Hope and Ben Laoghal away to the south-west. Melvich stands on a height above the bay of that name, and overlooks the mouth of the Halladale River; the Thurso road turns south up the strath to cross the Bridge of Halladale, climbs

PLATE VIII   EVENING LIGHTS ON BEN HOPE AND LOCH H

Ben Hope is the most northerly s

ERLAND

Photograph by R. M. ADAM

oo feet in Scotland

northward once more towards the coast, and crosses the height of Drumhollistan into Caithness.

4. Altnaharra to Hope Lodge, 20 miles. This road provides the shortest route from Central Sutherland to Durness.

Leaving Altnaharra by the Tongue road the walker crosses the Mudale River and soon afterwards turns left at the cross-roads. The route is up the left bank of the river and of its tributary the Amhuinn Beag, climbing gradually out of the strath to a height of 507 feet, and passing the lower end of Loch Meadie, which stretches for 4 miles to the north. Beyond Loch Meadie is the pass to Strath More, a green oasis among the mountains, which extends northwards to Loch Hope. The road at first keeps high along the eastern wall of the strath, from which one looks across the river to the distant lodge of Gobernuisgach standing at the mouth of Glen Golly. At Altnacaillich, where it crosses the burn of that name, it is close to the Strath More River: the burn flows from the heights of Ben Hope, and has splendid waterfalls on its course. Two miles further on a rough road to Eriboll diverges to the left, crosses the river by a ford or ferry, and mounts steadily to the heights overlooking Loch Eriboll. A steep descent with a dangerous bend leads down to the Durness road close to the village of Eriboll. This road is not fit for cars, and the deep ford across the Strath More River is almost always impassable. The main road continues northwards, below the steep west face of Ben Hope and along the east shore of Loch Hope to Hope Lodge, where it joins the Tongue-Durness road. A keeper's house at Hope is the only dwelling met with until Hope Lodge is reached.

5. Altnaharra to Bettyhill, 23 miles. This road follows the north shore of Loch Naver, and is pleasantly wooded in parts; it commands fine views of Beinn Cleith Bric (Klibreck), rising across the water. Turning north into Strathnaver, it passes the house of Dalharald on the east side of the river, where was fought the great battle between Scots and Norsemen. Some miles further on is Syre, where

a road goes off eastwards to Kinbrace. At Skail, 2 miles beyond Syre, is the post-office of Strathnaver and the grave of Saint Maelrubha (Maree) of Applecross, who was martyred by Vikings in the year 722. A low mound in a green field beside the Naver marks his resting place, and is still known as the Red Priest's Grave. The grey stone which stands at its head still shows an incised cross, and there is a legend that when the Naver reaches the grave Strathnaver will again become populous. It is said that at times the river-banks have been carefully built up to prevent the fulfilment of the prophecy!

North of Skail the valley widens out, and the river winds sinuously from side to side of its green trough, passing under the bridge at Rhifail and down to Invernaver, where it is crossed by the road to Bettyhill. The Tongue road goes off up the hill-side 2 miles south of this bridge; Bettyhill is a mile to the north, above the eastern bank of the river.

6. Keoldale Hotel to Cape Wrath, 12 miles from ferry. A ferry crosses the Kyle of Durness from a stone pier a quarter of a mile west of the Keoldale Hotel. When the tide is low it may be necessary to embark from the rocks further to the north. On the far side of the Kyle the road ascends past the ferryman's house and winds along above the Kyle for 2 miles, descending to cross a river close to the cottage at Dail. This road is narrow, rutted and exceedingly rough and stony, but it is used by the motor lorry belonging to the lighthouse and by at least one car. Cyclists will find it heavy going in places, but quite practicable.

Fording the river at Dail, close to a plank bridge, the road climbs inland along the hill-side and descends to Loch na Innse Odhar, beside which stands the last house on the road to the Cpae. Beyond the cottage a gate must be passed, and then the road ascends along the flank of Meall Sgribhinn to reach a height of 551 feet. From this point one looks northwards to the sea, which is visible beyond the cliffs in the distance: an outlying reef, visible even from so far away, is a silent witness to the dangers of this coast. Cape Wrath is not visible; it lies behind the brown hills in the north-west.

The road drops steadily for 2 miles, passing the letter-box which marks the track to the shepherd's house at Cearbhag, down by the shore, crosses the Chearbhaig River, climbs out of the glen, and winds across the moors for 3 miles to the lighthouse. From the last mile of road there are extensive views along the coast to the south, where tall cliffs and outlying stacks rise from a desolate shore, and the solitary island of Bulgach lies in the offing. The lighthouse itself is not seen until one is close upon it; it stands on a rock plateau with the deep sea on two sides; above it on the cliff is the now disused Lloyds' signal station. The views along the north coast extend to Strathy Point, Dunnet Head and the Orkneys, while in the south-west Lewis and Skye are often to be seen.

(b) *By Hill-tracks*

1. From the head of Loch Eriboll to Loch Dionard and Durness, 16 miles. This route penetrates Strath Beag at the head of Loch Eriboll, crosses to Strath Dionard, and commands fine views of the craggy east face of Foinne Bheinn.

Leave the Eriboll-Durness road at the head of the loch, below Creag na Faolinn, and go south by the cart track up Strath Beag. In about a mile a path turns west, fords the river and goes up its western bank, curving round the base of Conamheall to reach the Beallach na h'Imrich. The track crosses this pass to Strath Dionard, and comes to an end at the house of Carrachandubh, close to Loch Dionard. The next 4 miles are down Strath Dionard to the cottage at the foot of Ben Spionnaidh: there is no path and the way lies along the east side of the river between the slopes of Foinne Bheinn and of Gran Stacach. At the cottage is the beginning of a track which joins the Durness road at the Drochaid Mhor, which is 4 miles south of Durness.

2. Durness to Portnancon over the hills, 5 miles. This is a short-cut to the Portnancon ferry along a " peat road."

The track leaves the main road at the head of Sango Bay, and heads south towards Meall Mheadonach. Its course can be seen on the hill-side in the distance. Crossing the Smoo Burn near its outflow from Loch Mheadonach, it turns south-east and makes for the pass between Ben Ceannabeinne and Meall Mheadonach. The cart road ends at the summit of the pass, and the walker must find his own way down to the road, which is clearly visible below. Portnancon pier and ferry are reached by a short branch road to the shore a short distance to the south.

3. Round Whiten Head, about 17 miles. A fine day's walk is that round the cliffs of Whiten Head from Inverhope to Melness. There is no regular path and the going is rough, but the sea-views and cliff scenery are very fine.

Leave the Durness-Tongue road at Hope Bridge and take the path down the right bank of the Hope River to the cottage at Inverhope. From this point the coast-line must serve as guide, the burns being crossed at the most convenient places. The cliffs are highest along the north coast, where a spur of Ben Hutick drops abruptly to the sea from a height of 935 feet, and a number of high promontories stand out into the ocean. The entrance to Loch Eriboll, with its islands, and the coast to Farrid Head are well seen, but Cape Wrath is hidden. Keeping east and south-east along the cliffs one turns south to cross the Melness River at Dalnafree, from whence a cart track leads to the Melness road. Melness is a long straggling township standing on the hill-side along the western shore of Tongue Bay. It is reached from Tongue by means of the ferry, or by car round the head of the Kyle.

4. Head of Loch Hope to Kinloch (Tongue), 8 miles. This is a fine tramp round the northern base of Ben Hope. The path leaves the road at the head of Loch Hope and goes north and then north-eastward, gradually ascending to 955 feet, and commanding magnificent views of the north-west face of Ben Hope. Bending east and then south-east it descends to the low country at the head of the Kyle of Tongue, joining the Tongue road close to Kinloch

Lodge. This track crosses the watershed between Durness and Tongue and fords a great many streams.

5. Crask Inn to Loch Choire and thence to Dalnessie and the Lairg road, through the Beinn Armuinn Forest, 20 miles. This track traverses the western portion of the Beinn Armuinn Forest, and gives a near view of Beinn Cleith Bric from the south-east. It may also be covered in the reverse direction, starting from Lairg. It should not be used during the stalking season.

Take the track leading east from the Crask Inn along Strath a' Chraisg, and continue over the Beallach Easach to the head of Loch a' Bhealaich. Leave the path, cross two streams and proceed by the *southern* shore of the loch as far as the narrows where it joins Loch Choire. Here is the head of another path which leads south up the Allt Coire an Fhearna, climbs over the east flank of Meall an Fhuarain, and reaches the head-waters of the Allt Gobhlach. The latter stream is then followed southwards for nearly 6 miles to Dalnessie, on the Brora River. From this place, which stands on the west bank of the Brora, a track goes westwards, crosses the Feith Osdaill, and follows the line of that stream to the point where it crosses below the main road, 6 miles north of Lairg.

6. Crask Inn to Kinbrace Station, by Loch Choire and Loch Baddanloch, 27 miles. This is a useful through route connecting the roads of Central and East Sutherland. As far as Loch Choire Lodge it is by a hill-track, but onwards to the public road near Baddenloch Lodge the way lies along an estate road.

Go east from the Crask Inn by Strath a' Chraisg and the Beallach Easach to Loch a' Bhealaich, continuing along its north shore and on by Loch Choire to the lodge at its head. From Altalaird, near the head of Loch Choire, where the path ceases, the walker must make his way round the shore to Loch Choire Lodge, where an estate road begins. Bending north-east and again south-east (a path cuts across the bend and shortens the distance), the road passes along the northern base of Beinn Armuinn,

slants north-east to Loch Allt an Fhearna, and circles round
to the south-east corner of Loch Baddanloch. This is a
broad sheet of water lying in the Baddanloch Forest, and
is connected by a narrow channel with Loch a' Chlair,
which is in its turn joined to Loch nan Cuinne (Rimsdale)
in a similar manner. These lochs lie at a height of 394
feet and form the source of the Helmsdale River. At
Baddanloch Lodge the estate road joins the public road to
Kinbrace, which passes Loch na Moine and leads along
the Helmsdale River to the railway station.

7. Loch Choire Lodge to the Laird road, by the west
side of Beinn Armuinn, 17 miles. This path leads through
the heart of the Beinn Armuinn Forest and crosses several
passes. In conjunction with the route from the Crask to
Loch Choire Lodge it would afford a long but magnificent
day's walk of 27 miles. In that case it would be more
convenient to start from Lairg by car or bus, leaving the
road at 6 miles north and ending the walk at the Crask Inn.

From Loch Choire Lodge a track leads south into the
hills, along the western slopes of Creag na h'Iolaire, and
over a high pass to the head-waters of the Allt an Seilich
Bige. This stream is followed downwards for 4 miles,
where another path goes south at right angles to the first,
turns sharply west to climb a spur of Sithean Fhreiciadain
(the Watch Hill of the Fairies), and again bends south to
cross a stream and reach the Crom Allt (Crooked Burn).
Following this stream down to its junction with the Allt
Gobhlach, the track joins the path described in Route No.
(b) 5, and leads by Dalnessie to the Lairg road.

CHAPTER XVII

THE HIGHLANDS OF EASTER ROSS, FROM BEN WYVIS TO BEN DEARG

MAPS.—*O.S. Popular Edition,* 1 *inch, sheets* 20 *and* 27.
Bartholomew's Half Inch, sheets 55 *and* 58.

THE town of Dingwall stands at the head of the Cromarty Firth, on the edge of the fertile coast lands of Easter Ross. A Royal Burgh with long centuries of history behind it, and the county town of the shire of Ross and Cromarty, it is a busy agricultural centre and the railway junction for the West Coast. Its Norse name of Dingwall is a reminder of the days when the jarls of Caithness and Orkney held their " Things," or assemblies for law-making, at this southern centre of their rule. Long before the days of the Norsemen the district had been a centre of population, for the hill-fort of Knockfarrell close by was a great native stronghold. The Gaelic name of the town is Inbhir Pheofharain, for the little River Peffery flows past it into the Cromarty Firth.

At Dingwall the roads to the north and the west diverge, the former going along the coast by Evanton, and thence east to Invergordon and Tain. The direct route to Sutherland, however, leads north from the bay of Alness, and climbs over the hills down to the Kyle of Sutherland, and on to Invershin at its head. From Invershin an important road leads up the Oykell River to Oykell Bridge along the northern boundary of Ross-shire, continuing to Inchnadamph and Lochinver. A second road goes north to Lairg, and thence by two diverging routes into North-west Sutherland. The West Coast road from Dingwall goes past

Strathpeffer to Garve, where it branches off to Achnasheen and Loch Carron in the south, and to Braemore and Ullapool in the north-west.

Within the great triangle formed by the Dingwall-Loch Broom and the Dingwall-Invershin roads is a broad expanse of rugged hill country through which runs no main road. Along its north-west side rises a group of lofty mountains; from Ben Dearg, behind Braemore, they extend northward through Eididh nan Clach Geala (the Hill with the Garment of White Stones) to Seana Braigh (the Ancient Hill), and the peaks of the Freevater Forest to the east. Among these hills are several fine mountain lochs, lying at the foot of mighty precipices such as Creag an Duine of Seana Braigh, which soars for nearly 2000 feet above Loch a' Choire Mhoir, and the great cliffs which rise from Loch a' Choire Ghranda between Ben Dearg and Cona Mheall. Ben Dearg is the highest mountain north of the Garve-Ullapool road; its rounded summit is prominent in the north when crossing the Dirrie More, and can be seen from the road beyond Ullapool.

In the south-eastern angle of this region the wide-spreading range of Ben Wyvis stands isolated above the low country at its base. The position and enormous extent of this mountain make it the most prominent object in the landscape when seen from Inverness and the coastal regions; it is said that passengers by rail from Inverness to Wick have Ben Wyvis in sight for fully half a day. The mountain, when seen from a distance, has little but its size to recommend it; it lies as a long brown ridge across the northern sky, and is very seldom entirely free from snow. To those who will explore its eastern corries it offers wild and rugged scenery, and the view from its summit plateau at 3429 feet is very fine indeed.

To the north of Ben Wyvis is the Kildermorie Forest, with its heights of Ben an Eun and Creachan nan Sgadan, which expands to the east into a long crescent of mountains, sheltering the deep hollow in which lies Loch Glass. From this loch flows the River Glass, which reaches the sea to the east of Evanton, after its mile-long passage of the Black Rock gorge, a chasm 130 feet deep. Beyond Loch Glass is the parallel glen containing Loch Morie (Loch of Mary), from which flows the Averon, or Alness River. Above Loch Morie it is called the Glasath, as coming from a small loch called Loch nan Glas Ath which lies far up its long and winding glen. This glen divides Kildermorie from Diebidale Forest, whose mountains extend north towards Strath Carron, and west to Glen Calvie and Glen Mor.

Strath Carron is a wide and populous valley which stretches westward from the Kyle of Sutherland along the course of the River Carron. At Amat, where the strath proper ends, is the foot of Glen Mor, whose head lies high up in the mountains to the south-west, at the Lodge of Deanich. Deanich stands at a height of 1000 feet in the heart of the mountains of Easter Ross at a point where three glens meet; though far from any main road it is an important crossing place for hill paths. Glen Mor, coming from the north-east, forms the eastern boundary of the Freevater Forest, whose lonely peaks of Carn Ban, Bodach Mor and Bodach Beag are untrod, except by stalkers and gillies, from one year's end to another. Westward from Glen Mor the shorter Glen Beag extends to its head, high up in the angle formed by Seana Braigh and Eididh nan Clach Geala. The lonely cottage of Glen Beg stands by the stream 3 miles west of Deanich Lodge, and further on the glen narrows to its head. To the north-west is a wild and rugged pass, 2400 feet high, leading over into Glen a' Cadha Deirg (Glen of the Red Pass), and thence to Glen Achall and Ullapool. There is no path out of the head of Glen Beag, but two steep tracks lead down into the head of the glen on the west.

From Deanich Lodge another path leads southwards over the shoulder of a hill into Strath Vaich, and thence to the Garve-Ullapool road. This is the valley which extends south from Loch Toll a' Muick, along the east side of the mountains of Tollomuick and Strathvaich

Forests; a private road runs down it from Lubachlaggan, south of Loch Toll a' Muick, and past Strathvaich Lodge to join the county road. As part of the Conon Basin hydro-electric scheme a dam will be built about 2 miles south of Loch Toll a' Muick, thus forming a new loch extending up to, and beyond, the head of Loch Toll a' Muick. Parallel to Strathvaich on the east is the shorter Strath Rannoch, penetrating into the Inchbae Forest and connected with Strathvaich by a path across the hills at its upper end.

The mountains of Easter Ross are to-day under deer and are therefore uninhabited, except for occasional stalkers' houses and the shooting lodges in each forest. Only along Strath Carron in the north, and at various places along the bordering roads, are houses and crofts and churches to be seen. To the east of Garve, where the low country begins, the face of the land is changed; Strathpeffer, Dingwall, Evanton, Alness and other towns and villages stand along the roads, for this is no longer the Highlands but the eastern coastal lowlands. Many of the eastern glens were in former years well populated, but the era of so-called " improvements " which began after 1760 necessitated the clearance of many of these poor folk, who were turned out under circumstances of great hardship to make room for sheep. In other cases their small holdings were consolidated into large farms and the occupants thrust forth homeless to shift for themselves. Kildermorie, Culrain, by the Kyle of Sutherland, Glencalvie near Strath Carron, and Gruinards in Kincardine Parish, were all cleared of their population, as were the uplands of the Balnagown estate, for Sir John Lockhart Ross of Balnagown was the originator of the " clearance " system in Ross-shire. If not so widely remembered as are the Sutherland Clearances, these Ross-shire evictions probably caused equal hardship, and were bitterly resented by the victims. So bitter was the feeling that an attempt was actually made to drive out of the county the hated sheep which were the cause of the trouble; it was necessary to call out troops before the disturbances were quelled. This was in the closing years of the eighteenth century, but the last evictions took place in 1854, nearly a century after the inception of the system.

COMMUNICATIONS

Rail.—The L.M.S. line from Inverness to Garve passes along the southern edge of the district, with stations at Dingwall, Achterneed and Garve. Strathpeffer, on a short branch line, and Novar and Alness on the line to the north, are also stations from which the hills can be approached.

Road Services.—The daily mail service between Garve and Ullapool, and that between Lairg and Oykell Bridge, both serve the outer fringes of the district. The passenger motor service from Invershin, which runs daily from June to September, and on Tuesdays, Thursdays and Saturdays during the rest of the year, may also prove of value to walkers.

Several lines of motor buses pass through Dingwall on their way north from Inverness; these may be useful to reach the eastern side of the district.

ACCOMMODATION

Hotels at Garve, Altguish, Strathpeffer, Dingwall, Evanton, Alness, Ardgay, Inveran, Invershin and Oykell Bridge, also at Ullapool.

Other accommodation at Strathpeffer, Dingwall, Evanton, Alness and Ullapool.

Youth Hostel at Ullapool.

WALKS

By Hill-tracks

1. Ullapool to the head of Glen a' Cadha Deirg and back, 28 miles. Leave Ullapool and go up to Loch Achall by the route described in Chapter XIII., and up Glen Achall as far as Rhidorroch Old Lodge. Cross the river to the south bank, then bend left and cross the stream which flows into it from the south. A track goes south into the hills from this point, crosses one burn and in 2 miles reaches

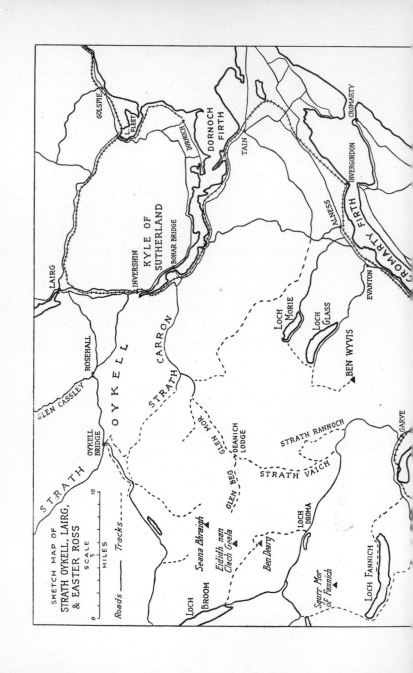

SKETCH MAP OF
STRATH OYKELL, LAIRG,
& EASTER ROSS

SCALE

0   5   10
MILES

Roads ———— Tracks ------

the north side of a second, on a slope above Glen Douchary. Here it is necessary to descend into the glen and cross the Douchary River, afterwards proceeding south along its eastern bank. The river comes from Glen a' Cadha Dheirg, a deep narrow glen with precipitous sides which continue round its head. At the head of the glen, in gullies which strike up the cliff face, are two steep paths, leading to a grassy incline at the southern side of Seana Bhraigh, which can easily be ascended from this point. The northern face of the mountain consists of almost sheer precipices, dropping to the little Loch Luchd Coire in the hollow below, and of the projecting headland of Creag an Duine, which rises from Loch a' Choire Mhoir for nearly 2000 feet.

The return can be made by the same route, or by Inverlael. In the latter case the way lies round the head of Glen a' Cadha Dheirg, without descending into it, and west past Loch a' Cadha Dheirg to the little Lochan Sgeirich, and down the nose of Druim na Saobhaide to the ruined house at Glensguail. Thence to the road at Inverlael is 1½ miles. The total distance by this route from and to Ullapool would be 30 miles.

2. Altguish Hotel to Ardgay, by Strathvaich and Strath Carron, 27 miles. This route leads through the heart of the mountain district, and connects the road to Ullapool with the head of the Dornoch Firth. The first part of the route and the last 10 miles are along a road, so that the walk can be materially shortened by availing one's self of a motor vehicle down Strath Carron.

Take the Garve road for 1½ miles and turn up Strath Vaich along the road marked " Private," past the schoolhouse and along the eastern bank of the Strathvaich River. At the cottage of Lubriach, where a path diverges to cross the hill to Strath Rannoch, the road crosses the river to reach the lodge of Strathvaich, and immediately recrosses to the east bank and goes north to Loch Toll a' Mhuic. Keeping the loch on the left the track runs along the foot of Beinn a' Chaisteil, bends north-east to climb over the divide, and descends to Deanich Lodge at the head of Glen Mor. Here the path crosses the Glen Mor River and joins a rough road leading down that glen along the north side of the stream. Upper Glen Mor is narrow and hemmed in by steep mountain walls; at its lower end the road and the river traverse a wooded gorge and come down to the Alladale River, which flows out of the Freevater Forest to the west. The road crosses the Alladale and turns east through the woods of Amat Forest, keeping beside the Carron River, which here makes a wide curve to the north. This river, which is born at the mouth of Glen Mor of the Alladale and the Glen Mor Rivers, receives two more feeders from its right bank as it flows along the edge of the woods, and shortly after joins the Black Water not far from Amat Lodge. The Black Water comes from Strath Cuilionach in the north-west, and has passed the manse of Croick and the church; along its eastern side goes a hill-track to Oykell Bridge.

Crossing the Black Water by Amat Lodge our road joins the main road, which leads north-east down Strath Carron. A mile further on is the bridge across the Carron leading to the church and cottages of Baileandounie, and along the southern side of Strathcarron down to the sea. Passing down the widening strath past Wester Greenyards, Downie and Gledfield House, the road reaches the village of Ardgay, standing at the inner end of the Dornoch Firth, with its railway station known as Bonar Bridge. Across the water to the north-east is the Sutherland town of Bonar Bridge.

3. Alness to Oykell Bridge, by Strath Rusdale and Amat, 30 miles. This is a long cross-country route from south-east to north-west. The first 9 miles as far as the head of Strath Rusdale, are along a road, and might be covered by car, thus reducing the day's mileage to more reasonable proportions. If it were possible to secure a night's accommodation in the vicinity of Amat or Baileandounie, the walk could be spread over two days, and might be extended to Altnacealgach, on the road to Lochinver.

Leave Alness by the road going north from near the station along the east bank of the Alness River, and at $2\frac{3}{4}$ miles from the start turn to the left at the cross-roads by Dalnavie smithy. This road leads up the well-wooded and populous glen of the Alness River, passes Ardross Castle which stands between road and river, and turns north-west up the narrower Strath Rusdale. Now the road begins to climb; it passes through a wood at the head of the strath, beyond which the hills close in and the track bends round to the north-west. It is 4 miles from the far side of the wood to Lochan a' Chairn, where the summit level is reached, the track climbing steadily along the eastern side of the glen. At the lodge among the trees to the north of the loch the height is 1357 feet; then the path descends towards the Salachie Burn, curves west along the hill-side, and passes between Carn Dubh and Carn na Gobhlaig-beithe to drop down the hill-slopes into the head of Glen Calvie. Coming down to the water-side it follows the eastern bank of the Water of Calvie for 2 miles, crosses a bridge to the west side, and goes on past Glencalvie Lodge to the Carron River. This is in turn crossed by a bridge and the road leads through the woods past Amat Lodge, where it crosses the Black Water, and joins the road to Croick. Turning west along this road past the church and manse of Croick, the route leads north-west up Strath Cuilionach along the true left bank of the river. Five miles beyond the manse of Croick a path diverges to the north, climbs over the spur of a hill, and drops down the hill-side into the Oykell valley. Passing the cottages of Amat (the second place of that name on the route), it fords the Einig River above its confluence with the Oykell, and leads up the bank of the latter to the hotel at Oykell Bridge. By diverging a little to the west at Amat one can cross the Einig by a bridge and rejoin the other route just before reaching the hotel.

4. Oykell Bridge to Loch a' Choire Mhoir, by Corrie-mulzie, and back, 22 miles. This route takes the walker into the wild country at the northern foot of Seana Bhraigh,

and the corries and lochs below it. The way lies up the Einig Glen as far as Duag Bridge, keeping to the southern side of the valley, by the route described in Chapter XIII., Route No. (*b*) 1.

Cross Duag Bridge and continue along the Dubhag River up to the Lodge of Corriemulzie and thence up the Corriemulzie River till it bends south and is joined by the Allt a' Choire Bhuidhe. The track crosses the latter, and shortly afterwards fords the Corriemulzie River and leads along the hill-side to the shore of Loch a' Choire Mhoir, which lies at a height of 1000 feet at the foot of the projecting headland of Creag an Duine. Beyond the loch Coire Mor runs east into the hills, with steep cliffs above, for another 2 miles, ending as a cul-de-sac at the base of Carn Ban. South-west of the loch, in a high corrie between Seana Bhraigh and Creag an Duine, is the tiny Loch Luchd Coire, a dark tarn amid impressive surroundings.

To see these lochs from above and to walk along the long line of cliffs from Seana Bhraigh eastwards the walker must climb Seana Bhraigh. This can best be done by returning to the ford a mile north of Loch a' Choire Mhoir, and ascending the northern slopes of the mountain to the summit. The return can be to Oykell Bridge by the outward route, or to Inverlael by that described in Route No. 1 of this chapter. If the walker can manage to find his way over to Glen Beag he can reach Deanich Lodge and thence walk down Strath Vaich to Altguish Inn. This may not, however, prove too easy, and should only be essayed when plenty of time is available.

5. Evanton to Alness via Loch Glass and Loch Morie, 24 miles. This walk enables the visitor to see something of the north spur of Ben Wyvis, and of the two mountain lochs of this district.

Take the road leading up the north bank of the River Glass to Kinloch at the lower end of Loch Glass, leaving the main road in Evanton at the north side of the bridge. By some cottages half a mile along the road a footpath diverges to the left, and leads along the river where it rushes through the deep and narrow chasm known as the Black Rock. It is in places only 12 feet wide and as much as 130 feet in depth. The road crosses to the south bank of the river at Eileanach Lodge, continues past Kinloch and skirts the south-west shore of Loch Glass for 2 miles as far as Wyvis Lodge at its head. The loch lies between high mountains at a height of 713 feet; from the centre of its south-western shore rises Feachdach (3018 feet), the north-east spur of Ben Wyvis. On the further side are Meall Mor, Meall Beag and Meall an Tuirc (Boar's Hill), which separate Loch Glass from Loch Morie. The road ceases at Wyvis Lodge, from which a footpath continues round the head of the loch and over the north-west slopes of Meall Beag down to Loch Morie.

Loch Morie is less shut in by the hills than the neighbouring loch; it is not so large and lies at a lower level. At its head is the ancient chapel, Cille Mhuire, dedicated to the Virgin Mary, after whom the loch is named. Further back, on the edge of its plantations, stands the lodge of Kildermorie, from which a track leads eastward to Strath Rusdale. The road from the lodge leads round the head of the loch and skirts its south-west shore, then runs in an easterly direction along the hills to the south of the Alness glen, bends southwards through the woods of Dalreoch, and crosses the Ardgay road at Contullich, a mile from Alness.

6. Ascent of Ben Dearg, by Loch a' Choire Ghranda, about 24 miles. This is not a hill-path route, but it provides the best way to see the magnificent surroundings of Loch a' Choire Ghranda, and to reach the summit of Ben Dearg. For this information about the route the writer is indebted to the ex-President of the Scottish Mountaineering Club, the Reverend A. E. Robertson, who is well acquainted with the district in question. The route is one of those described in the " Northern Highlands " guide book issued by the Scottish Mountaineering Club, which is illustrated with many fine photographs of mountain scenery.

Ben Dearg can be climbed from several centres, but Altguish is the most convenient inn from which to approach the mountain. It should be noted that a dam is going to be built, in connection with the Conon Basin hydro-electric scheme, near this inn to form a new loch about four miles long and reaching to within about one mile of Loch Droma. The present course of the road west from the inn will be submerged. The road to Braemore will, however, continue to be the start of the route to Ben Dearg, and should be followed to a point about a quarter of a mile from the Garve end of Loch Droma, where a deer path goes north-east across the shoulder of a hill and passes to the west of Loch a' Garbhrain. Climb the hill to the north of the loch known as Leac an Tuadh, from which a fine view of Coire Ghranda is obtained. Bear slightly west of north, descending a little, and again climbing to the level of the corrie, which is 1800 feet. Keep to the west side of the loch in the corrie, where the cliffs of Ben Dearg are very steep, and approach the loch at one point to within a few feet.

When at the head of the loch make for the pass up steep slopes, ascending to about 2600 feet, then turn sharply south-west and climb over rough ground to the summit. From here there is a magnificent view southward to the Fannichs and west to the Teallach mountains; across the corrie to the east is the fine peak of Cona Mheall, of 3200 feet, and to the north-west, above Coire Mathain Lathail, is the long saddle of Diollaid a' Mhill Bhric and the out-lying peak of Iorguill.

The descent may be made by way of Diollaid a' Mhill Bhric, dropping gradually down to the level of the moor at the head of Loch Broom, and thence by a steep descent into the glen of the River Lael. Inverlael Bridge, where the glen reaches the road by Loch Broom, is 6 miles from Ullapool: the whole walk from Altguish is about 24 miles, and it is better to make use of a motor vehicle for the road portion of the trip. It should be borne in mind that Ben Dearg and the whole district in which it stands are under deer, so that during the stalking season no climbing or tramping is possible. This applies also to most of the routes described which traverse deer forests, unless they are definitely rights of way. Even in that case it is wise to make enquiries from local residents before starting an expedition, since it may be possible to find alternative routes which will avoid any contact with stalking parties.

CHAPTER XVIII

STRATH BRAN, STRATH CONON AND GLEN ORRIN

MAPS.—*O.S. Popular Edition, 1 inch, sheets* 26 *and* 27.
Bartholomew's Half Inch, sheets 54 *and* 55.

ACHNASHEEN stands on the watershed of Ross-shire at the head of Strath Bran; its full name of Druim Achadh na Sine means the Ridge of Storm Field, and the place is open to all the winds that blow. It is the junction of the roads to Loch Maree, Torridon and Gairloch and that down Glen Carron to Strome Ferry, and possesses a good hotel and a post-office. The road to Strome Ferry bends south at Achnasheen and leads by the shore of Loch Gowan over the divide and on into Glen Carron, skirts the north shore of Loch Sgamhain and runs alongside the railway past Glencarron Station to Achnashellach. From the southern side of Glen Carron rise the slopes of Moruisg (3026 feet), a broad-based mountain which is the highest point in the Glencarron Forest. From Luib, 3½ miles south of Achnasheen, a track goes east across the river and the railway and through the hills to Scardroy Lodge, at the head of Loch Beannacharain, where it joins the road from Strathconon.

Strath Bran extends east from Achnasheen in a wide, shallow valley, down which runs the Bran River. The isolated mountain named Fionn Bheinn stands north of Achnasheen, but is better seen from further east; to the south the shapely Sgurr a' Mhuilinn (pronounced Scoor Vullin) rises on the borders of Strath Conon. Though of no great height, this mountain is probably one of the most familiar of the Ross-shire peaks; it is prominent in every view from the hills near Dingwall and Strathpeffer, and is well known by sight to railway travellers on the Inverness-Kyle line. Passing the station of Achanalt the road and the railway skirt the northern shore of Loch Achanalt, which is succeeded by the long narrow Loch a' Chuilinn, where road and rail diverge. Here the strath has become less bleak; the hill-sides and river-banks are tree-clad, and houses are beginning to appear. At Grudie Bridge the road crosses the Fannich River, which flows from the high-lying Loch Fannich behind the hills to the north, and joins the Bran 2 miles above its entry into Loch Luichart. Loch Achanalt, Loch a' Chuilinn and Loch Luichart will be affected by the Conon Basin hydro-electric project. This scheme will, when completed, necessitate the rebuilding of a few miles of railway, the present course of which will be submerged.

Loch Luichart is a crescent-shaped loch some 5 miles long, stretching from Strath Bran almost to Strath Conon. As the road and railway only pass along its northern shore for a short distance, before going east to Garve, it is less known than the majority of lochs of its size, and its shores are free from motor traffic. A path leads along its southern banks to Scatwell, in Strath Conon, connecting the latter with Loch Luichart Station. The River Bran, which enters the loch at its western end, issues from it as the Conon, and hurries over a series of rapids to its junction with the Meig, coming from Loch Beannacharain in the western mountains.

Strath Conon is the longest of the three Ross-shire glens which converge at the head of the Cromarty Firth. From its head at Loch Beannacharain to Conon Bridge, near Dingwall, it is 23 miles long, and is continued westwards by Glen Fhiodhaig for another 8 miles. Glen Fhiodhaig is a narrow mountain glen beginning at the southern base of Moruisg; at its head stands Glenuaig Lodge, past which flows the River Meig. This stream rises in the hills near by, flows down the glen to Loch Beannacharain, and through that loch, passes down the long narrow valley of Upper Strath Conon and mingles its waters with those of the Conon near Scatwell. The Meig, and not the Conon, is the River of Strath Conon, while the Conon is itself in reality the Bran. Below their confluence the united Meig and Conon flow east into the low country, and are joined at Moy Bridge by the Blackwater, flowing from Strath Garve and Loch Garve through the lovely wooded country near Strathpeffer. Further on, south of Brahan Castle, the River Orrin comes in from the south, and the Conon, by this time a broad and stately river, makes a bend to the north to fall into the Cromarty Firth below Conon Bridge.

The Orrin has its source in the mountains to the north of Loch Monar; it flows east through two small lochs and begins its course down Glen Orrin at the foot of Beinn Mheadhoin (Ben Vane), only 4 miles to the south of the head of Strath Conon. Glen Orrin is a glen of the uplands, treeless and bare, and much higher than its northern neighbour. Even at 2 miles from its foot the floor of the glen is 700 feet above the sea, and at its head the height is 1000 feet. The river describes a semicircle when leaving the uplands, passes through the woods south of Fairburn Castle and rushes over the Orrin Falls above the bridge at Aultgowrie.

Glen Orrin was never the home of a dense population, but Strath Conon of old was full of houses. The valley is sheltered and well adapted to the growing of fruit; honey was at one time produced in great quantities, and the Meig yielded plentiful supplies of salmon. These were caught in wicker baskets suspended over the Falls, or were speared by the inhabitants, for in the days before the " Clearances " fishing was free to all. After the Rising of the 'Forty Five, the proprietors of Strath Conon lost their estates, which remained for many years in the hands of commissioners and creditors, with disastrous consequences to the native inhabitants. Then, in the nineteenth century, came the Ross-shire " Clearances," when Strath Conon was depopulated to make way for sheep, so that, except in the low country to the east of Scatwell, the valley is to-day thinly peopled.

Eastward from Garve and Scatwell, along the Black-water, and the Conon, and the Orrin, is a tract of broken wooded country, neither Highland nor Lowland in character, which extends eastwards to merge into the coastal plain. Diversified by wooded heights, such as Tor Achilty, and by high ridges such as that of Knockfarrell and the Cat's Back, the district is rich in beautiful views; its lochs include Loch Garve, Loch Kinellan and the lovely Loch Achilty in its frame of woods, as well as Loch Ussie, into which the Brahan Seer is said to have thrown his divining stone. The district was from early days a favourite place of residence; it is to-day rich in castellated mansions and country seats, such as Brahan Castle, Castle Leod, Fairburn Tower and many others. Strathpeffer is now the chief centre of population; it is an inland watering-place with medicinal springs, situated half-way between Garve and Dingwall. Its large hotels and summer visitors have made it an English spa rather than a Highland village, and it is too far from the mountains to serve as a base for walkers. Ben Wyvis can, it is true, be ascended from Strathpeffer, but even that mountain is better approached from Evanton or Garve.

From very early times the district between Garve and Dingwall has been the scene of notable happenings. The ridge of Knockfarrell, overlooking Strathpeffer, still shows traces of the great fort which once crowned it. Near the southern end of the ridge, known as the Cat's Back, is the Beallach nan Corr (Crane's Gap), where the Munros, under Sir William Munro of Fowlis, were defeated by the Macken-zies in the fifteenth century. It was in the swampy fields near Strathpeffer in 1487 that Kenneth Mackenzie of Kintail routed the Macdonalds under Alexander of Lochalsh, a defeat which was the first step in the sapping of Clan Donald's power. Thirty-five years before, at Beallach nam Brog of Ben Wyvis, the Dingwalls, Rosses, and Munros fought a fierce battle with the Mackenzies, when both sides lost heavily.

COMMUNICATIONS

Rail.—The L.M.S. line from Inverness runs by Dingwall, Achterneed, Garve, Loch Luichart and Achanalt to Achnasheen and thence to Kyle of Lochalsh. There is a short branch to Strathpeffer.

Road Services.—Motor-bus services connect the district with Dingwall and Inverness and serve Strath Conon.

ACCOMMODATION

Hotels or inns at Achnasheen, Garve, Strathpeffer, Clachuile, Achilty, Conon Bridge, Muir of Ord and Milltown (Strath Conon).

Other accommodation at Achanalt, Strathpeffer and Muir of Ord.

Youth Hostel at Strathpeffer.

WALKS

(a) *By Road*

1. Strathpeffer to Scardroy Lodge, by Strath Conon, 20 miles. South by the main road to Contin, then north to cross the Blackwater and past Achilty Inn, turning west from the Garve Road to reach Loch Achilty. The road circles the north shore of the loch and goes south, through the woods, to cross the Conon, and turn right up the river. Passing along the edge of the Scatwell Woods the road climbs over a hill, with the confluence of the Meig and the Conon on the right, and descends somewhat to the south bank of the Meig. From the hill there is a fine view up the Conon to the foot of Loch Luichart in the north. For 6 miles from Little Scatwell to Milltown the way lies along the river, crossing at Bridgend to the north bank. For part of its course the Meig runs in a deep gorge, with narrow rock sides; this is called the Black Rock, like the more famous gorge at Novar. At Milltown, where there is a small hotel, the road bends south-west and continues for 5 miles up the wooded strath, bends to the west to reach the foot of Loch Beannacharain, and passes up the north

side of that loch to its head. Scardroy Lodge stands beside
a plantation just beyond the head of the loch; from it a
road, which shortly afterwards becomes a track, goes up
Glen Fhiodhaig to Glenuaig Lodge. A second track leads
north-west over a pass to Luib in the Achnasheen district.

2. Muir of Ord to Garve, via Urray and Moy Bridge,
12 miles. This is the most direct route from Beauly and
Inverness to Garve and the west. Muir of Ord is a rather
featureless town with a long straight street, and is an
important cattle mart.

Take the road which leads north-west past Urray
Church to the bridge over the Orrin, beyond which it
turns sharply to the west and runs dead straight to Marybank, 2 miles distant. Turning at right angles to the north
it leads down to the River Conon, which is crossed at Moy
Bridge, beyond which the way again lies west, across a
bend of the Blackwater, which is crossed close to Achilty
Inn. For the next 3 miles the road passes through open
woods, climbs up past the Falls of Rogie, which are off the
road to the right, and over to Loch Garve, which is reached
after the descent of a long gradual slope. Here we come
in sight of the railway, which has kept to the opposite side
of the wide strath, and now comes to run close to the road
along the south shore of Loch Garve. This is a fine sheet
of water about 2 miles long; across it to the north-west
is seen the entrance to Strath Garve, down which comes
the Blackwater from the heights of the Dirrie Mor. Garve
Station is just beyond the loch; here the road crosses the
line, and reaches the hotel and village of Garve. If this
walk is taken during the spring or early summer the hill-
sides and open country to the east will be gay with broom
and whin, which seem to flourish here. The distant views
of the mountains at the head of Strath Conon as seen from
the road near Bridge of Orrin are very striking.

(b) *By Hill-tracks*

1. Luib (Achnasheen) to Scardroy Lodge, 6 miles.
Luib is on the road to Strome Ferry, about $3\frac{3}{4}$ miles south

of Achnasheen. A track goes east across the river, crosses the railway close to the end of Loch Gowan, fords the stream which flows into that loch from the south, and climbs south-west into the hills along the course of the stream. Just beyond the ford it is joined by another path coming from the cottage of Inver, which stands between the railway and Loch Gowan. This second path leaves the main road opposite the head of Loch Gowan, fords the stream and reaches Inver along the east shore of the loch. It is an alternative to the route via Luib. Keeping south-east along the hill-side, the path climbs to 1300 feet over Carn Chaorain, and descends along the Scardroy Burn into a glen on the far side of the pass. Scardroy Lodge stands beside a plantation at the head of the two-mile-long Loch Beannacharain, along the north shore of which goes the road to Strath Conon. South of the loch is a group of mountains culminating in Bac an Eich (2791 feet), beyond which is the upper end of Glen Orrin.

2. Milltown (Strath Conon) to Achanalt, 5 miles. This is a rough road connecting Strath Conon with Strath Bran. It begins by the school at Milltown and goes north through the Strathconon Woods, climbs to 898 feet along the western flanks of Meall Bhad Ghaineamhaich, and bends north-west along the head-waters of the Allt Bail a' Mhuilinn. All this time the eastern slopes of Sgurr a' Mhuilinn have been in sight across the stream on the left. Reaching the summit at 942 feet, the road begins its descent round the northern flanks of Carn Garbh and presently arrives on the south shore of Loch Achanalt, which is circled to the west. Just before entering the loch the River Bran describes a loop to the south, across which a bridge has been thrown. Leaving the track to continue westwards, the walker bound for Achanalt should cross this bridge and make for the railway station which stands in full view to the north. The old hotel, now a private guest house, is by the road-side not far away.

3. Loch Luichart Station to the Clachuile Inn, 11 miles. This is a beautiful walk along the loch and down past the

Conon Falls, and along the Conon River to the inn. It
could form the first part of a fine tramp from Strath Bran
to Struy, in Strath Glass.

Leave the station at Loch Luichart and go south by
the road which soon bends to the east and follows the hill-
slopes above the loch. Beyond the head of the loch the
path crosses the foot of Glenmarskie and goes down the
west side of the Conon, past the rapids known as the Conon
Falls, to ford the Meig above its junction with the Conon,
and to join the road a little further on. The road leads
south-east and then east along the edge of the woods, with
the Conon close by on the left, passes the end of the road
to Loch Achilty and goes on to Clachuile Inn, which stands
beside the road $1\frac{1}{2}$ miles west of Marybank.

4. Clachuile Inn to Struy (Strath Glass), 13 miles. Go
east along the road as far as Marybank, turning south by
the road to the Orrin Falls, which skirts the grounds of
Fairburn and crosses the Orrin below the Falls. Half a
mile beyond the bridge two roads or tracks diverge to the
right and a road to Muir of Ord to the left. Take the
second track on the right, which leads west along the
lower slopes of a wooded hill for nearly 2 miles, where two
paths diverge to the south-west. Take the more southerly
of the two, which goes down the hill-slopes into Glen
Gowrie, fords the river and climbs over the ridge to the
south, past the eastern flanks of Beinn a' Chlaonaidh,
towards Strath Glass. Descending the southern slopes,
and passing between two small lochs, the path leads down
to the woods and joins the main road to Struy close to the
gates of Erchless Castle. Struy Bridge and village, with
its small hotel, are reached by walking west for rather
more than a mile.

5. Clachuile Inn to Milltown (Strath Conon), by Glen
Orrin, 18 miles. This is a somewhat circuitous walk which
enables the little-known Glen Orrin to be visited, and brings
the walker to the small hotel at Milltown by way of Upper
Strath Conon.

East along the Scatwell road, and then south to the

north bank of the Orrin near Fairburn House. From this
point a path goes south-west along the north bank of the
river and leads up Glen Orrin past Cabaan to Luip-
maldrig. Here it turns to the north-west and goes over a
pass of 1099 feet, past Loch Airidh Lochain, to descend
through the woods of Upper Strath Conon to Inverchoran,
near the foot of Loch Beannacharain. At Inverchoran the
Meig River is crossed to the main road, which leads down
the strath for 4 miles to Milltown. An alternative route is
by the path which keeps to the opposite, or east side of the
river, leading through the woods to Dalbreac Lodge,
where a road begins which goes across the river to Milltown.
For the greater part of the way this is a very lonely route,
with little shelter in case of bad weather. It should always
be traversed from east to west, if possible, so that the sun
may light up the western mountains in the forenoon and
be behind the walker for the last few miles down Strath
Conon.

CHAPTER XIX

INVERNESS TO FORT AUGUSTUS AND THE CORRIEYAIRACK PASS

MAPS.—*O.S. Popular Edition, 1 inch, sheets* 37 *and* 42.
Bartholomew's Half Inch, sheets 51 *and* 55.

THE town of Inverness stands at the northern end of the Great Glen, where the River Ness flows into the Moray Firth. It is built along the banks of the river at some distance from the sea, where the Ness flows swiftly through its wide green strath; to the west are low wooded hills, terminating in Craig Phadrig; eastwards the land slopes gradually towards Drummossie Muir. The foot of Loch Ness is 6 miles to the south-west of the town, with which it is connected by road and river; the Caledonian Canal which adjoins the latter for 3 miles, parts company at the Hill of Torvaine and curves round the western outskirts of Inverness to reach the canal basin at Muirtown. Then it passes through the last lock and joins the Beauly Firth, the land-locked western extension of the Moray Firth.

A low sandy promontory separates the canal mouth from the estuary of the Ness; on its northern side is the ferry station of South Kessock, from which there is regular communication to North Kessock in the Black Isle across the narrow tidal strait. The Black Isle is a large irregularly-shaped peninsula between the Firths of Cromarty and Moray; from Craigton Point, east of North Kessock, its coast extends north-eastwards to the Sutors of Cromarty, at the narrow entrance to the Cromarty Firth. Half-way along this stretch the finger-like promontory of Chanonry Point juts out into the Firth, leaving only a narrow channel between it and the opposite headland of Ardersier, on which stands Fort George. Along the south-east shore of the Firth, from Inverness to Fort George and on to Nairn, Forres and Elgin, stretches a belt of level country, for this is no longer the Highlands, but the Lowlands of Moray. Along this level strip goes the road to Elgin and Aberdeen, and the railway to Forres and Grantown; it was, until the making of Wade's roads in the eighteenth century, the approach to Inverness from the south.

Standing athwart the road to the north and west, Inverness has always been the Gateway to the Northern Highlands, and is to-day the centre to which a wide area of country, from Skye to Sutherland, looks for many of the necessities of life. Its pre-eminence has in late years been challenged by Fort William, but the northern town is the capital of Inverness-shire, and still maintains its position as the capital of the Highlands. As a railway centre it is of considerable importance, for all traffic from the east and the south must pass through Inverness to reach the north and the west. Perth and Aviemore on the main L.M.S. line to Edinburgh, with Aberdeen, Elgin and Forres on the L.N.E.R. line to the east, are connected by fast trains with Inverness, from which other branches lead west to Kyle and north to Wick and Thurso.

Five important main roads converge at Inverness, and a sixth goes north, across Kessock Ferry, to Cromarty and the Black Isle. These are the road from Nairn and Elgin along the coast, the great south road from Perth and Aviemore, the two roads to Fort Augustus along opposite shores of Loch Ness, and the main road along the Beauly Firth to Dingwall and beyond. As the main streets of the town are far from wide, the traffic during the summer and autumn season severely strains their resources, and that of the single bridge which carries the road across the River Ness. Outside the principal shopping centres, Inverness has many fine wide walks, some along the river-bank to the wooded islands which form a pleasure ground in the river, others along the terraces below the ridge on which the modern " Castle " stands. The neighbouring heights of Craig Phadrig, Dunain Hill, and Tomnahurich offer opportunities for easy and pleasant walks, and there are fine views from the shore of the Firth to the north-east, looking across to the Black Isle and westward to the mountains of Ross-shire.

As a centre for hill-walkers, however, Inverness is not so well situated as Fort Augustus, which stands among the mountains at the upper end of Loch Ness. Once known as Kilcumin, and later as the fortress intended to guard the Great Glen, it is now a small town beside the locks of the Caledonian Canal, containing a nineteenth century Benedictine Abbey. Here is also the terminus of the railway from Spean Bridge, which was closed to traffic in December, 1933. The Abbey stands on the loch-side between the Canal and the River Tarff; it was founded in the 'Eighties of last century on land gifted by the Lord Lovat of the day, who had acquired the old fort from the Government. Southward from Fort Augustus is Glen Tarff, a narrow wooded valley penetrating into the hills of the Culachy Forest; down it comes the rough track which is the degenerate successor of the road built by General Wade two centuries ago. This road began at Dalwhinnie, near the head of Loch Ericht, crossed to the Spey valley and made its way, by a series of zigzags, up the eastern slope of Coire Yairack and over the pass of that name at a height of 2507 feet. Intended as a link in the system of military roads which were to tame the Highlands, it was actually used by the army of Prince Charles Edward on his victorious march to Edinburgh in 1745. The way over the pass is now only fit for foot-passengers, for it is more than a century since the road was abandoned to the elements; for walkers it still provides an exhilarating approach to the Great Glen, with extensive views from the higher sections.

Loch Ness is nearly 24 miles long, and averages 1 mile in width; it is one of the deepest lochs in the Highlands, and its waters have never been known to freeze. From its head at Fort Augustus it extends in a north-easterly direction to Bona Ferry, where the short reach known as Loch Dochfour begins. Although almost the whole length of its shores is finely wooded, their regularity and lack of distinguishing features detract from its beauty as a whole. The eastern shore runs almost unbroken from Dores to Fort Augustus; only the little bays of Inverfarigaig and Foyers relieve the sameness of the banks. The western side is less regular; its two rivers have widened their mouths into the fine bays of Urquhart and Invermoriston, and the broad-topped mountain of Meallfourvonie helps to lend dignity to the hill forms. Except for this height there are no mountains of any size along Loch Ness; it is to the south, behind Fort Augustus, that the higher ranges begin.

Of the two roads from Inverness southward along Loch Ness, that on the western side has been widened and made more suitable for fast motor traffic, and is therefore no longer so attractive as it once was. It goes south-west from Inverness along the base of the wooded ridge bounding the Ness valley, reaches the loch-side at Lochend, passes the road to Abriachan on the right and continues along the shore, well above the water, to Urquhart Bay. Here it takes a wide sweep inland past Drumnadrochit, leaving the road up Glen Urquhart on the right, swings back past Lewiston to the loch shore, where the fine ruin of Urquhart Castle stands on its promontory at the southern point of the bay and goes on to Invermoriston. Again bending inland at this place to pass the hotel of Invermoriston and to cross the bridge over the rushing river, the road swings down past the pier and follows the loch shore for a further 5 miles to Fort Augustus.

The road on the east side of the loch is that built by General Wade to connect Fort William with Fort Augustus and Inverness. Coming north from Spean Bridge by the east side of Loch Lochy it was continued along the east side of Loch Oich, entering Fort Augustus from the south. Leaving the Fort and rounding the extreme south corner of Loch Ness, the road climbs a steep hill and descends to Glen Doe, crosses by a bridge and ascends a second steep hill to Loch Tarff. Passing along the southern shore of this loch and still continuing to climb, the road goes east and reaches its summit level at a height of 1275 feet. It is here at the highest point of an elevated plateau, with desolate mountains to the east; northward are two large lochs, and to the west, hidden in its long deep trench, lies Loch Ness. For 3 miles the road falls gradually to the hotel at White Bridge, one of the best fishing centres in the Highlands, which stands at the head of Strath Errick, on the Fechlin River. This river soon changes its name to Foyers, and winds northwards through wooded country towards Loch Ness, finally turning west to plunge over the Falls of Foyers and down to the loch. The road follows the river for some miles, keeping to its eastern bank, but turns off above the Upper Falls to go north-east down Glen Liath to the Pass of Inverfarigaig. This is a short wooded defile leading west to the shore of Loch Ness, with high tree-clad rocks on each side; down it rushes a brawling river.

Above the shore at Inverfarigaig the road divides into three branches, one leading south along the loch to Foyers, another going inland through the " Lake District " of Inverness-shire and the third along the shore to Dores and Inverness. The last is our route, which still follows the line of Wade's road of 200 years ago, hugging the shore all the way to Dores. It is a pleasant road, tree-shaded and cool, with the loch water close by on the left hand; at Dores it leaves Loch Ness and goes north-east, passes through the shady roads of the suburbs and enters Inverness along the river bank.

Loch Oich lies to the south-west of Loch Ness; it is 4 miles long, and is the next link in the chain of lochs which form so great a part of the waterway of the Caledonian Canal. On its western side are the woods of Invergarry and the mouth of the Garry River, with the ruins of Invergarry Castle. The main road, widened and improved, goes down this shore. On the opposite side of the loch the hill-sides rise abruptly above the shore, hardly leaving room for the passage of the old military road and the railway. This is the route for walkers, who are not likely to encounter any motors, and can enjoy in peace the lovely views across the loch.

At the south end of Loch Oich the two roads join and go forward as one to Spean Bridge. It is not quite a mile to the upper end of Loch Lochy, the third of the lochs in the Great Glen. This is a loch of different character, a stern, fiord-like water-lane with lofty mountains rising from its farther shore. On a windy day, with black waves rolling up from the south-west, Loch Lochy resembles an arm of the sea; the trawlers and drifters which frequently pass through it help to support the illusion. The road passes the head of the loch not far above the water-level, and goes south, gradually climbing past Letterfinlay and Invergloy and over the hill to Spean Bridge. Across the water on the western shore is the opening to Loch Arkaig, and the " Dark Mile " by Achnacarry, where Lochiel still resides. At Spean Bridge we are back in Lochaber and almost in the shadow of Ben Nevis.

All through the ages Inverness has played its part in the history of Scotland; it was the capital of Brude, the Pictish monarch, when Columbia made his way up the Great Glen on his missionary journey to the Picts. Brude may have resided in the Dun on Craig Phadrig, or on Tomnahurich; he ruled the north from Cape Wrath to Perthshire, and from Aberdeen to Skye. Legend tells how the Druids raised a tempest on Loch Ness, and how Columba in his small boat put out into the teeth of the wind and sailed triumphantly up the loch. In later years there was a royal castle at Inverness; it changed hands several times during the War of Independence, was razed by King Robert Bruce and rebuilt by James I. The town was taken and sacked by the Lord of the Isles in the fifteenth century, in reprisal for his capture by King James when attending a meeting of chiefs at Inverness.

James III. and James IV. both visited Inverness and stayed in the castle; Queen Mary also came north, but was refused admission by the governor of the castle, who afterwards paid for his temerity with his life. Taken by the Jacobites at the time of the 'Forty Five, the castle was finally blown up by their forces; the present building on its site was erected in the early years of the nineteenth century. Of the great " Citadel " erected by the troops of Cromwell during their occupation of Inverness very little now remains except the clock tower; it was built of stone brought from the old cathedral of Fortrose and the ruined priories of Beauly and Kinloss.

The burghers of Inverness took no part in the feuds of the clans; they stayed at home when the Munros fought a desperate battle with the Mackintoshes at Clachnaharry, to the west of the town. This was a matter of the road collop, or cess payable by cattle lifters to the clan through whose lands the spoils were driven home. The amount demanded by the Mackintoshes had been considered exorbitant, and payment refused by the Munros: in the battle which ensued the men from Moy got the worst of it, though both sides suffered heavily. Inverness was surrounded by the territories of the powerful Fraser clan, whose chief, known as MacShimei, ruled from Dounie Castle, on the Beauly River. Their lands extended far up the Farrar to Loch Monar, and included the Aird and part of Strath Glass. In the south-east they had wide possessions along Loch Ness-side, stretching down to Kilcumin (Fort Augustus) and beyond. It was at the head of Loch Lochy, on ground now covered by the loch, that the Frasers met with dire disaster in 1544. This was the Battle of the Shirts, fought on a hot July day against the Macdonalds and Camerons; the Frasers were on their way home after an expedition in the west, and were followed up and attacked by John of Moidart and his men. Outnumbered and outgeneralled, the Frasers turned gallantly to bay and were almost annihilated in the bloody conflict which ensued.

There were no roads in the Great Glen for nearly two hundred years after the Battle of the Shirts; the clansmen wore brogues of untanned hide, and moved easily along the hill-tracks. The wonderful march of Montrose from Kilcumin to Inverlochy was made through the mountains in deep snow, and could only have been carried out by Highland fighters. When General Wade, sent north by the Hanoverian Government in 1725 to pacify the Highlands, began the construction of his great roads, he was copying the Romans; his first road was that from Inverness through the Great Glen to Fort William. Later, in 1731, a road was built from Fort Augustus over the Corrieyairack Pass to Speyside and Dalwhinnie, attaining a height of 2507 feet at the summit. It is one of the ironies of history that the army of Prince Charles Edward should have been the first to use the new road in war, at the outset of his campaign against Sir John Cope.

The possibilities of a waterway through the Great Glen had been recognised for many years before the Caledonian Canal was opened in 1882. Its total length of 62 miles includes 38 miles through the three lochs of Lochy, Oich and Ness. Until the 1914-18 War a steamer ran weekly from Glasgow to Fort William and Inverness, carrying passengers and cargo. There is a passenger steamer service from Banavie to Inverness during the summer months, the journey being done alternately from south and north on successive week-days. If somewhat leisurely this is nevertheless the most satisfactory way to view the scenery of the Great Glen, and should be tried by all visitors. The motor-buses which have to a great extent supplanted the steamers are, from the tourist's point of view, a sorry substitute.

COMMUNICATIONS

Rail.—Inverness is a junction on the L.M.S. line, with services to all parts of the country. There is no longer any passenger service on the L.N.E.R. to Fort Augustus.

Steamer.—A passenger steamer runs on alternate week-days during the summer season from Banavie to Inverness, and from Inverness to Banavie.

Road Services.—Regular services of motor-buses are in

operation from Inverness to Fort Augustus and Fort William, to Beauly and Dingwall, Wick and Thurso, Nairn, Elgin and Aberdeen.

ACCOMMODATION

Hotels at Inverness, Drumnadrochit, Invermoriston, Fort Augustus, Foyers, White Bridge, Invergarry and Spean Bridge.

Other accommodation at Inverness, Drumnadrochit, Lewiston, Invermoriston, Fort Augustus, South Laggan, Gairlochy and Spean Bridge.

Youth Hostels at Buntait, at the western end of Glen Urquhart, Inverness, and Alltsaigh on Loch Ness.

WALKS

(a) *By Road*

1. Drumnadrochit to Invercannich, 12 miles. In addition to the roads already described down the Great Glen to Fort Augustus, there is a road from Drumnadrochit up Glen Urquhart and over to Invercannich in Strath Glass. This road leaves the Inverness-Invermoriston road at the bridge below the Drumnadrochit Hotel (Druim na Drochaidh means " The Ridge of the Bridge "), and leads west up wooded Glen Urquhart along the north bank of the River Enrick. Passing the end of the road which goes up past Loch na Ba Ruaidhe and over to Glen Convinth and the Aird, the Invercannich road ascends gradually to Loch Meiklie and leads along its northern shore towards the open moorlands, leaving behind the fertile hill-sides of Glen Urquhart with its many houses and farms. Two and a half miles beyond the loch, where a bridge leads across the river and westward to Corrimony, the road bends to the north-west and ascends to the summit at 708 feet. All about here is wide wind-swept moorland, with extensive views to the mountains of the north and west; below is the long trough of Strath Glass, into which the road descends by a long slant down the hill-side. From the hill one looks

across at Cannich, clustering round its hotel and post-office on the far side of the broad level valley; a bridge carries the road over the Glass and past the church and school to the cross-roads. By keeping straight on instead of turning at the bridge the walker will come to Tomich, with its hotel, by a route already described in an earlier chapter.

2. Drumnadrochit to Lovat Bridge, near Beauly, 12 miles. The last route took the walker into the head of Strath Glass: by turning off to Glen Convinth he can reach the foot of that strath not far from Beaufort Castle. This road leaves Glen Urquhart a mile to the west of Drumnadrochit Hotel, climbs very steeply out of the glen past Lower Gartally, and still climbing, reaches a height of 850 feet above Loch na Ba Ruaidhe. Crossing the summit level past a second loch, it reaches the head-waters of the Red Burn and descends into Glen Convinth. Crossing the Belladrum Burn close to the houses at Convinth the road leads directly north for nearly 3 miles, bends north-west to its junction with a road coming from the west, and goes north-east to Ballindoun, which stands beside the Beauly River, where four roads meet. Half a mile to the north-east the road joins the Inverness-Beauly road on the edge of a wood, a mile short of Lovat Bridge.

Note.—From Abriachan on Loch Ness-side, 9 miles from the town, a road leads up a very steep slope past Loch Laide and over into Glen Convinth, joining the previous route at a bridge 2 miles to the south of Ballindoun. The distance from Abriachan to Lovat Bridge by this route is a little more than 9 miles.

(b) *By Hill-tracks*

1. Loch Laggan Hotel to Fort Augustus, by Corrieyairack, 21 miles. This route should properly begin at Dalwhinnie, on the railway from Blair Atholl to Kingussie, and be followed along the modern road to Cat Lodge, and thence westward along the Spey to Glen Shirra Lodge, where the track from Loch Laggan Hotel is joined. This makes the walk too long for a normal day's tramp, and it is preferable to start from the hotel or from Kinlochlagan,

which can be reached, if desired, by walking from Dalwhinnie on the previous day. Walkers from the Youth Hostel at Loch Ossian can reach Kinlochlaggan by way of Ben Alder and Glen Pattack.

Leave the Tulloch road about 100 yards east of the Loch Laggan Hotel by a rough track which leads north by west up the hill-side, passes through the woods by Loch Crunachdan and in front of Glen Shirra Lodge to join Wade's road at a point a little to the south of Shirramore. Turning west along this road we pass Shirramore, then the cottage of Garvamore, and cross the Spey by Garva Bridge. Rising and falling along the north bank of the Spey to the cottage of Melgarve, the road fords a burn and soon begins to climb in earnest. Going along the hill-side along the Glen of the Yairack Burn, the track again turns west and climbs up the face of the hill which forms the head of the corrie. The zigzags by which the road ascended are now grass-grown scars in the hill-side, but there is no difficulty in reaching the top and continuing to the summit of the pass itself. Here, at a height of 2507 feet, one can look back towards Strath Spey, or climb Corrieyairack Hill a mile to the north for the sake of the view from its 2922-foot summit. Continuing our route towards the west we obtain, in clear weather, a magnificent view across the Great Glen, with mountains and lochs innumerable in sight. The track descends the northern side through the Culachy Forest to Alt Lagan a' Bhainne, crosses the new bridge erected by the Scottish Rights of Way Society, and goes down the western side of the Tarff glen and past Culachy House to join the main road from the south, 1½ miles from Fort Augustus.

2. Laggan Locks to Gairlochy, by the west side of Loch Lochy, 11 miles. This path along the unfrequented side of Loch Lochy provides a short route from Loch Oich to Loch Arkaig. It leaves the road at the head of Loch Lochy, crosses the canal at the Locks, and bends south round the head of the loch to Kilfinnan. Below this hamlet, on ground now covered by Loch Lochy, is the

site of the Battle of the Shirts, mentioned above. Beyond
Kilfinnan the road becomes a path and leads south-west
along the base of the mountains to Clunes at the entrance
to the " Dark Mile." To the west lies lovely Loch Arkaig,
with its memories of the 'Forty Five; the road bends west
to round the bay, crosses the Arkaig River, and winds
south along the shore to the lock bridge at Gairlochy.
These mountains of Loch Lochy are rugged and steep;
they rise in storm-channelled red slopes from the loch
shore, and form the eastern wall of the Glengarry Forest.
Along their base, on the day after Culloden, came Prince
Charles Edward, hurrying to the West Coast in the hope
of finding a ship for France.

INDEX

T   U